Serious Fraud and Current Issues

FRAUD LAW: BOOK ONE

Sally Ramage is the author of

International Trade	ISBN 0-595-32164-4
Civil Liberties in England and Wales	ISBN 0-595-32427-4
Legal and Regulatory Framework for Businesses in the UK	ISBN 0-595-32428-2
Intellectual Property	ISBN 0-595-32927-6

and many law enforcement articles written for periodicals: Accounting Technician, Law In A Box, MONDAQ, The Criminal Lawyer and PoliceOne.com

She is a member of the

Association of International Accountants
European Corporate Governance Institute
Society of Legal Scholars
Chartered Management Institute
National Union of Journalists

She has presented papers at Academic Conferences and is busy preparing for four conferences this year, as well as teaching compliance subjects as a visiting lecturer at the University of Wolverhampton, United Kingdom.

Serious Fraud and Current Issues

Sally Ramage

iUniverse, Inc.
New York Lincoln Shanghai

Serious Fraud and Current Issues

iUniverse books may be ordered through booksellers or by contacting:

iUniverse

2021 Pine Lake Road, Suite 100
Lincoln, NE 68512
www.iuniverse.com
1-800-Authors (1-800-288-4677)

ISBN-13: 978-0-595-35678-2 (pbk)
ISBN-13: 978-0-595-80155-8 (ebk)
ISBN-10: 0-595-35678-8 (pbk)
ISBN-10: 0-595-80155-2 (ebk)

Printed in the United States of America

Contents

Preface xi

Acknowledgements xiii

Tables of statutes, law cases, treaties etc xiv

CHAPTER ONE—AN EXPLANATION OF UK FRAUD 1

    Abstract *1*

    The Concept of Serious Fraud *1*

    More Case-law on the offence of conspiracy to defraud *2*

    Fraud is not classed as an offence by statute *3*

    The common law offence of conspiracy to defraud *5*

    A critical analysis of the UK fraud offence as proposed *8*

    The State and Fraudster *12*

    The motive in fraud *15*

    Crime and punishment *15*

    The fraud offence classification *16*

    Criminals classified *16*

    Responsibility and Culpability *18*

    The fraudster as a psychopath *19*

    Serious Fraud and senility *19*

    Statistics on fraud *20*

    Senility and fraud *22*

    The McNaughten Rules of the UK *23*

    Punishment of Fraudsters *23*

    Morality and fraud *24*

    Culture and fraud *25*

    Why do we still have fraud today? *28*

    Conclusion *30*

    Appendix One: Analysis of 49 SFO cases between 1999 and 2003 .... *31*

    Appendix Two: Population in prison under sentence by offence group and sentence: *33*

        England and Wales, 30 June 2002 .... *33*

Appendix Three: Crime statistics 1950 ....*34*

Appendix Four: R v Pound Green and Others (2004) unreported *35*

Appendix Five: R v Peter Young (2003) unreported *36*

Appendix Six: R v Mitchell Kirkup and Others (2004) unreported *37*

Bibliography *40*

   Books *40*

   Articles *44*

CHAPTER TWO—CURRENT ISSUES IN THE LAW OF FRAUD PROSECUTION *45*

Issue 1—Extradition in Criminal Cases *45*

   (a)—Trial in Absence *45*

   (b)—Extradition in Fraud Cases (Steen) *46*

   (c)—Corporate Advances *48*

Issue 2—The New Extradition Treaty between UK and US *71*

   ENRON extradiction request for three bankers—the British Chapter *71*

Issue 3—Trans-National Organised Crime *74*

   Trafficking *74*

Issue 4—Financial Systems do not stop Fraud *86*

   UK Consolidated Financial Regulatory System *86*

Issue 5—American Illegal Securitisation—Banking in the Unregulated Mortgage Market *103*

   American Mortgages (Fannie Mae) *103*

Issue 6—Immoral Markets *116*

   Carbon Credits Market *116*

   *The Carbon Credit Markets—Western Financial Opportunity Born out of
   Potential Global Crisis due to Centuries of Western Pollution* *116*

Issue 7—Terrorism and Sabotage *126*

   *An Examinatisn of the Formerly Largely Unregulated Global Charity Sector and
   the Impact of Anti-Money Laundering and Anti-Terrorism Legislation* *126*

CHAPTER 3—SHORT ARTICLES ON CONTEMPORARY TOPICS *137*

3.1—What is Fraud? *137*

3.2—The Test for Deception *138*

3.3 Common Frauds *139*

3.4—Fraudulent Evasion *140*

3.5—Fraudulent Trading *142*

3.6—Document Destruction 143

3.7—Cartels 145

3.8—Charity Bill 146

3.9—European Company 147

3.10—Revealing Facts—Computer Crime Conference 150

3.11—International Accounting Standards 151

3.12—Serious Fraud Office 157

3.13—The Fraud Offence 159

3.14—Money-laundering and trafficking 163

3.15—Fraud conference 2004 164

3.16—United Kingdom transfer pricing legislation among transfer pricing developments in other countries. 167

3.17—Compulsory whistle-blowing in EU financial markets 170

3.18—The Electronic Invoice 172

3.19—Terrorism and the Accounting Community 174

Appendix—Prevention of Terrorism Act 2005 177

About the Author 203

Preface

This volume and the second volume, of five planned volumes of a series of books on the law and fraud, will be published simultaneously.

Book One is divided into three—a detailed introduction to criminal law which deals with fraud, explaining why we do not yet have a fraud law in the United kingdom, the second consisting of some serious issues surrounding fraud, and the third part being a set of contemporary topics, subjected to the modern style with no footnotes, each article being concise and simply written.

Book Two deals with legal issues such as the right to silence of a suspect. The law of Germany, France and New York and Illinois is discussed and compared with English law to give a good perspective of fraud in the developed world. The very fact that I shall be producing five volumes speaks for itself that fraud is a huge problem and seems to have become accepted as part of our culture, with roots of fraudulent behaviour running deep into the fabric of finance and account ancy. There is nothing new under the sun, as the saying goes, and fraud is as common today as in centuries past, man's ingenuity and cunning only growing sharper.

Fraud is big business and it rots the fabric of finance and accountancy, as it is exercised by all day trading of bonds, junk bonds, loans. Twenty-five years ago, fraud was said to be rapidly expanding and illustrates itself by shady deals, fraudulently converted cash. Fraudsters who are active, especially electronic fraud, do in fact treat the use of fraud as serious "business" and the execution of frauds as "work", much like other criminals treat their activities as their "job"! We have recently seen the post-mortem of **Worldcom** and **Enron**, whose executives faced and still face imprisonment for theft, dishonesty, illicit trading, corruption and simply cashing other people's cheques. Identity theft poses a frightening thought of being taken in by crooks. If twenty-five years ago it was estimated that the amount of fraudulent cash around the world at any one time more than equalled the Gross National Products of several third-world countries, it would not be believed—a damning indictment indeed.

I took advantage of the fact that people seem thrilled to hear about frauds, like murders. What the thrill is I don't know, but I have prepared works that will use your attention to discuss law enforcement and the consequences of breaking the law by committing frauds. Like many people's cupboards, the behind-the-scenes situation in many respectable establishments and personalities is deeply murky and full of fraud. It is hoped that one will read this book from cover to cover and take stock of one's moral position. With an estimated £45 billion of fraud committed in the UK alone in the year 2003, we are now the world's second biggest fraud industry, only Germany's fraud being ahead of ours.

Other books published are

1. *UK Steel Industry & International Trade*, ISBN 0-595-32164-X
2. *Civil Liberties in England and Wales*, ISBN 0-595-66572-1
3. *Legal and Regulatory Framework for Business in the UK*, ISBN 0-595-32428-2
4. *Introduction to UK Intellectual Property*, ISBN 0-595-32927-6

These days my world consists entirely of writing legal articles, books and chapters and teaching legal and regulatory subjects to university business students, writing law enforcement articles used by PoliceOne.com for police training, and taking students to moot competitions, writing critiques and judging university internal moots. There is hardly any time left for sleeping!

Sally Ramage
20.3.2005

Acknowledgements

My grateful thanks go to Brian Mitchell, Dean of the School of Legal Studies, University of Wolverhampton, who treats everyone, including myself, with kindness and dignity. Always in control without arrogance or chauvinism, he always has a good word to say when I show him my work. It is an inspiration that helps me to carry on when I feel like wilting under the burden as I work through many a night because there are just not enough hours in the day.

I am always grateful for the challenge of bringing the business school students up to speed in the law and I glow with satisfaction when I see astonishing results of the highest quality; and I remind them and remind myself—you get out of your life what you put in. *Tout le monde vient a celui qui sait attendre.* All things come to those who know how to wait.

List of Encouragers

Although not a contributor, Andy Sinclair, Editor of *The Criminal Lawyer*, Tottel Publishers, keeps in touch with all of its contributors, of whom I am one. He is also a night owl and is known to email at 3 in the morning with queries.

William Micklethwaite, European News Editor of the *Bloomberg Internet Legal Newsletter* at http://www.Mondaq.com/ has encouraged me to continue with writing articles.

Marc Grainger and Fritha Sutherland from the Publishers Scott McMillan in London are good people who appreciate my efforts. We work to a strict schedule and I feel really at ease working with them each month at http://www.accountingtechnician.co.uk/

I have learnt much from the young university students as I experiment to make my lectures interesting; I coax them; I try out different ways to engage them in the subject; chalk and talk, Power-point slide shows, clip-art, art, pictures, cuttings, computer sessions, discussions, group effort, diatribe…In this day and age, some of them still call me "Miss"!

Of course I must acknowledge the help and support of Charles Muller, editor and publisher at http://www.Diadembooks.com/—a good and Christian man whose encouragement has been deeply appreciated.

I have seen wickedness; I have seen people who will deceive without batting an eyelid; I have heard dangerous deceits. I know how difficult it must be to try to change people who have no conscience—heartless people consumed with greed. I shall die at peace if I make even one ripple in that deep dark river of evil, that black hole of greed.

Tables of statutes, law cases, treaties etc

UK statutes

Agricultural Credits Act 1928, 11, 162

Anti-Social Behaviour Act 2003, 28

Anti-terrorism, Crime and Security Act 2001, 128, 136, 175, 180, 195

Business Names Act 1985, 82-83

Charities Act 1993, 127, 136

Coinage Act 1971, 11, 162

Companies Act 1985, 4, 11, 41, 81-83, 126, 136, 139, 142-143, 156, 161

Company Directors Disqualification Act 1986, 142

Computer Misuse Act 1990, 11, 162

Criminal Justice Act 1987, 4-5, 11, 80, 83, 140, 157, 161-162

Criminal Justice Act 1988, 5, 11, 140, 162, 192

Criminal Justice Act 1993, 6, 9, 139, 160, 171

Criminal Justice and Court Services Act 2000., 11, 162

Criminal Justice and Public Order Act 1994, 94

Criminal Procedure (Insanity) Act 1964, 23

Criminal Law Act 1977, 11, 162

Data Protection Act 1998, 150

Deeds of Arrangement Act 1914, 11, 162

Directors Disqualification Act 1986, 142, 171

Disability Discrimination Act 1995, 29

Enterprise Act 2002, 5, 11, 145, 162

Equal Pay Act 1970, 29

Extradition Act 1870, 47

Extradition Act 1989, 47

Extradition Act 2003, 80, 83

Finance Act 1982, 11, 162

Financial Services Act 1986, 4, 23, 36, 93

Financial Services and Markets Act 2000, 87, 147, 171

Forgery and Counterfeiting Act 1981, 5-6, 9, 11, 160, 162

Fraudulent Mediums Act 1951, 11

Gaming Act 1845, 2, 11, 137

Goods Vehicles Act 1995, 11, 162

Hallmarking Act 1973, 11, 162

Human Rights Act 1998, 12, 163, 179, 184, 190, 194

Insolvency Act 1986, 11, 162

Land Registrations Act 1925, 11, 162

Law Commissions Act 1965, 8

Law of Property Act 1925, 11

Limitation Act 1980, 11, 144, 162

Markets Abuse Act 2005, 94

Mental Health Act 1983, 11, 162

Nationality, Immigration and Asylum Act 2000, 83

Nationality, Immigration and Asylum Act 2002, 79, 195

Nuclear Material Offences Act 1983, 11, 162

Pensions Act 1995, 140, 147, 171

Police and Criminal Evidence Act 1984, 11, 162, 184, 188

Post Office Act 1953, 11, 162

Prevention of Terrorism Act 2005, 177, 188, 192, 195, 201

Proceeds of Crime Act 1995, 27

Proceeds of Crime Act 2002, 4, 80, 136, 140, 164

Protection of Depositors Act 1963, 11, 161

Public Interest Disclosure Act 1998, 172

Public Stores Act 1875, 11, 162

Race Relations Act 1976, 29

Road Traffic Regulation Act 1984, 11, 162

Road Traffic Act 1988, 11, 162

School Standards Framework Act 1998, 28

Sex Discrimination Act 1975, 29

Sexual Offences Act 2003, 79, 84, 163

Social Security Administration Act 1992, 11, 162

Stamp Duties Management Act 1891, 11, 162

Terrorism Act 2000, 122, 124, 128, 136, 175, 184, 194-195

Theft Act 1968, 2, 14

Theft Act 1978, 5-6, 9, 11, 138, 140, 160-162

Theft Amendment Act 1996, 11, 137, 162

Trafficking Victim's Protection Act, 84

Transport Act 1968, 11, 162

Unified European Act 1986, 124

Vehicle Excise and Registration Act 1994, 11, 162

Visiting Forces Act 1952, 11, 162

UK Case law

Arriva plc and First-group plc (3 December 2004) Competition Commission, 145

Attorney-General's Reference 6 of 2004, [2004] EWCA Crim 1275, 80

Balfron Trustees Ltd v Karsten Peterson & 8 Ors (2001) IRLR 758, Ch D, 163

Barings Futures (Singapore) pte Ltd v Deloitte and Touche [2003] EWHC 2371 (Ch), 32, 182

Bath Glass, Re [1988], 165

Brocklesby, James v Armitage & Guest (A Firm) (2001) 1 EGLR 67, 166

Cannane v J Cannane Pty Ltd (in liquidation) [1998] 153 ALR 163, 1, 23

Cronos Containers NV v Palatin [2002] EWHC 2819, 4

Derby v Weldon [1991], 172

Derry v Peek [1889] 14 App Cas 337, 1

Director of Fair Trading v Pioneer Concrete (UK) Ltd (1995), x, 145

Director of Public Prosecutions v Kent and Sussex Contractors Ltd [1944] KB 146, 6, 167

Guinness case in 1986, 144

Guinness plc v Saunders and Another [1987] BCC 271, 7

Guerra v Italy, (116/1996/735/932), 19 February 1998, 123

Fauntleroy, Henry (Trial of) 1824, 27

Income Tax Commissioners v Pemsel [1891] AC 531, 127

Infabrics Ltd & Ors v Jaytex Ltd (1981) HL [1981]) 1 All ER 1057, 144

Levin, Vladimir Re Levin House of Lords, 19/6.97, 48

Libyan Arab Foreign Bank v Bankers Trust Co. [1989], 88

Lopez-Ostra v Spain [1995] 20 EHRR, 123

Molins plc v GD SpA [2000] All ER (D) 107, 120

O'Connor, RJ v R [2004] EWCA (Crim) 1295, 2

OPRA v Peter Lavender (2002), 141

R v Benmerzouga and Meziane [2003], 6

R v Bhatt [2003] Canterbury Crown Court (unreported), 151

R v Chauhan; R v Holroyd [2000] CA (Criminal Division), 4

R v Clive Smith [2001] unreported, 19

R v Clucas and O'Rourke [1959] 1WLR 244, 2

R v Cushion [1997] 150 ALR 45, 2

R v Ghosh [1982] QB 1053, 3, 5, 8

R v Freeman & Hodgekinson [2003] unreported, 24, 41

R v Hayward, Jones, Purvis [2001] The Times. Feb 14., 48

R v Horseferry Road Magistrate's Court, ex parte Bennett [1994] 1 A.C. 42, 48

R v Jones, AJ HL [2002] 2 WLR 524, [2002]2All ER 113 CA (sub non R v Hayward, Jones and Purvis), 46

R v ICR Haulage Ltd [1944] KB 551, CA, 6

R v McDonnell [1966] 1 All ER 193, 7

R v Mitchell, Kirkup, Mason & Chapman [2004] unreported, 17

R v Olibutan [2003] The Times Nov 7, Court of Appeal, Criminal Division, 27

R v P & O European Ferries (Dover) [1990] 93 Cr.App. R72, 7

R v Pound, Green and others [2004] unreported, 35

R v Preddy, 8

R v Rosser [2003] unreported, 27

R v Steen, Andrews and Alexander [2003], 45

R v Theroux [1993] 2 SCR 5, 2

R v Peter Young [2003] unreported, 25, 36

R v Zlatie [1993] 2 SCR 29, 3

RBG Resources PLC v Rastogi (2002), 171

SASEA Finance Ltd v KPMG in 1999, 171

Scott v Metropolitan Police Commissioner [1975] AC 819 (HL), 2

Sears Group Properties Plc v Andrew Scrivener [1998] unreported, 7

Tax Commissioners v Pemsel [1891]AC531, 581, 127

Trail Smelter Arbitration, 33 Ajil, [1939], 182., 121, 124

Welham v DPP [1961] AC 103, 5

Wells Fargo Ltd v Citibank [1991], 88

Whitehouse v Jordan [1980] 1 All ER 650, 82 83

Woodland-Ferrari v UCL Group Retirement Benefits [2002], 141

United Nations

Abolition of Forced Labour, Convention 1957, 77

Illicit Trafficking in Narcotic Drugs and Psychotropic Substances, Convention against (Vienna) 1988, 77

Prevent, Suppress and Punish Trafficking in Persons, especially Women and Children, Protocol to 2000, 78

MARPOL Convention, 119, 124

Prevention of the Sale of Children, Child Prostitution and Child Pornography, Programme of Action, 78

Refugees Protocol, 71

Rights of the Child, Convention 1989, 77

Rights of the Child, Declaration 1959, 77

Suppress and Punish Trafficking in Persons, especially Women and Children, Protocol to Prevent (2000), 78

Suppression of Traffic of Persons and the Exploitation of the Prostitution of others, Convention on 1949, 78

Transnational Organised Crime, Convention against, 75

EU materials

Directive 2000/25/EC, 117

Directive 2001/115/EC, 172

Directive 2003 which makes it a criminal offence to send unsolicited e-mails, 171

Directive 2004/35/EC, 117

EEC/93/1836 (an environmental management and auditing scheme for European industry), 116

EEC/92?1973, 116

Employee Involvement Directive, 148

European Company Statute, 147

Euratom. Directive 75/436, 116

European Arrest Warrant, Framework Decision, 73

European Union Convention Regulation 1992, 73

Financial Instruments Markets Directive, 171

Illegal Immigration and Trafficking Directive, 74

Interest and Royalties Directive (2003/49/EC), 148

Jurisdiction and the Enforcement of Judgements in Civil and Commercial Matters, Convention on, (Brussels Convention) 1968, 148

Market Abuse Directive 2003/6/EC, 93

Prospectus Directive, 109, 113-114

Regulation EEC/93/1836, 116

Re-insurance Directive, 88

Risk-Based Capital Directive, 88

Solvency Directive, 88

Supervision of Credit Institutions on a Consolidated Basis, Directive 92/30, 88

Treaty of Rome in 1958, 88

other European

European Convention on Human Rights, 45, 47, 150

Guerra v Italy, (116/1996/735/932), 19 February 1998, 123

Lankhorst—Hohorst GmbH v Finanzampt Steinfort (Case C-324/00) [2003] STC 607, 169

Lopez-Ostra v Spain, (1995) 20 EHRR 277-300. ECHR, 123

Vcalan v Turkey ECJ Application 46221/99, 46

US statutes

Anti-terrorism and Effective Death Penalty Act of 1996, 78

Bank Secrecy Act 1970, 91

Declaration on the Rights and Duties of Man 1795, 123

Depository Institution Management Interlock Act 2000, 110, 113

Employee Retirement Income Security Act, 106

Exchange Act, 106

Graham-Leach-Bliley Act 1999, 113

Home Ownership Security Act 2003 (New Jersey), 109

Immigrant Responsibility Act 1996, 83

Internal Revenue Code, 129

International Emergency Economic Powers Act 2001, 136

International Money Laundering Abatement and Financial Anti-Terrorism Act 2001, 109, 113

Maine Truth in Lending Act 2004, 109

Massachusetts Predatory Home Loan Practices Act 2003, 109

Money Laundering Act 1986, 91

Nebraska Mortgage Bankers Registration and Licensing Act, 109

New Jersey Home Ownership Security Act 2002, 109

Non-Profit Integrity Act 2004 (US), 129

Oklahoma Anti-Predatory Lending Law New Jersey Home Ownership Security Act, 109

Patriot Act 2003, 91

Pledge Protection Act 2004, 79, 84

Predatory Home Loan Practices Act 2003 (Massachusetts), 129

Property 5, 73 CJS, section 963(h)(3)(b), 128

Sarbanes-Oxley Act 2002, 71, 113

Set-backed Securities Facilitation Act 2002 (Delaware), 113

Tax Code 2003, 129

Tax Reform Act 1986, 168

Trafficking Victims Protection Act 2003, 79

Truth in Lending Act 2004 (Maine), 109

United States Code, Title 18, 71

US law reports

Department of Justice v Muldrew, Darby and Bermington., 71

Edwards v Phillips, 373F.2d 616 (10th Circuit), 128

Humanitarian Law Project v United States Department of Justice, (2003), 352 Fed 382(9th Circuit), 136

Madigan v Telemarketing Associates (2003), 129

Montessori School of Paris, Inc. v Commissioner, 75 T.C.480(1980), 136

United States v Muldrew, Giles Robert Hugh Darby and David John Bermington, 72

Canadian materials

Anti-Terrorism Act 2001, 109, 113, 136

Criminal Code, 42, 130-131, 136

Criminal Code (amendments) 2001, 136

Foreign Missions Amendment Act 2001, 136

Proceeds of Crime Act 2001, 136

Public Safety Act 2001, 136

Public Safety Act and Proceeds of Crime Act., 130

Other national and international materials

Basle Capital Adequacy Accord 1988, 89

Basle II Capital Accord 2004, 89

Basle Revised Concordant on Principles for the Supervision of Banks' Foreign Establishments, International Legal Materials, 89

Bustament Code (some Latin American countries), 122

Commonwealth Scheme for Mutual Assistance in Criminal Matters 1986, 122

European Convention of Human Rights 1950, 28

Extradition Treaty 2003 US-UK (still to be ratified by the US), 73

Extradition Treaty 2003 UK-US, 71

Financial Action Task Force, 71, 91, 128

Full Mutual Assistance Treaty UK-US, 73

Geneva Convention on Long-Range Trans-boundary Air Pollution 1979, 124

German Federal Civil Code (amendments) 2002, 136

Havana Convention on Private International Law 1935, 122

International Convention on Civil and Political Rights, 71

ILO Convention 180, 83

ILO Convention 182, 77

IMF Report on Financial Stability Assessment Programme Protocol to Prevent, Suppress and Punish Trafficking in Persons, Especially Women and Children, in 2000, 79

Kyoto Protocol to the Climate Convention 1997, 117

MARPOL Convention 1995, 124

Memoranda of Understanding (between banking supervisors) with Korea, 95

Mortgage Bank Act 2004 (Germany), 113

Mortgage Bankers Registration and Licensing Act 2004 (Nebraska), 113

Mutual Assistance Treaty Switzerland-US, 113

OECD Corporate Governance Convention 1998., 113

OECD Money Laundering Code, 94

OECD Transfer Pricing Guidelines 1995, 94

Rio de Janeiro Declaration on Environment and Development, 123

Trial Smelter arbitration case Trail Smelter Arbitration, 33 Ajil [1939], 121, 182

CHAPTER ONE

AN EXPLANATION OF UK FRAUD

Abstract

This chapter explores the concept of serious fraud and fraud and fraudsters in society. It will explain the concept of fraud with the emphasis being on the fraud which is called economic or white-collar crime. It concludes this section of the chapter with a critical analysis of the UK's fraud offence bill.

Fraud in society is explored as is the mind and culpability of the fraudster, showing that fraud does not spring from one root cause but from a number of sources ranging from status and financial frustration, inadequate socialisation, conflict of cultural values and even genetic deviations and greed. Fraud is a crime and so crime has to be analysed to discover how fraud fits in.

The Concept of Serious Fraud

Fraud is defined in the Oxford Dictionary[1] as "the quality of being deceitful; criminal deception; the using of false representations to obtain an unjust advantage or to injure the rights or interests of another; a dishonest trick".

English law does not provide a definition of fraud, nor is there a substantive offence of fraud in criminal law[2]. Common law fraud consists of "a false statement of fact which is made by one party to a transaction to the other knowingly, or without belief in its truth or recklessly without caring whether it be true or false, with the intent that it should be acted upon by the other party and which was in fact acted upon".[3]

'Fraud' involves the notion of detrimentally affecting or risking the property of others, their rights or interests in property, or an opportunity or advantage which the law accords them with respect to property. Conversely it is not fraud to detrimentally affect or risk something in or in relation to which others have no right or interest or in respect of which the law accords them no opportunity or advantage.

Fraud is perceived by some[4] as criminal and unethical behaviour and the term 'white-collar crime' is often used as an alternative to the word fraud[5]. White collar crime is sometimes classed as crimes of the rich, sometimes as organised crime, or crime of an organised and pre-meditated behaviour, whilst others might view those same as the problems which arise when a business created for an honest purpose, is turned into a criminal one. All this suggests that there is no single wide field of white collar crime or economic crime or business crime but that the word "fraud" gives a rough imagery rather than a fixed definition of this type of activity.

---

1. Oxford English Dictionary, 2003, Oxford University Press
2. In a recent case, Cannane v J Cannane Pty Ltd (in liquidation) [1998] 153 ALR 163 at 172, the judge said "It is notoriously difficult to provide an exhaustive statement as to what is involved in the concepts of 'fraud' and 'intent to defraud'.
3. Derry v Peek [1889] 14 App Cas 337 at 374.
4. Page F, "What is fraud?", New Law Journal, 28th Feb 1997. In this article the writer says that fraud is not yet universally recognised or understood as a crime in the way that theft is because for many centuries it was purely a civil matter.
   Waters, T, "Fraud in prospect and hindsight", Fraud Intelligence, Jan 2002. In his article, Mr Waters says that the UK authorities are currently "grappling with difficult questions concerning the definition, prosecution and regulatory treatment of fraud".
5. See Croall, H, (1992), "White Collar Crime", Open University Press, at pg19.

In Illinois, however, fraud is much less precisely defined. Fraud in Illinois law does not specify itself but is the term generally used for deception, not necessarily with the result of financial loss. The Illinois Supreme Court held in Re Eugene Lee Armentrot and others[6] that "Fraud encompasses a broad range of behaviour, including anything calculated to deceive, whether it be by direct falsehood or by innuendo, by speech or by silence, by word of mouth or by look or gesture. Fraud includes the suppression of the truth, as well as the presentation of false information". Here, fraud is defined as anything calculated to deceive and it is clear and well established Illinois law.

Not only does English law not define fraud, there is no substantive offence of fraud in English criminal law even though there are offences that cover fraudulent activity and fraudulent conduct involving deception and dishonesty. The contemporary term "fraud" can cover a wide spectrum of criminal activity ranging from minor offences such as benefit fraud to sophisticated frauds involving complicated financial transactions and large sums of money. The offences of theft and deception are contained in the Theft Acts 1968 and 1978. There is also the common law offence of 'conspiracy to defraud' and the offence of 'fraudulent trading[7]'. An English example of the offence of deceit is the case of R v Clucas and O'Rourke[8] in which Clucas and O'Rourke were convicted of a number of offences of fraud in wagering. They had operated a scheme whereby one of them would contact a bookmaker giving a false name and pretend to be engaged on a works contract. He would ask the bookmaker to accept bets on behalf of men on a building site. When there were winnings, Clucas and O'Rourke collected them; when there were losses of any substantial amount, they moved on to another place. Section 17 of the Gaming Act 1845 provided that "every person shall, by any fraud…in wagering on the event of any game, sport, past-time or exercise, win from any person to himself, or any other or others, any sum of money or valuable thing, shall be deemed guilty of obtaining such money or valuable thing by a false pretence." The question put to the jury was, "Were the accused at the time they made these bets with bookmakers intending to cheat and defraud those bookmakers by not paying losses?" The jury decided they were. Clucas and O'Rourke's deceit was the concealment of their intention to move on without paying if they lost on the bets.

More Case-law on the offence of conspiracy to defraud

In later case-law, in the case of R v Cushion[9], Justice Williams said that fraud really means no more than dishonesty. This upholds the broad meaning of fraud consisting of the two elements of dishonesty and deprivation but not deceit as was given in the 1975 case Scott v Metropolitan Police Commissioner[10]. Yet the element of deceit, though not included in the Scott case, was classed as an element of fraud in the case R v Theroux[11] when Justice McLachlin said: "To establish the actus reus of fraud, the Crown must establish beyond a reasonable doubt that the accused practised deceit, lied, or committed some other fraudulent act. It will be necessary to show that the act is one which a reasonable person would see as dishonest. Deprivation or the risk of deprivation must then be shown to have occurred as a matter of fact. To establish the *mens rea* of fraud the Crown must prove that the accused knowingly undertook the acts which constitute the falsehood, deceit or other fraudulent means, and that the accused was aware that deprivation could result from such conduct."

---

6   In re Eugene Lee Armentrout, Jay Robert Grodner, Charles A. Petersen, Kim Edward Presbrey, William H Weir and William John Truemper, Jr, 99 Ill.2d 242 [1983]

7   An example of which is the case R J O'Connor v R [2004] EWCA (Crim) 1295, in which a managing director of a company organised a scheme whereby he would post shirts to previous customers, whose bank details he had kept, and charged then for these shirts without sending out any documentation with the goods explaining the basis upon which it had been sent, whether or when the recipient would be charged for it or how he should go about rejecting or returning it; he was found guilty and appealed on the grounds of no case to answer and on fresh evidence that was not given at trial, but his appeal was dismissed.

8   R v Clucas and O'Rourke [1959] 1WLR 244

9   R v Cushion [1997] 150 ALR 45

10   Scott v Metropolitan Police Commissioner [1975] AC 819 (HL)

11   [1993] 2 SCR 5

In the case of R v Zlatie[12] it was held that non-disclosure can constitute fraud if the non-disclosure could be viewed by a reasonable person as dishonest. Such failure to disclose information would be with the intention to cause pecuniary loss to the other party. Case-law supports criminal sanctions for fraud when it means: to deprive by deceit or to dishonestly deprive, negligent misrepresentation which puts the property of others at risk, and false representation to obtain an unjust advantage. Today, the criminal law test used in fraud cases is the test for dishonesty only and is the 1982 decision of the Court of Appeal in R v Ghosh.[13] It has two strands, those being that the defendant's actions must not only be dishonest by the ordinary standards of reasonable and honest people, but that he must also have realised that his actions were dishonest according to those standards.

Fraud is not classed as an offence by UK statute

English courts still have not ventured to lay down precisely what constitutes fraud.[14]

Fraud in its many forms may be said to be any behaviour by which one person intends to gain a dishonest advantage over another. It includes such diverse acts as extortion, embezzlement, forgery, unfair competition, commercial espionage and other white-collar crimes; and serious frauds consist of the most serious of these types of crime, namely complex embezzlement, long firm frauds and commercial and organised crimes.[15]

It can be said that, reduced to its basic level, fraud follows an incremental pattern limited only by the perpetrator's greed, opportunities and success or otherwise in concealing previous losses. Greed is the motivation.[16] Concealment is an essential part of most large-scale, prolonged frauds, this being concealment of losses, concealment of blame, misrepresentation[17] or manipulation.

Clinard and Yeager (1980)[18] called it organisational crime and Farrell and Swigert (1985)[19] studied the complex organisations in which such crimes are committed. Such organisations usually have high reputations and the crime of serious fraud is perpetrated as an ongoing illegal activity as explained by Sutherland.[20] Such corporations are organised around a common goal to achieve profit and adopt a structure that is the most efficient and rational means of maximising this goal.

---

12 [1993] 2 SCR 29

13 R v Ghosh [1982] QB 1053.

14 Editorial, New Law Journal, 21 May 1999, "The definition of fraud" states that the most disturbing revelation of the 1999 Fraud Advisory Panel's annual report is that, 13 years after the Roskill Report, there is still no clarity as to how best to tackle the growing menace of white collar crime. There is no legal definition of fraud and government departments, professional bodies, business organisations and the police all have their own working definitions. The article states that "even within the police there is no agreed definition or consistent recording practice. The City of London police statistics are analysed by value according to type of fraud, but the Metropolitan Police statistics use the number of cases per type of fraud. The West Yorkshire Police figures cover six-monthly periods and are broken down between three offices and are analysed by victim type…."

15 Geis, G, Meir, RF, Salinger, LM, "White Collar Crime", 3rd ed, 1995, Free Press.

16 In Croall, H, (1992), "White Collar Crime", Open University Press, at pg 73, Croall asserts that "..As in the case of conventional crime, a combination of individual, cultural and structural factors must be considered and white collar crime cannot simply be attributed to greed, acquisitiveness or even capitalism and its associated values. Greed or a desire for success may well provide initial motivations…"

17 Spencer Bower, "Actionable Misrepresentation", 4th ed, 2000, pp108-9
"A representor may have acted on inquiry or materials which would not have satisfied a person of normal intelligence, much less a trained judge, but this counts for nothing if the belief—the individual being who he was—really and truly existed. Belief is nonetheless belief because it is irrational".

18 Clinard, MB & Yeager.P.C, "Corporate Crime", 1980, Free Press New York.

19 Farrell, RA & Swigert.V.L, "The corporation in criminology: new directions for research", 1985, Journal of Research in Crime & Delinquency, 83-94.

20 Sutherland, EA, "White collar Crime", 1949, Holt, Rinehart and Winston.

Fraud as an offence as stipulated by the Home Office. Although there is no statutory offence of fraud in the United Kingdom, the Home Office sets out the offences that it considers are offences of fraud in *Counting Rules for Recording Crime*, a Home Office Publication in April 2003, some of which are financial fraud offences which this work will concentrate on, these being

False statements by Company Directors, etc. under Theft Act 1968 section 19

"..an officer of a body corporate or incorporated association (or person purporting to act as such), with intent to deceive members or creditors of the body corporate or association about its affairs, publishes or concurs in publishing a written statement of account which to his knowledge is or may be misleading, false or deceptive in a material particular..."

-   Common law offence of conspiracy to defraud;

-   Carrying on business with intent to defraud under section 458 of the Companies Act 1985 and Fraudulent Trading under the same section

-   "…any business of a company is carried on with intent to defraud creditors of the company or creditors of any other person, or for any fraudulent purpose.".[21]

-   fraudulent misappropriation of funds under the Proceeds of Crime Act 2002[22]

-   Engaging in a course of conduct which creates a false or misleading impression as to the market in or the price or value of investments, contrary to section 47(2) of the Financial Services Act 1986[23]

-   Obtaining pecuniary advantage by deception (apart from cheque and credit card fraud) under Theft Act 1968 section 16

-   Conspiracy to defraud (apart from cheque and credit card fraud) under Common Law and Criminal Justice Act 1987 section 12

---

21   A recent case of Fraudulent Trading was <u>R v Freeman and Hodgkinson [2003]</u>. The case concerned the failure and bankruptcy of the tank container manufacturer Universal Bulk Handling Ltd . This was a loss making business whose performance was fraudulently hidden by the two defendants.. The company was formed in 1958 and became a wholly owned subsidiary of Hadleigh plc in 1990, after which business was poor and the defendants began to falsify the accounts, concealing the true state of affairs from Hadleigh plc and the auditors. In 1999 Hadleigh carried out an investigation which led to the discovery of Universal Bulk Handling's fraudulent trading, an overall discrepancy of £11.5 million between what the accounts declared to be owing to the company and what in fact the company owed to both its suppliers and its customers, which caused Hadleigh to be placed into receivership.

22   An example of such a case is <u>Cronos Containers NV v Palatin [2002] EWHC 2819</u>. The defendants were Mr and Mrs Palatin and Klamath Enterprises SA. Mr Palatin owned the shares of Klamath. Mr Palatin in 1994, defrauded the claimants by causing 5 separate payments from one of the claimants' customers to be paid into an account at Barclays controlled by the Palatins. The monies were then used to improve a property owned by Klamath.

23   An example is the case of <u>R v Chauhan; R v Holroyd [2000] CA (Criminal Division)</u>. In this case the defendants engaged in a course of conduct which created a false or misleading impression in the company's (International Food Machinery plc) accounts thereby permitting the company to proceed to flotation when it would otherwise have not been able to do so, and created a false and misleading impression as to the value of the shares in International Food Machinery plc, and backdating sales contracts and inflating stock values to make the company seem more profitable than it was.

- Suppression, etc of documents, under the Theft Act 1968 section 20

- Evasion of Liability by Deception, under Theft Act 1978 section 2

- Assisting another to retain the benefit of criminal conduct, under Criminal Justice Act 1988 section 93A

- Concealing or transferring proceeds of criminal conduct, under Criminal Justice Act 1988 section 93C

- Cartel offences, under The Enterprise Act 2002 sections 183 and 185

- Forgery, under Forgery and Counterfeiting Act 1981 section 1

- Copying a false instrument, under Forgery and Counterfeiting Act section 2

- False Accounting under the Theft Act 1968 section 17(1)

"..a person dishonestly with a view to gain for himself or another or with intent to cause loss to another—

(a) destroys, defaces, conceals or falsifies any account or any record or document made or required for any accounting purpose; or

(b) in furnishing information for any purpose produces or makes use of any account, or any such record or document as aforesaid, which to his knowledge is or may be misleading, false or deceptive in a material particular…"

These are some of the classifications which the police in the United Kingdom use for bringing charges of fraud. Although an analysis of the charges brought by the SFO in five years cases to 2003 show that the SFO used only five charges in total, they being, the charge of fraudulent trading in 18% of these cases, false accounting in 14% of cases, theft in 12% of cases, corruption in 8% of cases, the remaining cases, 48%, brought on the charge of conspiracy to defraud. The analysis proves that the Serious Fraud Office uses most commonly the charge of "conspiracy to defraud". This most used charge therefore deserves examination.

The common law offence of conspiracy to defraud

A person who agrees with one or more other persons by dishonesty[24] to deprive a person of something which is his or to which he would be or might be entitled, or to injure some proprietary right of another person[25], is guilty of conspiracy to defraud[26] in common law.

Following the implementation of section 12 of the Criminal Justice Act 1987, the Director of Public Prosecutions issued guidance as to the circumstances in which it would be appropriate to prefer a charge of conspiracy to defraud.

"Where an indictment contains counts alleging substantive offences and a related conspiracy count, the prosecution must justify the joinder or be required to elect to proceed on the substantive or conspiracy counts. Where substantive counts meet the justice of the case a conspiracy count will rarely need to be added but may be added where the substantive counts do not represent the overall criminality of the case. Where a Crown Prosecutor is

---

24 The meaning of dishonesty is given in R v Ghosh [1982] QB 1053
25 See Scott v Metropolitan Police Commissioners [1975] AC 819.
26 The meaning of defraud is found in Welham v DPP [1961] AC 103.

proposing to lay a conspiracy count, before doing so he should give consideration to the risk of the trial being lengthy and complicated or otherwise causing unfairness to defendants."[27]

The maximum penalty provided by section 12 Criminal Justice Act for the offence of conspiracy to defraud is ten years.[28] The charge of conspiracy to defraud is much used today because in a conspiracy to defraud charge it is only necessary to prove the essentials of a charge. Tax evasion schemes, for example, are particularly likely to be caught by conspiracy to defraud charge. To bring complexity to the charge, conspiracy to defraud can occur over more than one territory. An agreement formed in one territorial area may be aimed at people in another area or other areas, or may reach into such areas in the course of its performance. This is an aspect of criminal conspiracy that has made it difficult to relate to the theory of territoriality which has so much influence on common law rules concerning the administration of criminal justice. The Criminal Justice Act 1993 makes provision for such problems by making provision about the jurisdiction of courts in England and Wales in relation to certain offences of dishonesty and blackmail.

It states that Group A offences are offences under the Theft Act 1968, under the Theft Act 1978, under the Forgery and Counterfeiting Act 1981 and under common law offence of cheating in relation to the public revenue. It states that Group B offences are conspiracy to commit Group A offences, conspiracy to defraud, attempting to commit a Group A offence and incitement to commit a Group A offence. It does not matter whether such a guilty person is British or not, as long the offence had effect on England and Wales and gives extended jurisdiction over certain conspiracies. If persons conspire to defraud and that fraud is to be committed abroad, as long as they conspire in the UK, they can be charged with an offence, although they planned to commit the offence in other countries. Before the Criminal Justice Act 1993, they would only be charged in the UK if they conspired to defraud in the United Kingdom, even if the conspiracy to defraud occurred abroad.

This legislation was used in 2003 to convict two Al-Qaeda fund-raisers to 11 years imprisonment.[29] The two defendants had conspired to defraud persons and companies in the United Kingdom in order to commit other crimes abroad. The judge said to Benmerzouga and Meziane,[30] "You have both been convicted by the unanimous verdict of the jury of conspiracy to defraud in respect of banks and credit card companies and entering into a fund-raising arrangement for the purpose of terrorism."

But a charge of conspiracy to defraud, although the most used charge by the SFO, is no longer used in the form of the offence of conspiracy to defraud by a limited company, although this charge has been successfully used in the past in the case of R v I.C.R. Haulage Ltd[31] in which the appellant company and nine individuals were charged with conspiracy to defraud by overcharging. One of the nine individual defendants was the managing director of the company. The company was convicted and appealed and the appeal was dismissed. In his judgement, Justice Staple used another such case, Director of Public Prosecutions v Kent and Sussex Contractors Ltd,[32] to support his argument in which Lord Caldecote CJ said "The real point we have to decide…is whether a company is capable of an act of will or of a state of mind, so as to be able to form an intention to deceive or to have knowledge of the truth or falsity of a statement…The offences created by the regulation are those of doing something with intent to deceive or of making a statement known to be false

27 Crown Prosecution Service Practice Direction dated 9 May 1987.

28 In 1998, there were 1175 cases of conspiracy to defraud (in England and Wales) with an average sentence of 2 years. None of the convictions carried the full possible sentence of ten years. Source: Crime and Criminal Justice Unit (RDS), Home Office, October 2000.

29 "Al-Queda fundraisers sentenced to 11 years", Times Newspapers April1, 2003. It is to be noted that the maximum penalty for this offence is ten years. Home Office statistics show that, since 1995, there has never been any person sentenced for the full maximum sentence of ten years. Source: House of Commons Hansard written Answers for 25 Jan 2001.

30 The case was R v Benmerzouga and Meziane [2003]., unreported. The two men lived in Leicester and had collected the names and credit card details of almost 200 different bank accounts on computer disks and enveloped found littered around their homes and cars. The cards were sent to associates across Europe allowing them to fraudulently amass more than £200, 000 for terrorist causes.

31 [1944] KB 551, Court of Criminal Appeal

32 [1944] KB 146

in a material particular. There was ample evidence on the facts as stated in the special case, that the company, by the only people who could act or speak or think for it, had done both these things, and I can see nothing in any of the authorities to which we have been referred which requires us to say that a company is incapable of being found guilty of the offences with which the respondents have been charged." In the same case Justice Macnaghten said, "It is true that a corporation can only have knowledge and form an intention through its human agents, but circumstances may be such that the knowledge and intention of the agent must be imputed to the body corporate…If the responsible agent of a company, acting within the scope of his authority, puts forward on its behalf a document which he knows to be false and by which he intends to deceive, I apprehend that according to the authorities that my Lord has cited, his knowledge and intention must be imputed to the company."

Today, companies are prosecuted by bringing charges of conspiracy to defraud against identified senior individuals.[33] Whether this is the best course or not is yet to be settled. In the case of a one-man company, though, that man could not be charged with conspiring to defraud with the limited company, as was seen in R v McDonnell[34] where McDonnell was charged with conspiring to defraud with a limited company of which he was a sole director. Directors are charged instead of the company because in many cases the company concerned becomes insolvent at the same time and directors of an insolvent company will become liable to contribute to the assets of the company in liquidation, although this liability does not depend on fraud being proved.

A conspiracy to defraud charge (see the writer's survey results of SFO cases in Appendix 1) is often used because the SFO have been successful as it can more easily prove that one individual had the necessary *mens rea*, much like the corporate liability in R v P & O European Ferries (Dover)[35] which, though not a fraud case, was a case of corporate liability and in which it was established that it was necessary to be able to identify one individual who had the necessary *mens rea*.

The agreement to commit a crime of recklessness can be classed as a conspiracy because the central focus of conspiracy to defraud has been upon the requisite mutual state. So the scope of common law conspiracy to defraud is very wide.

The SFO has used the charge of conspiracy to defraud in cases of misleading the markets and insider trading. Insider trading is very difficult to prosecute and there are very few cases brought to trial in the United Kingdom. The Guinness case,[36] although it involved the manipulation of share price, was not brought to trial as an insider trading case but on charges of theft and false accounting. The Guinness case involved a financial operation to ensure that the Guinness share price was supported during the take-over bid for Distillers plc. The bid for Distillers was largely to be satisfied by Guinness shares and therefore the higher the price of Guinness shares, the fewer shares would have to be issued in consideration. It can be argued that this was a case of conspiracy to defraud, although this charge was not used in this case.

The 'conspiracy' can be argued to be as follows: During the period of the take-over bid in 1986, a very large proportion of Guinness shares were acquired by a group of supporters who were given company indemnity against loss; they were also given success fees. Among these supporters were the Guinness Pension Funds. These Funds were the Martins Fund which bought 36, 000 Guinness shares, the Irish Fund which bought 100, 425, 986 Guinness shares, the Senior Executive Fund which bought 87, 000 Guinness shares. Mr Roux bought 5, 000, 000 Guinness shares. Mr Parnes bought 2, 950, 000 Guinness shares. Mr Parnes was paid £3, 350, 000 in 1986 when he submitted an invoice for "Corporate Finance and Success Fee".

A conspiracy to defraud charge can also be brought as a private criminal prosecution as in the case of Sears Group Properties Plc v Andrew Scrivener[37] in which Sears sued the group technical director for conspiracy to defraud the company between 1991 and 1997, alleging that Scrivener conspired with suppliers to overcharge on contracts for fitting out retail premises. Sears claimed damages and an injunction restraining Scrivener from using or disclosing confidential information.

---

33   Pettet, B, "Company Law", 2001, Pearson Education Ltd. pg 32.

34   [1966] 1 All ER 193

35   [1990] 93 Cr. App. R 72

36   Guinness plc v Saunders and Another [1987] BCC 271.

37   Sears Group Properties v Andrew Scrivener [1998] unreported

The Law Commission reported[38] on the scope of creating a general offence of fraud that juries and all other parties concerned would find easier to understand that the charge of conspiracy to defraud. It proposed that the eight deception offences under the Theft Acts be meshed to cover the various actions alleged in serious fraud indictments. The Theft Act offences usually employed to prosecute fraud, overlap and are often criticised as being too technical.[39] The Commission said that the statutory offences do not always give an accurate picture of the fraud in question. The Commission quoted Lord Hardwicke

"Fraud is infinite, and were a court once to…define strictly the species of evidences of it, the jurisdiction would be cramped, and perpetually eluded by new schemes which the fertility of man's invention would contrive."

The new Fraud Bill does not model the fraud offence on the offence of conspiracy to defraud which it considers to be too wide. In arriving at a new definition of fraud, the Commission quotes Stephen[40]

"…two elements at least are essential…first, deceit or an intention to deceive or in some cases mere secrecy; and secondly, either actual injury or possible injury or an intent to expose some person either to actual injury or to a risk of possible injury by means of that deceit or secrecy."

The Commission stated that it accepts these two elements and adds that of dishonesty.[41] The new offence of fraud will not require proof of deception as the Commission rejects the concept of deception which must operate on the mind of the victim. The Commission stated that the concept of dishonesty in the fraud offence emphasises the act of the perpetrator and need not be proved to have caused the loss in question. So the offence of fraud would mean making a positive misstatement, or dishonestly making a false representation, or dishonestly failing to disclose information to another. In all cases, it is not necessary that any consequence is brought about by the fraud. The draft Bill does not contain any special defences and the offence has a maximum of ten years.

A critical analysis of the UK fraud offence as proposed

The UK's proposed fraud offence as recommended by the Law Commission[42] may appease the public who are dismayed by the rising rate of "fraud". The new offence will be based on misrepresentation, non-disclosure and abuse of trust. There is to be a new offence also of obtaining services dishonestly and this offence will not require the proof of misrepresentation and of non-disclosure as the fraud offence will require. The Law Commission had rejected the offence of conspiracy to defraud, stating that conspiracy is too close to dishonesty. This new fraud offence is compared with the old offence of conspiracy to defraud to see exactly what the differences are that warrant a new offence of fraud.

The full recommendations of the Commissioners are as follows

"FRAUD

1   Any person who, with intent to make a gain or to cause loss or to expose another to the risk of loss, dishonestly

(1) makes a false representation, or

38 Law Commission Report No. 276, "FRAUD—Report on a reference under section 3(1)(e) of the Law Commissions Act 1965, presented to Parliament in July 2002. This report examines the law on fraud, and in particular considers whether it is readily comprehensible to juries; is adequate for effective prosecution is fair to potential defendants; meets the need of developing technology including electronic means of transfer; and makes recommendations to improve the law in these respects.
39 For example, in the case of R v Preddy, appeals by the defendants against the accusation of mortgage frauds were allowed on the basis that the bank credits which they had been charged with obtaining under section 15(1) of the Theft Act 1968 were not 'property belonging to another'.
40 Stephen, "History of Criminal Law", 1883.
41 The concept of dishonesty is defined in R v Ghosh [1982] QB 1053
42 (Law Com No 276) Fraud Report on a reference under section 3(1)(e) of the Law Commissions Act 1965, presented July 2002, Cm 5560.

(2) fails to disclose information to another person which

   (a) he or she is under a legal duty to disclose, or

   (b) is of a kind which the other person trusts him or her to disclose, and is information which in the circumstances it is reasonable to expect him or her to disclose, or

(3) abuses a position in which he or she is expected to safeguard, or not to act against, the financial interests of another person, and does so without the knowledge of that person or of anyone acting on that person's behalf,

should be guilty of an offence of fraud.

2   Fraud should be triable either way, and on conviction on indictment should be punishable with up to ten years imprisonment.

OBTAINING SERVICES BY DECEPTION

3   Any person who by any dishonest act obtains services in respect of which payment is required, with intent to avoid payment, should be guilty of an offence of obtaining services dishonestly.

4   The offence of obtaining services dishonestly should be triable either way, and on conviction on indictment should be punishable with up to five years' imprisonment.

ABOLITION OF EXISTING OFFECNCES

5   All the deception offences under the Theft Acts 1968-1996, and conspiracy to defraud, should be abolished."

The new fraud offence has the *mens rea* of intention on the part of the defendant. Conspiracy to defraud is the attempting to defraud and the incitement to defraud—the same elements as the fraud offence. The fraud offence intends that all the deception offences under the Theft Acts and conspiracy to defraud will be abolished. But what of the cases where the offence occurred abroad?

At present the charge of conspiracy to defraud is the most used charge by the Serious Fraud Office because in a conspiracy to defraud charge it is only necessary to prove the essentials of a charge. (Tax and VAT evasion schemes, for example, are particularly likely to be caught by conspiracy to defraud charge). To bring complexity to the charge, conspiracy to defraud can occur over more than one territory. An agreement formed in one territorial area may be aimed at people in another area or other areas, or may reach into such areas in the course of its performance or plot. This is an aspect of criminal conspiracy that has made it difficult to relate to the theory of territoriality which has so much influence on common law rules concerning the administration of criminal justice. The Criminal Justice Act 1993 makes provision for such problems by making provision about the jurisdiction of courts in England and Wales in relation to certain offences of dishonesty and blackmail.

It states that Group A offences are offences under the Theft Act 1968, under the Theft Act 1978, under the Forgery and Counterfeiting Act 1981 and under the common law offence of cheating in relation to the public revenue. It states that Group B offences are conspiracy to commit Group A offences, conspiracy to defraud, attempting to commit a Group A offence and incitement to commit a Group A offence. It does not matter whether a guilty person is British or not, as long as the offence had effect in England and Wales and gives extended jurisdictions over certain conspiracies. If persons conspire to defraud and that fraud is to be committed abroad, as long as they conspire in the UK, they can be charged with an offence, although they planned to commit the offence in other countries. Before the Criminal Justice Act 1993, they would be charged in the UK only if they conspired to defraud in the UK, even if the conspiracy to defraud occurred abroad. The new fraud offence adjusts this 1993 Act. For instance, it deletes from section 2 Criminal Justice Act 1993, the parts relating to sections 15 and 16 of the Theft Act 1968 but it still leaves the following in section 2, namely that Group A offences are

-   section 1 Theft Act–theft,

-   section 17 Theft Act–false accounting,

-   section 19 Theft Act–false statements by company directors,

-   section 20(2) Theft Act–procuring execution of valuable security by deception,

- section 21 Theft Act–blackmail, and

- section 22 Theft Act—handling stolen goods.

This is ambiguous; it seems to mean that theft is not fraud, that false accounting is not fraud, that false statements by company directors are not frauds, that procuring execution of valuable security by deception is not a fraud, etc. The case of Barings Futures (Singapore) pte Ltd v Deloitte and Touche[43] is a case that illustrates the false statement by a company director. If an accountant signs off incorrect audits, those statements are false statements and a fraud.

At present, the common law offence of conspiracy to defraud can technically be committed by a limited company, even though this has not occurred since 1944 in the case of R v ICR Haulage Ltd[44] in which the limited company and nine individuals were charged with conspiracy to defraud by overcharging and in the case of Director of Public Prosecutions v Kent and Sussex Contractors Ltd[45] Justice McNaughten said "It is true that a corporation can only have knowledge and form an intention through its agents, but circumstances may be such that the knowledge and intention of the agent must be imputed to the body corporate...If the responsible agent of a company, acting within the scope of his authority, puts forward on its behalf a document which he knows to be false and by which he intends to deceive, I apprehend that according to the authorities that my Lord has cited, his knowledge and intention must be imputed to the company". On this matter of fraud by a company, the Law Commission's draft Bill is silent.

Looking at the mechanics of recording crime to see what will result from a new fraud offence—even in 1999—*The New Law Journal* editorial[46] said that "...there is not even an authoritative measure of the extent of fraud in the UK. Police and private sector estimates vary from £400 million a year to £5 billion and the Association of British Insurers puts the total at nearer £16 billion...Even within the police there is no agreed definition or consistent recording practice. The City of London Police statistics are analysed by value according to type of fraud. The West Yorkshire Police figures cover 6 monthly periods and are broken down...and analysed by victim type..."

The DTI submitted that 1, 000 persons were charged in 1993 with the offence "conspiracy to defraud" and that 321 were convicted in the UK[47]. In the UK Commons Hansard Written answers for 25 January 2001[48], the figures given for the common law offence of conspiracy to defraud were 1003, 1069, 1119, 1175 and 1174 persons charged during the years 1995, 1996, 1997, 1998 and 1999 respectively and that the actual convictions were 383, 477, 500, 466 and 420 respectively for those same years. In a population of over 63 million persons, this is hardly cause for alarm and the charge of conspiracy to defraud cannot be the culprit for the extent of fraud nor for the lack of conviction for fraud crimes.

The Home Office Counting Rules for Recording Crime[49] give the standard ways in which the Home Office counts fraud and forgery for the UK. For Home Office statistics, the following are counted as "fraud and forgery"[50]—

- frauds by company directors,[51]

- false accounting,[52]

---

43 [2003] EWHC 2371 (Ch)
44 [1944]KB 551
45 [1944] KB 146
46 Editorial, New Law Journal, 21 May 1999, Vol 149 No 6889 p 737
47 Memorandum submitted by Dr Elaine M Drage, Director, Trade Policy 2, DTI, to Select Committee on International Development, 2000.
48 http://www.parliament.the-stationery-office.co.uk/pa/cm200001/cmhansrd
49 Home Office Research Development & Statistics Directorate, April 2003.
50 Home Office Research Development & Statistics Directorate, April 2003.
51 Recorded as crime type 51-maximum sentence seven years.
52 Recorded as crime type 52-maximum sentence seven years.

- cheque and credit card fraud,[53]

- other frauds,[54]

- bankruptcy and insolvency offences,[55]

- forgery of drug prescription,[56]

- other forgery,[57] and

- fraud, forgery associated with vehicle or driver records.[58]

The new fraud offence is silent as to whether it makes the relevant sections of all these acts repealed, except that the proposed Fraud Act will that—

(1) abolish the common law offence of conspiracy to defraud, Criminal Justice Act 1988;

(2) the Visiting Forces Act 1952 section 3, would have inserted "the Fraud Act 2002"[59] in paragraph 3;(this is not included in the Home Office list under fraud);

(3) the Theft Act 1968 will have omitted s 15 and 16, and sections 24 and 25 will be altered;

(4) Criminal Law Act 1977 will omit section 5(2) ; (this is not counted by the Home Office as fraud);

(5) Theft Act 1978 will omit section 4(2)(a) and 5(1);

(6) Limitation Act 1980 will have section 5(b) altered ; (this is not counted as fraud by the Home Office);

(7) Finance Act 1982 section 11(1) will change ; (this is not counted by the Home Office as fraud);

(8) Nuclear Materials Act 1983 section 1(1)(d) is altered;(this does not feature in Home Office Counting rules ;

(9) Police and Criminal Evidence Act 1984 section 1(8)is altered;

(10) Criminal Justice Act 1987 section 12 is omitted ;(this is on the Home Office Counting rules);

In total, the new Fraud Act will repeal Theft Act 1968 sections 15, 15A, 15B, 16, 18(1), 20(3), 24A(3), Criminal Law Act section 5(2), Nuclear Material Offences Act 1983 section 1(1)(d), Criminal Justice Act 1987 section 12, Criminal Justice Act 1993section 1(2)(b) and 2(b), 5(b), 6(1) and 6(5)., Theft Amendment Act 1996 sections 1, 3(2) and 4 and Criminal Justice and Court Services Act 2000, schedule 6 paragraph 1

This will not clear up the confusion of recording fraud by the Home Office, not to mention the confusion that occurs when various police forces count crimes in various ways and so the public will be none the wiser about the true extent of fraud.

---

53 Recorded as crime type 53A.

54 Recorded as crime type 53B.

55 Recorded as crime type 55-maximum sentence seven years.

56 Recorded as crime type 60-maximum sentence ten years.

57 Recorded as crime type 61-maximum sentence ten years.

58 Recorded as crime type 814-maximum sentence two years.
    These offences counted under the eight above headings, comprise offences under the Theft Act 1968, Companies Act 1985, Protection of Depositors Act 1963, Theft Act 1978, Criminal Justice Act 1987, Fraudulent Mediums Act 1951, Public Stores Act 1875, Post Office Act 1953, Stamp Duties Management Act 1891, Agricultural Credits Act 1928, Gaming Act 1845, Law of Property Act 1925, Land Registrations Act 1925, Criminal Justice Act 1988, Social Security Administration Act 1992, Computer Misuse Act 1990, Enterprise Act 2002, Deeds of Arrangement Act 1914, Insolvency Act 1986, Forgery and Counterfeiting Act 1981, Mental Health Act 1983, Coinage Act 1971, Hallmarking Act 1973, Protecting the Euro Against Counterfeiting Regulations 2001(SI 3948/2001), Road Traffic Act 1988, Vehicle Excise and Registration Act 1994, Transport Act 1968, Goods Vehicles Act 1995 and Road Traffic Regulation Act 1984.

59 2002 having been the proposed date of the statute. The Bill is still at consultation stage.

According to the Home Office Counting Rules, the maximum ten year sentence now applies to the following offences:

53/1   False statements by company directors,

53/4   Giving false information knowingly or recklessly when applying for a Confidentiality Order, etc.

60/21   Forgery of a drug prescription or copying a false drug prescription

60/22   Using a false drug prescription or a copy of ac false drug prescription

61/2   Forgery or copying false instrument (other than drug prescription)

61/27   Possessing materials or dies to make counterfeit coins or note

61/31   Counterfeiting etc of dies or marks (other forgery etc)

Conspiracy to defraud at common law also carries the maximum of ten years sentence.

It can be argued that since conspiracy to defraud charge was only used in just over one thousand instances,[60] consistently, in recent years' figures, that, the offence is not the problem. It may be that the problem is one of evidence gathering, entrapment and breaches through inadequacies of following the PACE guidelines and prosecution presentation. The new fraud offence would still leave many other "fraud" offences under various statutes or the status quo. Is conspiracy to defraud trials lengthy because of the charge used[61] or because of prosecution defects in bringing a case to trial without breaching PACE or breaching the Human Rights Act 1998?

The State and Fraudster

Fraud has been with us and recorded even since the fourth legal code of King Edgar passed between AD 946 and 961. Some early records which survived were drawn from 1208[62] on the instructions of the bishop of Winchester. Thirteenth century auditors had a policy-making as well as a fraud-detecting role and there was even a school of business administration at Oxford by early thirteenth century. "Around this time there was much crime apart from fraud. There was much mugging and murders committed by gangs of youth, often the sons of rich citizens."[63]

All the way down to the fifteenth and sixteenth centuries there is recorded evidence of fraud and dishonesty. For instance, kings' goldsmiths used to regularly clip gold coins paid to merchants for their goods and services. By clipping the gold coins and retaining the clippings, the kings believed that the merchants would be fooled and that these kings would make handsome savings.[64]

Fraud was recorded as having taken place in the 17th century when high taxes were not enough revenue for government and exploited the rage for gambling by establishing a national lottery in England. It was vital to prevent fraud

---

60   House of Commons—International Development—Minutes of Evidence—Memorandum submitted by Dr Elaine M Drage, Director, Trade Policy 2, DTI—http://www.parliament.the-stationery-office.co.uk/cm200001/cmselect/cmintdev/39/0 25/06/03

61   Barbara Ann Hocking, "The fame, fortunes and future of the 'rump of the common law': Conspiracy to defraud and English Law", Justice Studies, Queensland, Australia 4058.

62   Danziger, D, Gillingham, J, "The year of the Magna Carta", 2003, Hodder & Stoughton.

63   "The year of the Magna Carta", 2003, D, Danziger, J, Gillingham.

64   "Anatomy of the economic crisis: tulip mania and today's speculation", (1982), http://www.workers.org/marcy/cd/samecris/eccrisis01.htm

and it is recorded that in 1710, twenty members of the lottery team sat on long, narrow tables to cut up the tickets, which were engraved in copper and printed by the sheet with intricate flourishes pricked out among the numbers. To guard against cheating, the sheets were firmly screwed down to the tables and cut with penknives, using perforated rulers so that the tickets had a jagged edge. When a winner claimed a prize, his ticket, and that held by the promoters, were put together to see if the two matched.[65]

In the 1720's the South Sea Company rose to financial and political prominence through political leverage and corruption. It was the age of risk. The South Sea advert [66]read: "Such persons as are desirous to be Proprietors may on Thursday next purchase permits…at five shillings each, at Baker's coffee house in Exchange Alley. N.B. No permits will be delivered for less than £1000 and not more than three permits to one person, to prevent their being engrossed by a few, as 'tis to be feared has been done lately".[67]

When prospective investors came, they were issued with a permit to take up a certain subscription with no details of how much or when and these permits were signed by fictitious names. Thinking that there were easy quick profits to be made, many invested millions of pounds in total, many using credit to buy more stock. But the company was doomed; it had no business plan and no market for its goods. The whole scheme was riddled with fraud and corruption and after this collapse, such new investment schemes became commonly known as "bubbles".

Forgery was rife, as narrated by Pierce.[68] There were two famous forgers, James MacPherson (1736 to 1796) who forged volumes for the Gaelic 'Ossian' poems for gain, and Thomas Chatterton (1752 to 1770) who forged the fifteenth century 'Rowley Poems' for gain. In late 1794 William—Henry Ireland began to forge Shakespeare on a massive scale and there is even a picture painted called "The oaken chest or the gold mines of Ireland" by John Nixon, painted in 1795, which depicts all of Ireland's family busy churning out forgeries. He forged 600 signatures to provide 'authentic' manuscripts by Shakespeare.

Later, in the eighteenth century, London, for instance, was described as lawless…In a book written by a Mrs D George[69], she quotes the City Marshall of 1718 who said : "Now it is the general complaint of the taverns, the coffee houses, the shop keepers and others, that their customers are afraid when it is dark to come to their houses and shops for fear that their hats and wigs should be snitched from their heads or their swords taken from their sides, or that they may be blinded, knocked down, cut or stabbed; nay the coaches cannot secure them, but they are likewise cut and robbed in the public streets, etc, by which means the traffic of the City is much interrupted."

Thirty years later, Henry Fielding, the pioneer Bow Street magistrate, took an equally gloomy view. He wrote a book whose title is "An enquiry into the causes of the late increase in robbers" in 1751. Fielding said "There is not a street in Westminster which doth not swarm all day with beggars, and all night with thieves. Stop your coach at what shop you will, however expeditious the tradesman is to attend you, a beggar is commonly beforehand with him; and if you should not directly face his door, the tradesman must often turn his head while you are talking to him, or the same beggar, or some other thief at hand, will pay a visit to his shop. I omit to speak of the more open and violent insults which are everyday committed on His Majesty's subjects in the streets and highways. They are enough known and enough spoken of. The depredations on property are less noticed, particularly those in the parishes within ten miles of London…These are however grown to the most deplorable height insomuch as the gentleman is daily, or rather nightly, plundered of his pleasure, and the former of his livelihood…The innocent are put

---

65 Balen, M, "A very English deceit", 2002, Fourth Estate.

66 John Strachan in an article in "History Today", April 2004, says that…"*Advertisements of the late eighteenth century are…fascinating and socially revealing. England in this period saw significant developments in advertising. Alongside the introduction of nationwide systems of product distribution and a growing awareness of the potential of brand marketing, advertisers became increasingly sophisticated in targeting specific audiences in terms of regions, social class and gender.*" This is also an indication of the economic well being of the time.

67 Newspaper advert as quoted in Balen's "A very English Deceit".

68 Pierce, P, "The Great Shakespeare fraud", May 2004, History Today.

69 George, MD, "London Life in the 18th century", 1930, .

in terror, affronted and alarmed with threats and execrations, endangered with loaded pistols, beat with bludgeons and hacked with cutlasses, of which the loss of health of limbs, and often of life, is the consequence; and all this without any respect of age or dignity or sex…Street robberies are generally committed in the dark, the persons on whom they are committed are often in chairs and coaches, and if on foot, the attack is usually begun by knocking the party down, and for the time depriving him of his sense. But if the thief should be less barbarous, he is seldom so incautious as to omit taking every method which he can invent to avoid discovery…How long have we known highwaymen reign in this kingdom after they have been publicly known for such? Have not some of these committed robberies in open daylight, in the sight of many people, and have afterward rode solemnly and triumphantly through the neighbouring towns without any danger or molestation…Great and numerous gangs…have for a long time committed the most open outrages in defiance of the law…There are at this time a gang of rogues, whose number falls little short of a hundred, who are incorporated in one body, have officers and a treasury; and have reduced theft and robbery into a regular system. There are members of this society of men who appear in all disguises, and mix in most companies. Nor are they better versed in every art of cheating, thieving and robbing, than they are armed with every method of evading the law…If they fail in rescuing the prisoner, or in bribing or deterring the prosecutor, they have for their last resource some rotten members of the Law to forge a defence for them, and a great number of false witnesses ready to support it…Among the beggars in the streets I myself have discovered some notorious cheats, and my good friend Mr Welch, the worthy High Constable of Holborn division, many more. Nothing, as I have been well informed, is more common among these wretches, than for the lame, when provoked, to use their crutches as weapons instead of supporters; and for the blind, if they should have the beadle at their heels, to outrun the dogs which guided them before".

There is much similar evidence which has been described by other authors, for example by the author LO Pike of 1876. There were parts of London which were given over to these criminals and such areas were their sanctuary until the end of the seventeenth century. There was a Sanctuary Act 1623 which prohibited sanctuaries. One such sanctuary for criminals was Whitefriars, an area between Fleet Street and the Thames. The Minories and Baldwin's Gardens, Gray's Inn Lane were other convenient refuges for hard pressed thieves. An Act was passed in 1696 to make it an offence to resist arrest in such privileged places. The criminals moved to Surrey and another act was passed in 1722 to make it an offence to resist arrest. In 1724 it was made a transportable offence for any three persons to assemble to prevent the collection of debts in London.

During the eighteenth century, many courts, alleys and houses inhabited by thieves and beggars were gradually rebuilt. By this time drunkenness was rife and gin was plentiful. Distilling became the new English trade and it received special government grants. Prostitution became common. The first half of the eighteenth century was full of highwaymen such as Dick Turpin. Crime abounded well into the nineteenth century and the Industrial Revolution. Society was in transition as towns grew rapidly. Crime was increasing in quantity but decreasing in violence. During the inter-war years there was a steady rise in crimes against property. In 1933 there was the Children and Young Persons Act which provided a more humane approach towards the young offender. But crime today, regardless of quantitative change is more serious today because of the increase in organised crime. Poverty was not the driving force in increased crime and many thieves, as thieves of ages past, are not driven to theft by the immediate pressure of necessity. Aristotle's statement holds good today as it did then: "There are some crimes which are due to lack of necessities…But want is not the only cause of crimes. Men also commit them simply for the pleasure it gives them, and just to get rid of an unsatisfied desire…The greatest crimes are committed not for the sake of necessities, but for the sake of superfluities."[70]

---

70 Aristotle, "Politics", translated by E, Barker, 1946, Oxford.

The motive in fraud

Fraud is often due to motives which are both qualitatively and quantitatively similar to non-criminal motives, and it is generally just as biologically normal as ordinary behaviour. Law-breaking which is petty fraud is so common that to determine who is guiltless might be as perplexing as the unanswered question of Pontius Pilate.[71]

But what is crime? Two authorities may disagree. The idea that the moral law is supreme and that crime is the breach of the established moral law implies that there are universal, supreme and permanently valid rules of conduct. But the criminal law is not universal. It is relative, both to time and place. What is forbidden by the law changes from year to year and is impressively transformed over longer periods or during times of terror, as in 2004, when the anti-terrorism laws of many countries derogates all the Conventions and Human Rights Treaties.

Elliot (1952) defines crime as "any act, or failure to act, which is forbidden or prescribed by law, the failure to abide by such law being punishable by fine, imprisonment, banishment, death, or other punitive treatment, as the particular state may prescribe."[72]

As related at the beginning of the chapter, eighteenth century England imposed the death penalty for all sorts of trivial acts: appearing disguised on the public highway, shooting rabbits, stealing anything from a person. Offences such as blasphemy, swearing, adultery and homosexuality were once crimes, for example, even though today they are not crimes.

Crime and punishment

Hart (1961) defines crime as an act or omission forbidden by law under pain of punishment,[73] and the term will be used in major or minor offences, and the word criminal is applied to all offenders who are punishable in criminal courts, these crimes including serious frauds. The theorist Austin said that it is irrelevant what a person believes, fears, or is motivated by, because whether he has an obligation to do something is defined, not in terms of these subjective facts, but in terms of the likelihood that the person having the obligation, will suffer a punishment at the hands of others in the event of his disobedience. Fraudsters like to think of themselves as people caught up in business decisions,[74] as the unfortunates of the commercial world but they are just criminals as are burglars, murderers and thieves.

Serious frauds are sometimes classed as white-collar crimes. There is a theory of 'white collar crime' by E.H. Sutherland. Sutherland (1939) put forward the theory that much white collar crime is not a breach of any kind of law or even the spirit of the law. It includes such things as falsehood in advertising, the manipulation of property markets and the sale of securities which are about to fall in value. He declared that all American statistics on crime at the time were misleading and incorrect because they almost completely ignored the high rate of lawbreaking among leading business and professional groups. He charged that arrests, convictions and punishments were reserved chiefly for the lower economic and social classes. Sutherland's research was into the far reaches of criminal activity among 70 of the 200 largest manufacturing, mining and mercantile corporations in America, where he found patent violations, restraint of trade, coercion, intimidation, espionage, financial manipulation and other unfair practices which he classed as white collar crime.[75]

---

71 Indeed, LM Hussey, in an article called "Twenty four hours as a law breaker", Harper's Magazine, March 1930, said that the lawlessness of the average citizen stems from the complexity of the law and from the fact that it is virtually impossible for the average person to keep informed of the law, even though the courts adhere to the notion that ignorance of the law is no excuse.

72 Elliot, MA, (1952) "Crime in modern society", Harper & Brothers, pg 14.

73 HLA Hart, "The concept of Law", 1961, Clarendon Press.

74 Croall, H, "White collar crime"1992, Open University Press, on pg 55, says "There are convincing arguments that large successful corporations and top executives may be less likely to commit offences as they have less need to offend and can pursue their goals legally." Croall refers to arguments by Box(1987) that "corporate crime need not occur".

75 Elliot, MA, (1952) "Crime in modern society", Harper & Brothers, pg 43.

Such crime may be the response to a high sense of duty towards an organisation or individual or group and it sometimes happens that an offender believes his act is right and proper although it is wrong in the sense that it is punishable by law. This result is unfortunate for the offender as well as for society since the acceptance by the lawbreaker of the fact that his offence is wrong and his punishment just is an identification of his will with the will of his fellowmen, and a step towards compensating persons he has injured by his offences.

The fraud offence classification

Official classification of the Home Office classifies UK fraud as offences against property without violence, and also as forgery and offences against currency. This legal and official approach differs from the scientific approach. The legal interest may depend mainly on the guilt of the accused and the differentiation of false trading or false accounting. The medical interest will be chiefly concerned with the personality of the offender[76], both generally and also at the time the crime was committed.

For medical purposes such crimes can be conveniently classified into acquisitive, aggressive, gregarious and suchlike, according to the instinct involved.[77] This approach directs immediate attention to the emotional qualities accompanying the crime and the disposition of the offender.

Official statistics do not allow any precise figure to be given concerning the number of criminals whose offences are attributable to any particular instinct. Not only is there overlapping but differentiation is often incomplete. The fraud figures cannot be taken at their face value, for, although the great majority of these offences are apparently acquisitive, the study of individuals often shows that a seemingly acquisitive offence is really due to self-preservation or parental instinct, and that some cases of theft are primarily sexual offences and are only incidentally associated with the aggressive or acquisitive instinct. Again, the figures relating to fraud are open to the criticism that they never can include frauds which are not reported to the authorities[78] or to the offenders who are not even suspected of committing crime. Criminals in general are usually classified as accidental, occasional or habitual and those classifications hold good for fraudsters.

Criminals classified

From a medical point of view criminals can also be classified broadly under the headings of normal, subnormal, mentally defective, psychoneurotic, psychopathic and psychotic personalities. But the groups overlap and no psychiatric classification is likely to give entire satisfaction.[79]

---

76 That the crime is classed as "behaviour" purports to its being medical-psychological, as is supported by Clinard (1983) who says that corporate crime can be defined as "illegal corporate behaviour which is a form of a collective rule-breaking....". pg 11, Croall, H, "White collar crime", 1992, Open University Press.
   By contrast, in seeing the offender-criminal as the user of the organisation, rather than the organisational goals making the defendant the offender, Wheeler and Rothman, in the 1993 Yale Project on white collar crime, demonstrated that "offences show greater sophistication, complexity and magnitude where the offender uses an organisation". pg xiii, Nelken, D, "White Collar Crime", 1993, Dartmouth Press. This implies that it is only the scale of the opportunities that inhibit the scale of the offences.

77 Elliot, MA, (1952), "Crime in Modern Society", Harper & Brothers, pages 102-149. Lambroso (1878) was a criminal anthropologist who studied prisoners and concluded that the criminal was a distinct anthropological type, a "born" criminal. The Jurist Garafalo (1914), contrary to Lambroso, said that criminals are characterised by psychological anomalies, eg deficient in pity, violent, etc. Ferri (1917) concluded that there were 5 classes of criminals—insane, born, habitual, occasional and passionate. Professor Gillin (1946)extended Ferri's classification to fourteen.

78 Mills (1970) argued not to pay too much reliance on crime figures alone, warning against an obsession with the matters of method to the exclusion of all others.

79 For instance, in Pearson's study of degeneracy, as adopted by American psychiatrists (Diagnostic and Statistical Manual of Mental

Criminality in general is sometimes roughly measured by the nature, number and variety of offences which have been previously committed.[80] The degree of turpitude in different classes of crime, as well as of different offenders in the same crime group, cannot be accurately assessed unless the individual offender and the circumstances associated with the crime are closely studied.

Criminality and turpitude are not measured necessarily by the prescribed legal punishment. For example, although murder must be punished with greater severity than theft, the murderer who is not insane and who has been reprieved is unlikely to repeat his offence when he regains his liberty, whereas the criminal tendencies of the thief not infrequently prompt him to steal again as soon as an opportunity to do so presents itself.

There is one school of criminology which considers that crime was forced upon those who became criminal because of their inherited traits.[81] But daily observation of human behaviour indicates that it is sometimes mainly endogenous and at other times chiefly exogenous. Studies show that the persistent criminal is on the whole more concerned with self in isolation than with self in the social setting and often shapes his behaviour in fantasy, rationalisation and projection.[82]

Disorders of the American Psychiatric Association) Antisocial Personality Disorder, as defined, consists of features of psychopathic symptoms and even of symptoms of defective persons as per the UK Mental Deficiency Act:

A.

1 failure to conform to norms with respect to lawful behaviours as indicated by repeatedly performing acts that are grounds for arrest;

2 deceitfulness, as indicated by repeated lying, use of aliases, or conning others for personal profit or pleasure;

3 impulsivity or failure to plan ahead;

4 irritability or aggressiveness, as indicated by repeated physical fights or assaults;

5 disregard for the safety of self or others;

6 consistent irresponsibility, as indicated by repeated failure to sustain consistent work behaviour or honour financial obligations;

7 lack of remorse, as indicated by being indifferent to or rationalizing having hurt, mistreated, nor stolen from another.

B. The individual is at least 18 years.

C. There is evidence of conduct disorder.

D. The occurrence of antisocial behaviour is not exclusively during the course of Schizophrenia or a Manic Episode. ("Genetics and Criminal Behaviour", by D Wassermann & R Wachbroit [2001] Cambridge.

80 Baldwin and Bottoms (1976) relied on statistics. Such statistics provided the means by which these researchers sought to measure the extent of crime in society. What is more they used such statistics to provide the basis of explanations of crime by relating crime levels to the features of social areas, such as types of housing tenure or to other trends in society such as changes in levels of unemployment.

81 That a lying is a personality trait can be asserted and that lying is a violation of trust in white collar crime is acknowledged. Shapiro (1990) said that "virtually all types of fiduciary relationships are vulnerable to misrepresentation, deception, exaggeration, omission, distortion, fabrication, or falsification of information by those in positions of trust.". Zukerman (1977) said that these misrepresentations may convey calculated lies and total fabrications. pg 16 Nelkon, D, "White collar crime", 1992, Dart Press. It can therefore be argued that violators of trust, liars, ie. white collar criminals, have a genetic propensity to becoming criminals.

Durkeim (1933), the sociologist, theorised that the intrinsic features of the social organisation of trust and its tendency to collectivise large numbers of principals means that the extent of harm from abuse of trust is likely to be large. He argued that society considers as dangerous those behaviour it responds to as criminal. It can be concluded that white collar crime is criminal behaviour because it causes great harm. But Durkheim's theory also postulates that crime is a consequence of defective social regulation and people deviate because the laws are so flawed that they offer few restraints or moral direction.

Durkheim's views that crime reflect inadequate laws can be rebutted, at least in American states, which have severe punishments for crime and the most imprisoned per thousand of population in the world's countries. See Global Report on Crime and Justice, United Nations Office for Drug Control and Crime Prevention., (1999), Oxford University Press.

82 The recent SFO case of R v Mitchell, Kirkup, Mason & Chapman [2004] unreported, illustrates this phantasy personality that committed this serious fraud in which these people made false claims about their credentials . Mitchell styled himself as an investment banker and the others made false claims about their expertise. They projected themselves as top flight business professionals to obtain £5 million in fee income whilst obtaining not one of the venture capital loans applied for by their clients in over five years. The company website, brochures, advertisements and its corporate video all carried the same illusion. Advertisements were placed in the Wall

That personality takes time to reach its full development and practical observations show that in a majority of cases as one gets older personality is a more important criminogenic factor than environment.[83] This can be borne out in the survey of the fifty serious fraud cases in the UK that show that the criminals in these cases are all aged over forty.[84]

Responsibility and Culpability

The term 'criminal responsibility' is concerned with acquittal on the grounds of insanity[85] or alternatively with conviction and punishment, and 'medical culpability' as used here is concerned with conviction and the degree of blameworthiness in cases of minor mental abnormality, which lies somewhere between that attached to the unlawful act of a normal person on the one hand and one who is insane according to the law[86] on the other. If an offender who is responsible in law for his act or omission commits a crime as the direct result of a recognised form of mental abnormality, a psychiatrist may consider to what extent he is culpable, and whether any medical recommendation should be made to the court on his behalf.

In the UK, in studies by East and Hulbert[87] in 1950, it was estimated that 80% of the prison population was normal[88] or not mentally diseased. In New York at the same time studies by Thompson showed that 89% of the New York prison

Street Journal, The Times newspaper, the Financial Times newspaper and other important newspapers. They pretended that they had successfully obtained loans for a $50 million timeshare and resort complex in Spain, a £27 million manufacturing plant in South Africa and a $10 million cellular phone project, among others. Clients were attracted from around the world. The case is a classic advance fee fraud case.

83   This contrasts with Edwin Sutherland's theory, or rather his combination of theories to which he gave the generic title 'Differential Association', an extract of which is as follows: "Criminal behaviour is learned. Criminal behaviour is learned in interaction with other persons in a process of communication. The principal part of the learning of criminal behaviour occurs within intimate personal groups. When criminal behaviour is learned, the learning includes (a) techniques of committing a crime, which are sometimes very complicated, sometimes very simple; (b) the specific direction of motives, drives, rationalisations, and attitudes. The specific direction of motives and drives is learned from definitions of the legal codes as favourable and unfavourable. A person becomes delinquent because of an excess of definitions favourable to violation of the law over definitions unfavourable to violations of the law. This is the principle of differential association. Differential associations may vary in frequency, duration, priority and intensity. The process of learning criminal behaviour by association with criminal and anti-criminal patterns involves all the mechanisms that are involved with any other learning. While criminal behaviour is an expression of general needs and values, it is not explained by those general needs and values since non-criminal behaviour is an expression of the same needs and values. Thieves generally steal in order to secure money, but likewise honest labourers work in order to secure money...." Source: "Crime and the Social Structure", pg 85, (1963), by John Barron Mays, Publisher Faber and Faber.

84   This is also borne out by Vincezzo Ruggiero in "Crime and markets", (2000), Oxford University press, pg 115, where he argues that fraud is a learnt behaviour over time, [the same as a maturing personality]. He says, "Contrary to F.Sutherland's (1949) theorization, deviant techniques and behaviours were not only learned [in Italian, French, German, British and Japanese corruption] by members of specific and homogeneous enclaves or professional groups, they were also translated into tools adaptable to a variety of social groups".

85   Peter Young case (see Appendix 5 for the facts of the case)

86   The UK 1957 McNaughten Rules laid down that juries could bring a verdict of guilty but insane if it could be shown that the offender was suffering from "some defect of reason due to disease of the mind, in consequence of which he either did not know the nature and quality of the act at the time he performed it, or did not know that the act was wrong". pg 115, "Crime and the social structure", (1963), Mays JB, Faber and Faber.

87   Sir Norwood East, (1951), "Society and the Criminal", Charles C Thomas Publisher,

88   Seabright.P, (2004), "The company of strangers", Princeton University press; review of book by The Economist 14th August 2004. That the majority of the prison population are normal can also be confirmed by modern studies of society and cheating, one such study being Paul Seabright's in which he states that modern society has developed over the last 10, 000 years due to two opposing traits : intellectual capacity for rational calculation and an instinct for reciprocity. An instinct for reciprocity, he states, is shown by a tendency to repay kindness with kindness and betrayal with revenge, even when rational calculation might seem to advise against it.

population was normal. This shows that there seems to be a large steady proportion of prisoners from any population who are just bad and law breakers, not sick. No similar studies have taken place in any country since the 1950's. Although these studies were of the prison population as a whole, these results can be argued to also represent the small proportion of the prison population that are fraudsters, since it can be argued that fraudsters are criminals in the common sense of the word.

What is normal?—Nathaniel Cantor[89] said: "Anyone who has achieved a dynamic balance between the need for self-expression and the need for self-repression has a normal personality. Such a person will possess a sense of internal freedom, a feeling of inner self-confidence, and a lack of disruptive fear…To accept fearlessly whatever life's circumstances bring is a sign of an emotionally mature personality…Who then is normal? None of us, is the answer."

Normality when applied to personality embodies the idea of a standardised average. But normal standards not only differ widely, they are variable and elusive, and concern intellectual processes, emotional reactions, and willpower. Personal intellectual processes clearly vary from time to time apart from the deteriorating effects of disease. The normal emotional level of ordinary men partly depends upon circumstance, and the emotional responses of an accused person in the witness box may affect the view of the jury regarding his guilt or innocence.

The fraudster as a psychopath

It is the psychopathic personality which is the most likely of personality disorders that fraudsters suffer from, reading the facts from case-law of serious frauds. Overholser[90] observed that before the law can be expected to recognise the group as calling for specialised treatment it will be necessary for psychiatrists to come to a better agreement on such cases. The criminal psychopathic personality may be defined as a person who, although not insane, psychoneurotic or mentally defective, is persistently unable to adapt himself to social requirements on account of abnormal peculiarities of impulse, temperament and character which may require specialised medical and rehabilitative treatment instead of, or in addition to, the ordinary methods of punishment before his social reclamation can be effected.[91]

The fraudster Clive Smith[92] was unfit to plead in a Serious Fraud Office case in 2001. He was charged with conspiring to defraud investors in the Richmond Oil and Gas flotation but at a preliminary hearing, it was claimed that he was mentally and physically unfit to stand trial and was separated from the main trial of other conspirators. The prosecutors tried to bring him back into the trial after they claimed that his health had improved but he could not be subject to new medical examinations without his consent.

Serious Fraud and senility

Fewer older persons commit indictable offences than the rest of the population as is illustrated by the following table:

NB: This way of analysing prison statistics has been discontinued.

He states that calculation without reciprocity favours cheating whilst reciprocity without calculation exposes people to exploitation. He claims that a stable society requires both traits in order to keep cheating and free-riding in check.

89   Cantor.N.J, (1932), "Crime, criminals and criminal justice", Holt, New York.

90   Dr Winifred Overholser was the Superintendent of St. Elizabeth's Hospital'. She occupied the uncontested position of leadership in the field of forensic psychiatry in America in the 1950's.

91   Sir Norwood East, "Society and the Criminal", 1949, Charles C Thomas Publisher. He states that it is impossible to know the number of psychopathic personalities in the population at large since many never reach the psychiatrist's consulting room and pass through life with their mental abnormality undeclared and unrecorded.(pg 174)

92   R v Clive Smith [2001] unreported.

Year	guilty	up to 21	21–30	30–40	40–50	50–60	over 60
1929	53332	21606	13529	9159	5321	2436	1271
1930	56766	23924	13989	9374	5526	2607	1346
1931	59366	24973	14761	10075	5694	2569	1294
1932	64958	27889	16481	10746	5696	2777	1369
1933	62660	26919	15576	10574	5573	2644	1374
1934	65736	30048	15344	10561	5589	2827	1367
1935	69849	34510	15199	10508	5571	2640	1421
1936	72785	36140	15467	11143	5806	2803	1426
1937	77529	39493	15974	11551	6024	2967	1520
1938	78463	39567	16392	11929	6063	2963	1549

Source: Home Office Criminal Statistics

Certain features appear. There is a marked reduction in the crime rate of elderly persons in the UK. But the survey (1999-2003)of UK serious frauds show a high percentage of older persons being convicted of serious fraud (forty five percent of all serious fraud cases) which is the inverse of the situation for non-fraud crimes, indicating that serious fraud is a speciality of older executives.

Of the convicted persons in the ten year period it was found that 10898 of those were aged 60 and over and had been convicted of larceny, embezzlement, forgery, fraud, receiving, coining, etc., ie 2% of all offenders.[93] These offences are often committed by professional criminals who have just gotten older. This is confirmed with the survey results of the SFO cases which showed that of the 49 cases that went to trial by the Serious Fraud Office of the United Kingdom between 1999 and 2003, 15% of defendants were aged 30 to 39, 40% were aged 40 to 49, 35% were aged 50 to 59 and 10% were over 60 years old. It also smashes Glueck's theory (1943) that many serious offenders do become minor offenders as they grow older.[94]

Statistics on fraud

The 2002 Home Office statistics of the prison population for England and Wales for the year 2002 (see Appendix 2)show that there were 48, 451 persons in prison, of which 1005 were imprisoned for fraud and forgery offences, a total of 2 % of the prison population . This is the same 2% of the prison population who committed embezzlement and fraud in the USA in 1950 (see Appendix 3). From other similar statistics it can be seen that there is a very small

---

93 This constant 2% of fraudsters in society from 1952 figures to 2003 figures supports the reasoning of Adolph Quetelet ("The constancy of crime", 1952) to postulate the existence of a "constant criminal propensity" in large groups.

94 Elliot, MA, (1952), "Crime in Modern Society", Harper & Brothers, pgs 333-334. Eleanor Glueck conducted studies on adult criminals over many years and concluded that maturity is an important factor in inducing willingness to abide by rules and regulations of a social group.

but steady ratio of persons in the population who commit fraud and that fraud offences are mainly committed by persons 30 years of age and over.[95]

The recent Serious Fraud Office prosecution of Guy Pound, Anthony Green and Peter Beard, Peter Hayward and John Parkinson(see Appendix 4)could be argued to be a case of senility as three defendants were aged 71, 72 and 76 years old. The defendants were professionals in the construction business who were contracted by the Talbot Village Trust to design and Build a number of projects. They were found guilty of perpetrating a £3.5 million fraud. No medical evidence was sought or given in this case.[96]

> "The difference between senescence and senility is that in senescence there are modifications in the person which must not be looked upon as disorders, while in senility there are actual alterations. Therapy is possible as a cure for senescence but impossible in senility."[97]

In criminal situations the welfare of the community must be considered as well as the personality of the offender, and there are views regarding the antisocial potentialities of law-breakers. If growing old is as natural a process as growing up, and senescence is the counterpart of adolescence, it becomes a matter of practical importance to differentiate criminal behaviour which is associated with senescence as a recent improvisation in the life history of the offender or the continuance of a long-established habit, from offences which are attributable to the functional or organic mental diseases of senility. It was the case that Saunders in the Guinness case was found to suffer from senile dementia.[98] The finding was

---

95 Types of crime committed at different ages (%)in 1953

Offence	under 17	17 to 29	30 and over
Breaking & entering	53%	35%	11%
Larceny	34%	31%	35%
Robbery	34%	55%	11%
Receiving	22%	29%	49%
Violence	8%	52%	40%
Sex	20%	31%	49%
Fraud & False pretences	4%	29%	67%

Source: Home Office Figures found in Jones. H, "Crime and the penal system", 1956, University Tutorial Press.
This table confirms that in middle age and old age there is a definite shift from the more overt forms of property crimes, such as robbery, and breaking and entering, to sex crimes, and violence, and more subtle types of property offence such as receiving, fraud and false offences. Criminality of old men lies in the fact that such criminals are committers of crime in which craftiness has an important place.

96 R v Pound and others [2004] unreported. Three construction industry professionals were convicted for defrauding the Talbot Village Trust in Dorset of £3.5 million through manipulation of building contracts. The fraud related to six contracts and involved invoicing for work not done and disguising inflated professional fees in the contracts. The defendants were professionals, Pound being a 71year old architect responsible for the planning, design and management of the projects, Green being a 76 year old Chartered Surveyor, Hayward being the 76 year old chairman of the construction company, Beard a 56 year old quantity surveyor and Parkinson a 60 year old managing director of the company. The quantity surveyors and the architect were responsible for measuring the work and for certifying that it had been constructed in accordance with the contract. They did this despite not all the work being done. This fraud was perpetrated over many years.

97 Goulstonian Lecture on "The Neurology of old age" by Macdonald Critchley. Quoted in "Society and the Criminal", by Sir Norwood East (1949) pg 78.t

98 Innes.J, (2002), "Law Lords reject Guinness Appeal", article in the newspaper New Scotsman 15.11.2002 . In the article Innes mentions Saunders' senile dementia diagnosis, but stated [without authority] that Saunders recovered in ten months.

only revealed during his imprisonment and should have been discovered and put to the court before trial. The Poole Trust case is an instance of the defendants being over 60 but perhaps suffering from senescence.

In serious criminal cases, when the police are unable to avoid delay in arresting a suspected offender, there may be special significance in the fact that in senescence the memory for recent events becomes impaired and reminiscence prevails. The reasoning power does not necessarily become less and often gains in strength and reliability until age is well advanced. Indeed the wisdom of age, founded upon experience, is sometimes so impressive that it cannot be set aside lightly as an imaginary or ephemeral quality. Although intellectual resilience and the receptivity for few new ideas are weakened in senescence, and decisions are reached with less alacrity than formerly, "there can be no doubt that the amount of crime in the later periods of life is diminished in part by the fact that conduct is more influenced then by knowledge, reason and restraint, and is less affected by opportunity, emotion and the stimulation of the senses".[99]

Senescence then, apart from its physical concomitants, is characterised by a gradual lessening of the intellectual, emotional and volitional attributes of mind whereby memory, perception, receptivity, attention, interests and other desires become restricted, less vivid and less compelling. It passes into senility when the impairment becomes excessive, the mental activities imperfectly synchronised, and when initiative, the ability to form well-considered opinions and sustained effort fails and social maladjustment results. Persons become less concerned with external events, they become increasingly egotistic, and their emotional life is impoverished. Dissatisfaction with their companions and surroundings marks the fact that the pleasures and obligations of former years have lost their appeal.

Senility and fraud

Senility can be differentiated from arteriosclerotic dementia in persons accused of crime. Arteriosclerotic psychosis persons have usually a sudden onset and show less intellectual impairment. A lowering of moral standards, alcoholic excesses and dishonest practices are common among persons with arteriosclerotic psychosis.[100]

In matters involving criminal responsibility in the aged regard must be paid to the fact that the conduct and mental condition of senile offenders should be compared with the standards of their former years as well as with the standards of so-called normal persons. Indeed, where mental abilities are strikingly superior in the prime of life, a perceptible amount of deterioration due to old age may sometimes, in a criminal charge such as serious fraud, escape recognition and they may be regarded as above the average of intelligence and ability for his years.

Aged criminals, especially fraudsters in the UK, have been for many years treated under a milder form of discipline than others.[101] The mental background of the ageing offender before trial is important, but does not receive any attention, even though the later period of life presents special problems to senescence and senility.

Senescence does not acquit the offender of responsibility, although in advanced cases bordering on senility there may be reason to consider that his mental condition modifies culpability to an extent which should be taken into consideration.

Tyler.R, (2000), "Examining physician suggests British home secretary misled Parliament in bid to release Pinochet", article published by the International Committee of the Fourth International on 18th January 2000; in this article Professor Sir John Grimley Evans acknowledges the incompetence of some doctors to reach an unequivocal and unanimous diagnosis of senile dementia.

99 Sir Norwood East, "Society and the criminal", 1949, Charles C Thomas Publisher, pg 83.

100 Sir Norwood East, "Society and the criminal", 1949, Charles C Thomas Publisher, pg 68.

101 The study of the Serious Fraud Office cases from 1999 to 2003 shows that of the 78 persons being defendants in the 49 SFO cases over 5 years,

   36   persons received sentences of between 1 and 2 years imprisonment,

   18   persons received sentences of between 3 and 4 years imprisonment,

   12   persons received sentences of 5 to 7 years imprisonment,

   2   persons received sentences of 8 to 10 years imprisonment and

   10   persons received less than one year imprisonment. In the UK these sentences are usually halved if prisoners behave well.

"In the early stages of senile or arteriosclerotic dementia, culpability according to medical standards may be modified; in advanced stages the accused may be properly considered insane according to the law."[102]

In all cases appropriate rewards or treatment can be selected only by taking into consideration with other facts what the aged offender was, as well as what he is. His weaknesses demand our understanding; they may claim our sympathy if not respect.

In only two of the UK's Serious Fraud Office prosecutions were the fact that someone was insane considered and one of these was the Peter Young case.[103] In November 1998 Young was charged with conspiracy to defraud and with offences under the Financial Services Act 1986(see Appendix 5). However, in December 2000, after hearing medical evidence in relation to Young's mental health in a Fitness to Plead hearing, a jury found that Young was under a disability and was unfit to be tried.

The McNaughten Rules of the UK

There is a requirement under the Criminal Procedure (Insanity) Act 1964[104] that in such a situation, evidence could be put before a jury in a Hearing of the Facts in order to determine whether the defendant did the act or acts alleged in the indictment. It was found that Peter Young did commit the fraud he was charged with. Usually, when an offender is found guilty but insane, he is committed to a mental hospital, during Her Majesty's pleasure. Because of this, the plea of insanity is usually entered by the defence only in murder cases.

Punishment of Fraudsters

Jeremy Bentham[105] looked upon crime as a prohibited act from which there resulted more of evil than of good. But what is crime? Clearly, the criminal law is concerned with crimes alone and not with illegal acts in general. To distinguish those breaches of the law which are crimes from those which are merely illegal without being criminal is to assume that crimes are wrongs whose sanction is punitive and is remissible by the Crown and since fraud is a crime in modern times, crime needs to be examined in order to understand fraud.

Crime is therefore a serious anti-social action to which the state reacts consciously by inflicting pain. It is prohibited by statutes and common law. It can be said that a crime is also an offence against morality, against a person's social duty to his fellow members of society and therefore renders the offence liable to punishment. Morality is so closely interwoven with social conduct and immorality with criminal conduct that it seems desirable to pursue the matter further.

Centuries ago, the operation of the law between subjects was not to punish so much as to assess the compensation to be paid to the injured individual.[106] As time went on the idea gradually developed, probably under ecclesiastical influence, that the infliction of punishment was necessary and that liability to punishment should depend upon moral guilt. The ecclesiastical

---

102 Sir Norwood East, (1949), "Society and the Criminal", pg 94, Charles C Thomas Publisher.

103 <u>R v Young [2003] unreported</u>.

104 The principle in this Act is known as the McNaghten Rules which state that the plea of insanity can only be sustained if the defence can show that the prisoner was labouring under such a defect of reason, from disease of the mind, that he (a) did not know the nature and quality of the act he was doing, or (b) did not know that it was wrong. To establish a defence on the ground of insanity, it must be clearly proved that at the time of committing the act the party accused was labouring under such a defect of reason from disease of the mind as not to know the nature and quality of the act he was doing, or, if he did know it, that he did not know he was doing what was wrong. The wording of the McNaghten Rules was determined by the fact that the case involved delusions. The insanity of a deluded person takes the form of false beliefs. Where delusions are not involved, the knowledge factor, on which the Rules lay much emphasis, is the important thing. The much greater importance of emotional disturbances of this sort in insanity, as against disturbances of "reason", is the irrational impulses of the unconscious.

105 Bentham.J, (1970), "An introduction to the Principles of Morals and Legislation", Oxford Clarendon Press.

106 This is in effect restitution, where the rights of the victim come into play. This means that the criminal makes good the damage or the loss he has inflicted upon his victim. This is perhaps the most primitive of all the elements of punishment, for it brings out in a naked form the personal interests involved.

courts used to impose cruel sentences and because of this they had to begin to take account of the mental functioning of the offender. This is the beginning of the doctrine of *mens rea* as a subject assessment of criminal responsibility, although moral guilt was measured by strictly objective considerations. The ecclesiastical courts were satisfied that what they considered to be immoral and wrong was in fact so and they attached a religious significance to their assessments. After they declared their awards, the only occasion in which an appeal could be made to the Deity by the judge today is embodied in the sentence of death.

So the criteria for immorality seems to depend on the fact that the conduct in question[107] in injurious to society when it is generally practiced. The conviction rate of such conduct[108] bears witness to the importance or not of such offences in the eyes of the jury.[109]

But the highest moral conduct, for example to provide well for one's own family by stealing millions of pounds from others, or a company director who falsely trades in order to save the jobs of thousands of employees, may result from motives which are themselves immoral. Without entering the realm of casuistry it can be said that a crime may occasionally be the result of altruism as in many fraud cases, especially in the crimes of false accounting and false trading.[110]

Morality and fraud

Modern society is not single minded when passing moral judgements and it is difficult to see what the norm is for moral behaviour.[111] Morality depends on tradition[112] and the potential fraudster is required to base his behaviour mainly upon that tradition. Taken together with the fact that we are all different and that we have little control over the bio-chemical factors which affect us and can give us inherited anti-social tendencies, crime may result if the tendencies of the individual and his environment outweigh the resistance which can be opposed to them.

---

107 Hart:H.L.A, (1961), "The concept of law", Oxford University Press, states " The Thomist tradition of Natural Law comprises the contention that .. there are certain principles of true morality or justice, discoverable by human reason and that man-made laws which conflict with these principles are not valid law…Some conceive morality not as immutable principles of conduct or as discoverable by reason, but as expressions of human attitudes to conduct which may vary from society to society or from individual to individual.. For a legal system to exist there must be a widely diffused…recognition of a moral obligation to obey the law…"

108 In Canada, for example, study on sentencing by Hagan (1988) show that managers are treated with disproportionate severity and employers with disproportionate leniency.. A survey of sentencing of fraud in England and Wales in 1987 showed that only 19 people(0.096% of all convicted fraudsters) received sentences in excess of 4 years for fraud. Levi, M, "Fraudulent Justice? Sentencing the business criminal.", "White Collar Crime, 1992, Dartmouth Press.

109 eg, the UK conviction rate for conspiracy to defraud was 3%, 4%, 4%, 3%, and 3% in 1995, 1996, 1997, 1998 and 1999 respectively. Source : House of Commons Hansard written answers for 25.1.2001.

110 The SFO June 2003 Universal Bulk Handling case is an example of this.
    R v Freeman & Hodgekinson [2003] unreported. Two company directors were imprisoned for fraud surrounding the collapse of Lancashire Universal Bulk Handling which had losses of £12 million. The company, formed in 1958, became a subsidiary of another company in 1990 and soon after experienced adverse trading conditions . They began to falsify the accounts, hoping to trade out of these difficulties, but deteriorated further each year until 1999 when the fraud was discovered. Instead of an average yearly profit of £2 million as stated, there was a discrepancy of over £11 million.

111 Elliot in "Crime in modern society" discusses norms of modern behaviour. She states "Norms of behaviour which define our conduct give rise to the stability of our social order. Hence it is often difficult for us to understand that the norms which are expressed in laws contribute to lawbreaking. The fact is that these norms may correspond to ethical concepts of legislators and be at the same time wholly unrepresentative of the behaviour norms of the lower economic and social classes which bulk so large in the group arrested and convicted for crimes."

112 Patrick Devlin in "The enforcement of morals", 1965, Oxford University Press, stated that society cannot live without morals, these morals being the standard of conduct which the reasonable man approves. He argued that a man who concedes the morality is necessary to society must support the use of those instruments without which morality cannot be maintained, these two instruments being teaching which is doctrine and enforcement which is law.

The primary concern of society, and the first duty of its legal instruments, is the protection of the majority from the misdeeds of the fractional minority and so we cannot afford to discriminate always between the variables which go to make up criminal behaviour. So as society, we deal with results for the sake of the general welfare. Society is jealous of its rights and is not ready to accept with equanimity the irresponsibility associated in a criminal court with insanity and some forms of mental defectiveness, or the lessened culpability which is apparent in some forms of mental abnormality.

Culture and fraud

An analysis of how different societies view and treat different acts of persons belonging to those societies show that deeds such as fraud can be seen to be a reflection of the society in which it is perpetrated and is given treatment according to the society against which it is perpetrated.

If, say in country A, serious fraud is much more common here than in country B, then an resident of country A is more likely to commit serious fraud than is a resident in country B. If in country A there are plenty of businesses and law finance and contract laws so that it is very easy to commit serious fraud in country A, and the opposite is true in country B, then if a resident of country A commits a serious fraud and I am the judge but I come from country B, in passing sentence, I am likely to give him the maximum sentence the law of country A allows. It can be argued that the fraudster from country A is under an environmental burden and so I am not fair in judging him by my standards.

Suppose that there are genetic differences between the residents of country A and country B in that country A's residents are better fraudsters because they have mental and physical capacities that make for people of great cunning, nerves of steel, skill in manipulation, then they must receive special consideration because they are unlike the people of country B. Suppose that country A has other environmental factors in that residents there raise their children to be fraudsters. Then fraud would be much more common in country A. And suppose that residents of country A are harder to socialise than is the human norm because of some genetic factor. Then they would have a greater tendency to fraud. That this theory could be applied to the situation of the UK and the US would be to explain why 50% the UK's Serious Fraud Office defendants receive sentences of 5 years imprisonment whereas in the US the sentences are in the region of fifteen to twenty years for serious fraud.[113]

So it can be argued that fraudsters are raised in the white collar families in society and can be classed as such and can be argued that they are a result of their environment. Croall[114] and also Sunderland give definitions of white collar crime.[115] It could explain why it is that a certain type of criminal behaviour is more common in a certain population due to the increased prevalence of skills in that population required for this type of crime and that opportunities abound for members of the white collar community to engage in this type of behaviour with impunity.

As to the genetic factors, if the desire to commit fraud has a genetic cause, the source of the desire can be argued not to be regarded as a mitigating circumstance. But if we are to make the same moral judgements for environmental factors as for genetic factors, then we must treat all person uniformly, irrespective of any factors. This would make a nonsense of law and cases such a R v Peter Young[116] would be tried and sentenced regardless of insanity. If we admit the factor of insanity, we must admit factors such as environment and genetics. But the law is slow to do this and seems to be afraid that psychiatry might understand the transgressor too well and might forgive too readily.

Jeremy Bentham clearly regarded such punishment as made to exceed the advantage of the offence.[117] He added, "the proportion between punishment and offences ought not to be so mathematically followed up as to render the

---

113 The Economist, "Bosses behind Bars", 12 June 2004.

114 Croall.H, (1992), "White collar crime", Open University.

115 Edwin Sutherland defined white collar crime as ".. approximately…a crime committed by a person of respectability and high social status in the course o his occupation.".White Collar Crime by Hazel Croall, 1992, Open University.

116 {2003} unreported

117 And as such the criminal law is more revengeful than rational and just and represents more hostility against the criminal than concern about the safety of society.

laws subtle, complicate and obscure."[118] Punishment can be argued to be evil[119] when it prevents an offender from providing for his dependants and when his work in the outer world is more valuable to society than his occupation in prison, when his family suffer because of his conviction, and when he leaves prison more hostile and embittered than when he entered it. To leave prison more hostile and embittered than when he entered cannot benefit society. This argument can be upheld by Elliot's assertion that laws reflect the norms of legislators which are not the norms of the lower economic and social classes "which bulk so large in the group arrested and convicted for crimes".[120] This argument, however, cannot be justified for fraudsters because of their relatively light punishment in the UK as compared with the US.[121]

Bentham considered that the evils of punishment were : the evil of coercion, ie, more or less painful privation; the sufferings caused by the punishment; the evil of apprehension, ie . the fear of prosecution; the derivative evil suffered by the offender's parents and friends. If punishment is viewed as a deterrence, it would reduce crime. The aim in deterrent punishment is to instil in the individual a regard for the law because of his fear of the punishment which will follow if he transgresses. This leads to an ethical question and that is, whether legally correct behaviour maintained for the reason of deterrence is worth having. We all of us are trained socially in the element of fear. These are the foundations on which we build our sentiments. They develop into sincerely held moral principles, to which, when they are matured, we cling in the face of the most appalling temptations and difficulties.

How severely are we justified in punishing criminals merely to reduce the amount of criminality? How far we go is going to be determined by our sense of compassion and decency. It follows that the more civilised a country, the more vigorous its restriction on punishment. This imposes a practical limitation upon the utility of very severe punishments. Where punishments are very severe, it is impossible to impose it and so it defeats its own ends. An example of this is the death penalty in the UK in the nineteenth century, which resulted in magistrates acquitting obviously guilty persons because they were not prepared to impose the death penalty for petty offences, but contrary to this theory is the evidence in America where capital punishment is rife in 48 of the 51 states and punishment for fraud can be as much as 50 years imprisonment cumulatively for various offences committed by one person.[122]

The affectionless psychopath, as most fraudsters are, is therefore an individual for whom the prudent calculation of gains and losses required by the deterrent theory would be quite impossible. It may be the reason for the lenient sentences to fraudsters in the UK. It is therefore surprising that fraudsters from other countries do not, as it were, 'forum shop' and come to the UK to do fraud.[123] Many observers have noted that criminals of this type, who constitute a substantial proportion of persistent offenders, are quite incapable of learning even from the experience of punishment, much less from the threat of it.[124]

---

118 Popper.K, (1945), "The open society and its enemies", Routledge and Kegan Paul.
   This call against mathematically equivalent punishment and thus suffering is well explained by the Philosopher Popper who insisted that "no symmetry between suffering and happiness, or between pain and pleasure advocates a negative as opposed to the traditional positive utilitarianism: 'Instead of the greatest happiness of the greatest number, one should more modestly demand the least amount of suffering for anybody; and, further, that unavoidable suffering should be distributed as equally as possible.'"

119 Hobhouse.L.T., (1922), "The elements of social justice", Faber and Fsber; Hobhouse states that punishment is evil can be upheld by philosophers from the time of Socrates who said that the infliction of evil upon anyone can never in itself be good.

120 Elliot, MA, (1952), "Crime in Modern society", Harper & Brothers, pgs 358-9.

121 Of the 5 years of serious fraud cases studied in the UK, 60% received between 1 and 2 years imprisonment sentence, 23 % between 3 and 4 years, 15 % between 5 and 7 years, 2% over 10 years.

122 USA Federal Sarbannes–Oxley Act 2002

123 Of the 78 fraud defendants to SFO cases over 5 years, only 3 were Australian, 2 were Nigerian and 2 were Irish, the remainder being British.

124 Doran, J, "Reinventing the wheeler dealer after a ban", Monday May 31, 2004, Times Newspaper.
   In this article, the writer states that after fraudsters are tried and sentenced, there are always more avenues for them to pursue such as mortgage broking, unregulated areas such as hedge funds or currency trading firms. It sites examples of fraudsters such as Jack Grubman, a former analyst of Salomon Smith Barney . He was fined $15 million to settle an investigation into his conduct. He now

Deep psychological studies of psychoanalysts such as Flugel[125] show that, nevertheless, deterrent punishments are the ally of the law-abiding individual in his struggle to keep his own anti-social wishes under control. He states: "The criminal, by his flouting of the law and moral rule, constitutes a temptation of the id [ie. To our own unconscious and primitive wishes]; it is as though we said to ourselves, 'if he does it, why should not we?' This stirring of criminal impulses within ourselves calls for an answering effort on the part of the super-ego, which can best achieve its objects by showing that 'crime doesn't pay'. This in turn, can be done most conveniently and completely by a demonstration on the person of the criminal. By punishing him we are not only showing him that he can't 'get away with it' but holding him up as a terrifying example to our own tempted and rebellious selves."

The limitations of deterrent punishments must still be borne in mind. There is much crime, especially of the more serious sort, on which it has little effect, and many criminals, particularly of the more persistent type, on whom it will make little impression. In the United Kingdom, punishment for fraud offences consists of imprisonment and also confiscation of the proceeds of fraud wherever possible. This is enacted in the Proceeds of Crime Act 1995 which can be seen as restorative justice. For example in a 2003 case, Lee Rosser[126] was handed consecutive prison terms in two trials concerning conspiracies to defraud investors in a 'malt whisky scheme' and a 'millennium champagne scheme'. The UK's Serious Fraud Office traced his assets and won a confiscation judgement. The court was told that through Rosser's fraud, the benefit from the fraud of £5 million, but that because he made a large number of cash transactions and his expensive lifestyle, his realisable assets were few. The court nevertheless ordered him to pay £519, 000. This case is similar to the case of R v Mitchell, Kirkup and others where the defendants had spent most of the proceeds of their fraud on a luxury lifestyle and there was practically none of the proceeds remaining.(see Appendix 6). Contrary to this obvious benefit from the fraud perpetrated, in the case of R v Olubitan,[127] the facts of this particular case bore no evidence that the conspirator received any pecuniary advantage from the conspiracy. Therefore the confiscation order was quashed.

The United Kingdom is different to the rest of the European Union in that the prosecutors apply for a confiscation order after a serious fraud conviction whilst in the rest of the European Union, a freezing order on assets is the opening gambit in most actions of suspected fraud. Such an EU freezing order is achieved through a criminal investigation presided over by magistrates. In England trusts are often used in which to protect assets from confiscation but a discretionary trust may be made to pay the creditors when the beneficiaries become bankrupt.

The 1824 case of the Trial of Henry Fauntleroy[128] for forgery illustrate that the criminal offences of fraud and forgery have been diluted from an offence which carried a sentence to hang, a capital punishment to the recent 2004 UK serious fraud case in which the lenient sentences of 120 hours of community service was passed.

The UK Proceeds of Crime Act 1995 resembles the informal German restitution and Mediation within the German Justice System except for the fact that it is a statute in the UK and an informal alternative procedure in Germany where, in adult penal law, the restitution order has been recognised since 1953 as a condition of probation and as a means of diversion by the prosecutor or judge.

In 1990, the offender-victim arrangement was introduced and since 1994, courts may reduce punishment, place an offender on probation, or refrain from punishing at all for offences punishable by up to a year in prison provided the

---

works as a consultant. Another example is Nick Leeson, the rouge trader who brought down Barings Bank after racking up losses of £850 million. He served 4 years in prison and now lives in the Irish Republic, making his living as a sought after guest speaker.

125 Flugel.J.C, (1950), "The psycho-analytic study of the family", London, Hogarth Press.

126 R v Rosser [2003] unreported.

127 R v Olibutan [2003] The Times Nov 7, Court of Appeal, Criminal Division.

128 Fauntleroy began as officer in his father's London bank in 1800. In 1814 economic conditions were bad and he began forging signatures of securities belonging to bank's customers, selling them and covering up the forgery by clever devices, constantly charging accounts at the Bank of England. His forgeries became more and more extensive, enabling Fauntleroy to live extravagantly. So extensive and so intricate were his forgeries that they covered a large number of customers and he used forgeries to cover forgeries. In 1824 his forgeries were discovered by the Bank of England. He was arrested, tried and was found guilty and sentenced to hang.

defendant has already compensated the victim or at least honestly attempted to do so before trial. The main difference between restitution and the offender-victim arrangement in German law and British law is that these restitution arrangements in Germany are alternatives to punishment whilst in the United Kingdom they are additions to punishment. In Germany the judge may decide on civil liability within the criminal proceeding but not so in the UK.[129]

Why do we still have fraud today?

As material prosperity increases, so crime increases. With rising standards in material prosperity, education and social welfare, there has been no related decrease in crime. On the contrary, crime has risen and is rising. There is increasing lawlessness[130] even among the young[131] and still among the old. Less poverty and more material prosperity did not automatically reduce crime.[132]

It can be seen that crime including fraud is not a simple phenomenon and does not spring from one simple root cause and so we cannot use the term fraud to carpet-bag a whole series of diverse and utterly different forms of behaviour. It is a heterogeneous phenomena and not a homogeneous. Fraud is not just wrong-doing or immorality. It is a socio-legal concept of much complexity. Its causes are multiple. Sociologically, it can be said to arise from a number of sources: from status and financial frustration, from inadequate socialisation in the home, from a conflict of cultural values, from residence in an under-privileged neighbourhood, from genetic derivations. There is no such thing as fraud in a very abstract philosophical notion, but pragmatically there are frauds and there are fraudsters. There is no such cause of fraud as such, only different types of fraud committed by disparate fraudsters.

Fraud, like all crime, is a result of a combination of psychological and sociological factors. There has been no follow-up study of fraudsters,[133] whether after psychiatric or medical treatment or after release into society.

Sociologically, present day society is irreligious, godless, materialistic, hedonistic, and given over to sexual indulgence and the pursuit of transient pleasures. There has been the loosening of family bond though industrialised cities and easy transatlantic travel, the sacrament of marriage having been denigrated and divorce being rife. These may be factors that lead to increasing fraud. On the other hand, the notions of social justice, equality of opportunity and individual dignity are more upheld now than in centuries past.[134]

---

129 It is interesting that a statistical comparison of frauds in the year 2000 in Germany, United Kingdom and France show that there were 895, 758 frauds in Germany, 318, 324 in the United Kingdom, 142, 583 in France, 371, 800 in the whole of the USA, translating into 10 per 1000 people, 5 per 1000, 2 per 1000 and 1 per 1000 persons respectively. Source:www.nationmaster.com

130 On Monday 16th August 2004, the UK Government announced that it would soon begin a regime of monitoring children of all persons that have ever been imprisoned with the aim of steering them away from crime because its surveys show that 50% of convicted criminals have children who themselves become convicted criminals. Source. BBC News 16.8.04 at 6pm. See also The Economist, 14 August 2004, page 66, "The evolution of everyday life".

131 See Schedule 26, paragraph 18(4) of the School Standards Framework Act 1998 which makes it a criminal offence to 'wilfully obstruct an inspector conducting an inspection in a children's nursery. See also the UK's Anti-social behaviour Act 2003. See Hamilton. S, (2004), "Highway robbery as thieves target £30, 000 caravans", Financial Mail, 15.8.04, in which the writer relates that thieves are targeting high-tech luxury models of caravans, often stealing to order for resale in markets as far away as New Zealand.

132 This reinforces Elliot's theory that a high crime rate is connected to a high standard of living. In "Crime and Modern Society", pg 280-1, she states "Part of stimulation to crime among lower class criminals stems from our standard of living…Man must work hard and compete with his skills or his brain power to achieve sufficient means to purchase these things. If he achieves all these gadgets he believes he is sharing in the good life, While many professional and learned Europeans never hope to own an automobile, virtually every skilled industrial worker in America can realise his desire to have one. Many unskilled persons lack the earning power to acquire automobiles, television sets, etc, however, and are constantly tempted to steal such items."

133 In 1949, Elliot in her book "Crime and Modern Society" stated (pg 137) "Professional crime is a business, a means of making money while engaged in activities specifically forbidden by law.."

134 The UK has the 1998 Human Rights Act and it had ratified the 1950 European Convention of Human Rights.

That society exists is sui generic. It is a thing, a noun. It is impersonal, objective and relatively stable and enduring. It is built up of a number of parts which together interweave to create solid social structures. These structures are our institutions, processes and organisations and they exist in relation to the individuals who make up the population. Without such structure, society could not exist.

In the general social structure certain ideas and notions become institutionalised and made semi-permanent, such as our laws and politics and economics. This study focuses on democratic states, not on fascist or totalitarian states. Germany, France, the United Kingdom, Illinois and New York are all democratic states. So there is a ground base for study of these societies and their fraudsters. The ideas, values and attitudes of such citizens are therefore influenced by the social forms in which these fraudsters are educated. But this does not mean that these individual fraudsters' minds and consciences were solely due to the social framework in which they live.

Although social structure does and has had influence on the individual minds of fraudsters, it is the same social structure that is reflected by the states' social institutions which embody and promote social philosophies that all of us, as society, believe to be right.

It can be argued that fraud, like all other human behaviour, is learned.[135] In a minority of cases, fraudulent behaviour arises more or less spontaneously as a result of individual illness or mental imbalance. But it in main, it exemplifies the fraudsters' normal behaviour. It is fraudsters' normal behaviour because it has motivations and goals just as the rest of society has motivations and goals as reasons for their behaviour. It is the fraudsters' normal behaviour because the fraudster responds in the fraudulent ways under pressures generated by the social structure just as the rest of society responds otherwise to the same pressures generated by the social structure which has one set of institutionalised goals, attitudes and motivations for all of us. So it cannot be that the social structure alone makes some people into fraudsters .Some people commit fraud because the social structure defines generally accepted values which these fraudsters cannot achieve unless they do fraud as an alternative route to achievement. To uphold this view is to say that society has the fraudsters it deserves or helps to create. The Serious Fraud Office cases illustrate the basic similarity and near identity of the economic roles of both legitimate and illegitimate business men.

The crime and fraud statistics over decades show a remarkable fact. Crime and especially fraud, is predominantly a male activity in our society.[136] This reflects the past male role of bread-winner. Males have over the centuries had experience of the careful husbandry of personal possessions, including women classed as chattels, this being part and parcel of social structure. With modern forms of social organisation,[137] and with equal opportunities laws[138] and anti-discrimination laws now in place, it remains to be seen if many women will join the ranks of fraudsters because of their newly acquired opportunities.

Malinowski[139] showed that in poor societies with few possessions, where property is handed down from father to son, fraud has little place. It is in huge industrial societies that fraud thrives. Western societies such as France, Germany, UK and US are infinitely complicated mass societies and have much fraud. It can be argued therefore that fraud does pay and people consider the risk worth taking. Strong social pressures in these societies are exerted through marketing on all

---

135 Sir Norwood East, in his book "Society and the Criminal" (pg 320, argues puts weight to this argument when he stated that "One of the most important causes of persistent criminality is habit, the stereotyped form of response to environmental circumstances and subjective conditions acquired by repetition. Habits enable many persons to face difficulties and conserve energy, but they may impose upon a tough-minded person action which takes the line of least resistance and a vicious circle may result: a particular situation arises, the consequential difficulty is repeated avoided and a crime is repeated committed."

136 The UK's very first female conviction for serious fraud occurred on Monday 14 June 2004 when a thirty five year old Goldman Sachs secretary was sentenced to seven years imprisonment for stealing four million pounds from her employer. Article by Adam Fresco, Times Newspaper, 15 June 2004.

137 Co-habitation of unmarried couples, single parents, homosexual partners who can adopt children, communes, etc.

138 For example, in the UK, the Sex Discrimination Act 1975, Race Relations Act 1976, Disability Discrimination Act 1995, Employment Equality Regulations 2003, Equal Pay Act 1970.

139 A criminologist who wrote "Crime and Custom in Savage Society", 1936, Kegan Paul.

of us to acquire more and more goods, more and more personal possessions. The economic buoyancy of these societies depends on consumer spending and waste is the key to prosperity. It can even be said, looking at the country crime rates, that there is an undoubted interconnection between high crime rates and economic success. The cultures studied here are undoubtedly the embodiment of materialism. The symbol of success is money and businessmen have high status and prestige. Sutherland's verdict is that American society is criminogenic.[140]

Prosperity in Germany, France, the UK and the US, can be said to exacerbate the necessity of fraud in societies which have institutionalised the goals of financial reward and free enterprise.

Conclusion

Although the word "fraud" had been bandied through the centuries, there has never been a legal definition of 'fraud' in English law. English offences of fraud are found in various Acts and are thus counted by the Home Office. The Law Commission has tried to suggest bringing all such offences under an umbrella offence of fraud, but to date, this is only a recommendation.

Socially, it has been found that fraud, that is deception and dishonesty as tested in the case R v Ghosh, is on the increase, and this increasing level of fraud does not support many of the theories of many criminologists. Sociologically, present day society is in great flux and it can be argued that fraud is learnt behaviour. That fraud is a trait of genetic propensity is being mooted again, this being a most controversial theory in the 1950's. The UK government most recent survey results, as announced in the media on 16th August 2004, reveal that over 50% of convicted criminals have offspring that are also convicted criminals. Further research is planned through the formal government tracking of all offspring of convicted criminals from now.

A sociological exploration of the environment around which major frauds have taken place brings to light the fact that serious frauds are committed mainly by older executives, mainly the more educated higher class of person, but that fraud on the whole remains a constant small percentage of all crimes (around 2%) committed by convicted criminals as was found in statistics since the 1950's.

---

140 Dr Sutherland made his initial indictment in his presidential address delivered at the 34th annual meeting of the American Sociological Society in Philadelphia in December 1939. (pg 39)"Crime and Modern Society", by M.Elliot (1952), Harper & Brothers Publishers.

Appendix One: Analysis of 49 SFO cases between 1999 and 2003

RESULTS OF ANALYSIS:

Offences	% of cases
fraudulent trading	18%
false accounting	14%
corruption	8%
conspiracy to defraud	60%

Defendants	30-39 yrs	40–49 yrs	50–59 yrs	over 60
	15%	40%	35%	10%

CASES WITH INTERNATIONAL ELEMENT   50%

Nationality of Defendants	Persons
British	71
Australian	3
Nigerian	2
Irish	2

GUILTY PLEA   32% of defendants

PRISON SENTENCES

less than 1 year	10 persons of 78
1–2 years	36 persons
3–4 years	18 persons
5–7 years	12 persons
8–10 years	2 persons

CASE DURATION from start to finish

10 years	1 case
7 years	5 cases
6 years	5 cases
5 years	11 cases
4 years	10 cases
3 years	9 cases
2 years	8 cases

Source: SFO press releases: www.sfo.gov.uk

Appendix Two: Population in prison under sentence by offence group and sentence:

England and Wales, 30 June 2002

Source: HOME OFFICE REPORT, "PRISON POPULATION", 2002.

EXTRACT

Offences	male	female	3–12 months	1–3 yrs	3–5yrs	5–10yrs	10 yrs and over
Robbery	5319	223	118	903	2049	2337	135
Theft	3391	164	1735	1249	449	117	5
Fraud	887	111	303	420	132	142	1

Appendix Three: Crime statistics 1950

Extract from statistics of prisoners in State and Federal prisons and Reformatories.

Source: Table 40 in Uniform Crime Reports, Annual Bulletin, 1950, FBI, US Dept of Justice, Washington.

Offences Charged	numbers		
	total	male	female
Robbery	19, 779	18, 930	849
Larceny	66, 031	58, 409	7, 622
Embezzlement and fraud	21, 439	19, 505	1, 934
Stolen Property	3, 289	3, 014	275
Forgery and counterfeit	11, 743	10, 395	1, 348

Appendix Four: R v Pound Green and Others (2004) unreported

A former architect to the Talbot Village Trust in Dorset was sentenced today at Southampton Crown Court. Guy Pound was jailed for three years' for his part in a £3.5million building contracts fraud.

Guy Pound and two quantity surveyors, Anthony Green and Peter Beard, were convicted at Winchester Crown Court on 16 February 2004. Green and Beard have already been sentenced. At Southampton Crown Court on 26 March 2004, they were each given prison sentences of 9 months, suspended for 12 months.

Confiscation proceedings against all three defendants are underway. A hearing date has yet to be confirmed.

The Talbot Village Trust ("the Trust") is a registered charity founded in the late 19th century. Its trustees are local landowners. It owns land in Wallisdown near Poole in Dorset. In the 1980s it began to sell some of its land to realise capital to finance developments for charitable projects on other parts of its land portfolio. The case centred on six construction projects undertaken between 1985 and 1995 amounting to £15 million. They include the construction of accommodation for the elderly and needy, hostels for Bournemouth University students, accommodation for Cheshire Homes and related road projects, all on Trust land. These contracts were commissioned through the Trust's agents, Savills of Wimborne, Dorset.

The three defendants provided construction-related services to the Trust. They fraudulently manipulated contracts by invoicing for work not done and disguising inflated professional fees in the contracts.

The SFO investigation, with the Dorset Police Commercial Branch, was opened in May 1999. The defendants were charged in June 2001 and the trial opened in January 2003. (Two other persons, senior executives in a Bournemouth building company, were also charged and tried but were acquitted).

Appendix Five: R v Peter Young (2003) unreported

In 1996 Peter Young was a fund manager at investment bank Morgan Grenfell in London. He joined the company in 1992. In 1994 he was given responsibility for a £300 million PEP fund called European Growth Trust. By 1996 it had become one of the largest unit trust funds in the country. At that time Young had responsibility for more than one billion pounds of investors' funds.

Certain regulations applied to the European Growth Trust. The fund could not hold more than 10% of the shares of any one company . It could invest no more than 10% of the fund in unapproved securities. The purpose of this regulation was to avoid over-exposure to riskier investments. Overseeing Young's compliance with the rules were Morgan Grenfell's internal compliance function and the trustees, General Accident.

In 1996 Morgan Grenfell discovered some irregularities with the European Growth Fund and Young was dismissed. The matter was referred to the Serious Fraud Office.

In 1998 Young was charged with conspiracy to defraud and with offences under the Financial Services Act 1986. In 2000, after hearing medical evidence in relation to Young's mental health in a Fitness to Plead Hearing, a jury found that Young was under a disability and was unfit to be tried. Thee is a requirement under the Criminal Procedure (Insanity) Act 1964 that in such a situation, evidence should be put before a jury in a Hearing of Facts in order to determine whether the defendant did the acts alleged in the indictment. The jury found that Peter Young committed the act alleged.

Appendix Six: R v Mitchell Kirkup and Others (2004) unreported

Five company executives were sentenced today at Leeds Crown Court having pleaded guilty to defrauding business victims of nearly £5 million in a worldwide advance fee fraud conducted through their Anglo American Group venture capital business based in West Yorkshire. They made false promises as to their ability to deliver finance projects amounting to US$24 billion.

The sentencing details are:

Paul Mitchell (born 27/8/61)	3½ years' imprisonment
Richard Kirkup (born 9/7/44)	3½ years' imprisonment
Angela Mitchell (born 27/12/59)	2 years' imprisonment
Mark Mason (born 11/6/61)	Community service order 120 hours
Victoria Chapman (born 22/4/66)	Community service order 120 hours

Anglo American Ventures Ltd was set up in early 1993 to assist businesses seeking start-up or "seed capital" and development capital. The defendants claimed both for themselves and for the company to have substantial expertise and success in the business of sourcing funding for commercial enterprises and that the company was established in its field. Anglo American advertised its service globally. A fee was required in advance to consider an application for capital. As time went by further fees were required from victims at different stages. However no venture capital was made available to any client within the five year trading period. The reality was that Anglo American neither had the expertise nor the ability to successfully fund or raise finance for projects. Nearly £5 million fee income had been generated for Anglo American. It was an advance fee fraud from the start.

The advertising prompted many thousands of potential applicants to ask for further details. Over 4, 000 of them were subsequently sent "Offers of Support" by Anglo American with a fee request ranging between one to ten thousand pounds depending on the scale of the venture required to be evaluated. Collectively these requests would have generated £13 million. Not all took the bait, but about eleven hundred did, sending in over £1½m in application fees alone from 78 countries. Many went on to suffer further and more costly deceptions at later fee paying stages of their applications. Some would proceed as far as joint venture plans requiring greater fees. There were 317 proposed and agreed joint venture plans and 79 paid up plans. Usually expressed in US dollars, they represented projects totalling $24 billion. The reality was that Anglo American only ever managed to connect three clients to nothing more than a bank loan and other financial assistance amounting to around £100, 000. This starkly illustrates the scale of the wild promises made by Anglo American.

Paul Mitchell and his wife Angela Mitchell, and Richard Kirkup were founding directors of Anglo American. Mark Mason, became a director at a later date. He knew Paul Mitchell and Richard Kirkup when the three had worked for the same life insurance company. Victoria Chapman had known Angella Mitchell when they both worked at an office interiors company. Chapman joined Anglo American as office manager, later becoming "assistant director". The company also employed staff in more junior positions who are not implicated in the fraud. The principals in the fraud were the Mitchells and Kirkup. Paul Mitchell was its architect. These three defendants were the most highly rewarded.

The original registered address for this imposingly named international finance operation was 9 Moor Knoll Drive, a modest house in East Ardsley, West Yorkshire. It was the home of the Mitchells. However the corporate stationery was modified to show the address as "Unit 9, Moor Knoll Drive". This was to give the impression of trading from offices on a business park. To add to the illusion of a global operation, company letterheads were adorned with the names of foreign cities "Los Angeles-New York-Hong Kong-Johannesburg-Geneva" to suggest offices and connections throughout the world. It was a fiction. There was no global presence.

Anglo American moved to office premises at Langham House, 140-148 Westgate in Wakefield in 1994 and later to a prestige location in Bond Terrace, Wakefield. They also used a Mayfair accommodation address to which potential victims would be invited to conduct business.

Anglo American Group Plc was created as the holding company for "Ventures" and also for a similar operation called Spiredale Ltd, but it was "Ventures" that brought in the bulk of the fees. (The Group Plc was not a stock exchange listed company).

The defendants made false claims about their credentials and the company's operations in their communications with clients. Paul Mitchell styled himself as an investment banker. Angela Mitchell and Richard Kirkup made similar false or inflated claims about their expertise. They projected themselves as top-flight business professionals. The clear intention behind this facade was to convince potential clients that Anglo American was an introducer to loan facilities of some substance and experience. Correspondence would cite claims of a team with over 20 years experience in funding projects world-wide. It was a fiction.

The company website, brochures, advertisements and its corporate video all carried the same illusion. Advertisements were placed in the Wall Street Journal, the European, The Times, the Financial Times and other significant business newspapers. The company website also drew in a lot of the income. The promotional video typifies the intended illusion. It included pictures of a power station with the caption "Location India–Financing a new power station—$150 million" to suggest it was an Anglo American assisted project. The power station neither had any connection with Anglo American; nor was it in India. It was the Drax power station in North Yorkshire.

Other video fictions include a $100 million coal mine in China, a $50 million timeshare and resort complex in Spain, a $27 million manufacturing plant in Southern Africa and a $10 million cellular phone project in Russia.

The Anglo American corporate brochure stated that the company had "successfully contracted joint venture projects totalling in excess of US$ 2 billion." Individual project requirements of up to $500 million were claimed to be deliverable. False career claims featured in the brochure for the Mitchells and for Kirkup. It also included a fabricated attestation from the company's (unidentified) solicitors and a bogus press release announcing a $50 million finance deal for production of edible oils in India, though no details were given for independent verification.

The brochure included a quotation from Shakespeare's play, Julius Caesar, to suggest the corporate ethos;

> "There is a tide in the affairs of men, which taken at the flood, leads on to fortune; Omitted, all the voyage of their life is bound in shallows and miseries. On such a full sea we are now afloat; and we must take the current when it serves, or lose our ventures."

With promotional tools and messages such as these, the fraudsters pulled in £4.8 million.

Clients were attracted from across the world. Advance fees were taken for a wide variety of business ventures. One example is a $6 million scheme for four exclusive menswear shops marketing a French designer brand in prestige locations—Covent Garden or Sloane Street in London; Rue St Honoré in Paris; Via della Spiga in Milan; Fifth Avenue or Madison Square in New York. Another example was a, $83 million basket of joint ventures through a broker in the Czech Republic. These were for a Rover car dealership, a shopping centre, a health clinic, a leasing business and a golf and hotel complex. Other examples further illustrate the diversity of the aspirant projects.

- Tourism projects in Austria;

- Mineral water production in Italy;

- Renovation of merchant ships in Greece;

- Powerboat business in the UK;

- Stud farms in France

- Financial restructuring of a company in Portugal;

- Tour operator in the USA;

- Ford car dealership in Brazil.

No project seemed to be too big or diverse for them to accept a fee. Their claim was that they had the right contacts for whatever the business.

This case is a classic example of advance fee hurdles; each jump either pulling in additional fees or making the applicants cut their losses and withdraw. Many applicants were referred to organisations listed in a published venture capital handbook who usually advised that that the venture was not practical. This therefore was a fruitless route for the applicants, most of whom had already explored the usual sources of loans. It was hardly the service expected of a supposedly well placed and experienced operation. Anglo American had no special contacts and no influence in the venture capital sector. Of the thousands of clients they attracted, only three received any financial assistance, one of which was a bank loan that could have been acquired through routine banking channels. These "successes" amounted to not much more than £100, 000. Conversely, there were many more examples of applicants being passed on to other so-called venture capital introducers in other countries who were known to the defendants and who also sought up-front fees from the applicants.

By the time the business ceased to trade in 1998, £4.8 million in income had been dishonestly obtained over the five-year trading period. Yet, despite the level of revenue, it had few assets. Pre tax profits were negligible. The defendants rewarded themselves handsomely. They sucked cash out of the business in the form of salaries, dividends and benefits, first class travel, a plush office and high quality motor cars. (Jaguar, Bentley, Porsche, BMW, Lotus and Aston Martin with private number plates AAG—for Anglo American Group, the holding company). When the business traded at a loss in 1997 they still continued to misuse the fee income.

Together, the Mitchels officially gained over £400, 000 (plus company benefits and facilities). Kirkup gained over £200, 000. Secretly, they shared £1 million siphoned off over the period of trading which they put in an Isle of Man bank account. This was concealed from the auditors, their own accounting staff, the Registrar of Companies and the Inland Revenue. False sets of accounts were filed on behalf of the company. Mason and Chapman were not found to have benefited from the secret £1 million, but they enjoyed good salaries, commissions and cars. The creation of Anglo American was found on one goal. It had been set up and operated from the start as a fraud for the benefit of the Mitchells and Kirkup and later also for Chapman and Mason who enhanced their earnings as turnover increased, knowing it to be a dishonest enterprise.

The Department of Trade & Industry received complaints from victims and commenced an investigation in October 1997. A court order shut down Anglo American in May 1998. The DTI had already alerted the SFO who launched an investigation in March 1998, jointly conducted with officers from the West Yorkshire Police fraud squad. On the 9th and 10th of that month, search warrants were executed at Anglo American's offices and the homes of the Mitchells and Kirkup. As an illustration of the reach of the fraud, investigations were conducted in seventeen jurisdictions by invoking mutual legal assistance arrangements and involving the cooperation of Interpol and many other overseas police forces.

All five defendants were charged in March 2002 with two counts of fraudulent trading in respect of Anglo American Group Plc and its "Ventures" subsidiary. A trial was scheduled for Leeds Crown Court on 26 January 2004, but just ahead of the opening the Mitchells pleaded guilty. The remaining three defendants considered their positions and by 10 February, changed their pleas. Kirkup admitted to the fraudulent trading charge. Chapman and Mason pleaded guilty not to fraudulent trading but to substantive counts of obtaining money by deception added by way of amendment to the indictment. Consequently, no trial accrued.

In passing sentences, HHJ Shaun Spencer QC said, "In terms of an example of greed, this case takes some beating". He commended the SFO and the West Yorkshire Police for the conduct of the investigation and the preparation of the case, citing in particular, officers DS Phil Hirst and DC Steve Butler and SFO case secretary Keith Billington.

Bibliography

Books

Abgrall. J, (2002)"Inside the mind of a killer", Profile Books.

Adams. S, (1984), "Roche versus Adams", Jonathan Cape.

Arlidge. A, Parry. J, Gatt. I, (1998), "Arlidge & Parry on Fraud", 2nd ed, Sweet & Maxwell

Ashman. C, Trescott, P, (1986) "Outrage", WH Allen London.

Ashworth. A, Emmerson. B, (2001), "Human rights and criminal justice", Sweet & Maxwell

Ashworth. A, (1995), "The criminal process", Clarendon Press.

Ashworth. A, (1991), "Principles of criminal law", Clarendon Press.

Balen. M, (2002), "A very English deceit", Fourth Estate.

Barchard. D, (1992), "Asil Nadir and the rise and fall of Polly Peck", Victor Gollancz Ltd.

Bar Council, (1989), "The quality of Justice", Bar Council London.

Barker. E, (1946) "Aristotle: politics", Oxford.

Bentham. J, (1970), "An introduction to the principles of morals and legislation", Oxford University Press.

Bevan. V, Lidstone. K, (1991), "Investigation of crime", Butterworths.

Bidwell. A, (1987), "Wall Street to Newgate", True Life Crime.

Bose. M, Gunn. C, (1989), "Fraud", Unwin Hyman.

Boulton. D, (1978), "The LockHeed Papers", Jonathan Cape.

Bower. S, (2000), "Actionable misrepresentation", 4th ed, Butterworths

Bower. T, (1998), "Maxwell the outsider", Mandarin Books

Brown. A, (2002), "Criminal Evidence and Procedure", 2nd ed, Butterworths

Bower. T, (1996), "Maxwell—the final verdict", Harper Collins.

Branch. T, Propper. E.M, (1982), "Labrynith", Viking Press New York.

Bresler. F, (1992), "Interpol", 1992, Sinclair-Stevenson.

Bromberg. W(1965), "Crime and the Mind", New York and London.

Burge. G, Ryan. C, (1993), "Corporate cannibals", Mandarin.

Calavita. K, Pontell. H.N, Tillman. R.H, (1997), "Big money crime", University of California Press.

Chinhengo. A, (1995), "Essential jurisprudence", Cavendish

Churchill. W.S, (1948), "The second World Was", Cassell

Clinard. M.B, Yeager. P.C, (1980), "Corporate crime", Free Press New York

Cohen. M.R, (1961), "Reason and Law", Collier Books

Connell. J, Sutherland. D, (1978), "Fraud—the amazing story of Dr Savundra", Hodder and Stoughton.

Cornwell. R, (1983), "God's banker", Dodd Mead & Co, New York.

Courtney. C, Thompson. P, (1996), "City lives", Methuen.

Croall. H, (1992), "White collar crime", Open University

Danziger. D, Gillingham. J, (2003), "The year of Magna Carta", Hodder and Stoughton.

Davie Report, (1995), HMSO

Davis N, (1992), "The unknown Maxwell", Pan Books.

Demaris. O, (1986), "The boardwalk jungle", Bantham Books.

De Reuck, A.V.S, (1968), "The mentally abnormal offender", Boston.

Devlin. P, (1965), "The enforcement of morals", Oxford Press

Dobson. P, Phillips. E, (2001), "Law relating to theft", Cavendish

DTI Report, Donaldson. D, Watt. I", (1997), "Guinness plc. Investigation under sections 432(2) and 442 of the Companies Act 1985", HMSO.

Duff. A, Garland. D, (1997), "A reader in punishment", Oxford University Press.

Elliot. M.A.(1952) "Crime in Modern Society", Harper & Brothers.

Etienne. P, Maynard. M, (2000), "The Infiltrators", Penguin Books.

Eysenck. HJ, (1970), "Crime and personality", London Paladin.

Fallon. I, Srodes. J(1987), "Takeovers", Hamish Hamilton.

Farrell. R,A, Swigert .V.L, (1985), "The corporation in criminology: new directions for research", Journal of Research in Crime & Delinquency, 83-94

Fay. S, (1996), "The collapse of Barings", Arrow Books.

Fleming. J, (2000), "Stripping away assets—as the scale of fraud around the world increases, both the law and the lawyers are running hard to keep up.", Nov 2000, Law Society Gazette, UK.

Fleming. R, Miller. H, (1994), "Scotland Yard", Signet.

Flugel.J.C., (1950), "The psycho-analytic study of the family", London Hogarth Press.

Fletcher. P, (2000), "Rethinking criminal law", Oxford University Press

Flew. A, (1973), "Crime or disease", Harper & Row, USA.

Forsyth. E, (1996), "Who killed Polly Peck", Smith Gryphon Publishers.

Franklin. P, (1990), "Profits of Deceit", Heinmann London.

Fraud Trials Committee Report 1986, HMSO

Genn. H, (1999), "Paths to justice", Hart Publishing, Oregon

Gilbert. M, (1986), "Fraudsters", Constable.

Giles. F.T, (1954), "The criminal law", Pelican Books.

Gillard. M, (1987), "In the name of charity", Chatto and Windus.

Glazebrook. P.R, (1989), "Statutes in criminal law", Blackstone Press.

Glover. E, (1960), "The roots of crime", International University Press.

Green. E.J, (1976), "Psychology of law enforcement", Wiley

Greenwald. J.M, (1997), "Document fraud", Loompanics Ltd.

Geis. G, Meir. R.F, Salinger .L.M, (1995), "White-collar crime", 3rd ed, Free Press, New York.

Graham Report, (1994), HMSO

Gurwin. L, (1983), "The Clavi Affair", Pan Books.

Hart. H.L.A, (1961), "The concept of law", Oxford University Press

Hobhouse. L.T, (1922), "The elements of social justice", Faber and Faber.

Hobson. D, (1999), "The national wealth", Harper Collins.

Hollin. C.R, (1989), "Psychology and crime", Routledge London

Holtman. J, (2001), "Criminal litigation", 9th ed, Jordans

Home Office Publication, (2003), "Counting Rules for Recording Crime", April 2003.

Home Office Statistics, (2002), "Prison Population, England & Wales", HMSO

Huntington. I, (1992), "Fraud: prevention and detection", Butterworths.

Inciardi. J.A, Siega. H.A, (1977), "Crime–emerging issues", Praeger Publications.

Irving. H.B, (1921), "Last Studies in Criminology", W Collins and Sons.

Jacobs. F.G, (1971), "Criminal responsibility", Weidenfield and Nicolson.

Jackson. M.W, (1986), "Matters of Justice", Croom Helm.

Jameson. K.M, (1994), "The organisation of Corporate Crime", Sage Publications.

Jones H, (1971), "Crime in a changing society", Penguin.

Jones. H, (1956), "Crime and the Penal System", University Tutorial Press.

Joseph. M, (1994), "The conveyancing fraud", Michael Joseph Press.

Jupp. V, (1989), "Methods of Criminological Research", Routledge.

Justice Bulletin Autumn(2003), Justice.

Justice Annual Report (2003), Justice.

Killick. M., (1998), "Fraudbusters", Indigo Press.

Kirk. D.N, Woodcock. A, (2002), "Serious fraud—investigation and trial", 3rd ed, Butterworths

Lacey. N, (1994), "A reader in Criminal Justice", Oxford University Press.

Law Commission Consultation Paper, (1998), "Legislating the Criminal Code: Fraud and Deception", April, 1998.

Levi. M, (1999), "Fraud: organisation, motivation and control", Ashgate Publishing

Lewis. M, (1989), "Liar's Poker", Coronet Books.

Lever. L, (1992), "The Barlow Clowes Affair", Macmillan London.

Littman. J, (1996), "The fugitive game", Little, Brown & Co.

Lukezic. J, Schwarz. T, (1990), "False Arrest", New Horizon Press.

Maguire. M, Morgan. R, Reiner. R, (1997), "Oxford Handbook of Criminology", Oxford University Press.

Maloney. T, (1994), "Royal Commission on Criminal Justice, Research Study 2, 3, 4:'Conduct of Police Investigations: Records of Interview, the Defence Lawyer's Role and Standards of Supervision'", HMSO.

Matthews. R, (1989), "Privatising Criminal Justice", Sage Publications.

Mays. J.B(1963), "Crime and the Social Structure", Faber and Faber.

McClean. D, (2002), "International Co-operation in civil and criminal matters", 2nd ed, Oxford University Press

McClusky. Lord, (1986), "Law, Justice and Democracy", Sweet and Maxwell.

McLagan. G, (2003), "Bent Coppers", Orion.

Milton. F, (1959), "In some authority", Pall Mall.

Moston. S, Stephenson. G.M, (1993), "Royal Commission on Criminal Justice, Research Study 22, 'Questioning and Interviewing of Suspects Outside the Police Station' HMSO.

Nelken. D, (1994), "The future of criminology", Sage Publications.

Neustatter. W.L, (1953), "Psychological Disorder and Crime", Christopher Johnson.

O'Shea. J, (1991), "The daisy chain", Simon and Schuster.

Norwood—East. Sir, (1949), "SOCIETY AND THE CRIMINAL", Charles C Thomas.

Pasley. F.D, (1966), "Al Capone", Faber and Faber.

Perry. F, (1979), "Reports for criminal courts", Owen Wells.

Pettet. B, (2001), "Company Law", Pearson Education Ltd.

Popper.K, (1945), "The open society and its enemies", Routledge and Kegan

Radzinowicz. L, (1961), "In search of criminology", Heinemann.

Raphael. R, (1994), "Ultimate risk", Bantham Press.

Raw. C., (1977), "Slater Walker", Andre Deutch.

Raw. C, (1992), "The Money Changers", Harper Collins.

Rimmington. S, (2001), "Open secret", Arrow Books.

Robinson. J, (1995), "The laundrymen", Pocket Books.

Rose. D, (1996), "In the name of the Law", Jonathan Cape.

Rosoft. S.M, Pontell. H.N, Tillman. R, (1998), "Profit without honor", Prentice Hall.

Ross. G, (1987), "Stung", Stoddart.

Ruggiero. V, "Crime and markets", (2000), Oxford University Press.

Rutherford. A, (1994), "Criminal Justice and the Pursuit of Decency", Waterside Press.

Schlesinger. S.R(1989), "Electronic Fund Transfer Systems Fraud", Paladin Press

Serious Fraud Office Annual Reports (1995), (1996), (1997), (1998), (1999), (2000), (2001), (2002), (2003), HMSO.

Schilit. H.M, (1993), "Financial shenanigans", McGraw Hill.

Sinclair. I, (1997), "Essentials of computer security", Bernard Banana Books.

Smith. J.C, (1960), "Criminal Case and Comment", Sweet and Maxwell.

Smith. P.G, (1970), "The crime explosion", Macdonald Unit 7 London.

Speakman. W.J, (1970), "Moriarty's Police Law", Butterworths.

Stasz. T.S, (1961), "The myth of mental illness", Harper and Rowe.

Sutherland. E.A, (1949), "White collar crime", Holt, Reinhart & Winston

The Royal Commission on Capital Punishment, (1953), HMSO London.

The Royal Commission on the Law relating to Mental Illness and Mental Deficiency", (1957), HMSO London.

Thoams. E, (1991), "The man to see", Simon and Schuster.

Thomas. G, Dillon. M, (2003), "The assassination of Robert Maxwell", Robson Books.

Thornton. P, (2003), "The prejudiced defendant: unfairness suffered by a defendant in a joint trial", Criminal Law Review,

Tobias. J.J, (1967), "Crime and Industrial 19th Century", Pelican Books.

Tomlinson. R, (2001), "The big breach", Cutting Edge.

Waldron. J, (1999), "Law and disagreement", Oxford University

Walker. C, Starner. K, (1999), "Miscarriages of Justice", Blackstone Press.

Wasserman. D, Wachbroit. R, (2001), "Genetics and Criminal Behaviour", Cambridge University Press

Welham. MG, (2002), "Corporate Killing", Butterworths

Widlake. B, (1994), "Serious Fraud Office", Warner.

Welham. M.G(2002), "Corporate killing", Tolleys Lexis Nexis.

Welsh. F(1999), "Dangerous Deceits", Harper Collins.

Young. M, (1991), "An inside job", Clarendon Press.

Zilboorg. G, (1955), "The psychology of the criminal act and punishment", The Hogarth Press.

Articles

Bhandari S, Gillett, F, "Fraud Watch", 2003, New Law Journal, Vol 153, No 7091

Doran .J, (31.5.2004), "Reinventing the wheeler dealer after a ban", Times Newspaper.

Economist, "Bosses behind bars", 12 June 2004.

Economist, Book Review, "The company of strangers" 14.8.04

Edgar. A, Jiwaji. A, "Legal Week", 10th July 2003, Vol 5 No 26

Hansard Written Answers, (2001), House of Commons.

Hussey. M, "I went twenty four hours as a law breaker", March 1930, Harpers' Magazine.

Innes. J, "Law Lords reject Guinness appeal", The Scotsman newspaper, 15.11.2002.

Sumners, J, Legal Week, 19th June 2003, Vol 5 No 23

Times, 23rd September 2003, "Keeping the profession's name clean"

Times 26th April 2004, "The fraudster may be the boss, not the PA", by Martin Waller.

Tyler. R, "Examining physician suggests British Home Secretary misled Parliament in bid to release Pinochet", articled published by International Committee of the Fourth International, 18th January, 2000. http://www.wsws.org/articles/2000/jan2000/pino-j18.shtml.

CHAPTER TWO

CURRENT ISSUES IN THE LAW OF FRAUD PROSECUTION

Issue 1—Extradition in Criminal Cases

(a)—Trial in Absence

Trial in absence: R v Steen, Andrews and Alexander [2003]

This was an Advanced Fee Fraud case brought jointly by the Crown Prosecution Service and the Serious Fraud Office. The defendants were charged in January 2000 and the case came to trial in January 2003, lasting until June 2003. This was an alleged fraud in which prospective borrowers were induced over 3 ½ years into paying an up-front fee in order to gain access to loans. In the course of this time, the defendants Alexander and Andrews received £1.5 million in administration fees and the defendant Steen received £2.5 million in due diligence fees from several hundred applicants.

They were found guilty of conspiracy to defraud and Steen, Andrews and Alexander were given prison sentences of 6, 5 and 2 years respectively.

In late May, during the trial, Steen absconded and fled to the Philippines and a warrant was issued for his arrest. The evidence against Steen had already been heard in court.

The judge mentioned the case of R v Hayward, Jones and Purvis[141] in deciding to continue the trial in Steen's absence. In the Hayward case the court had ruled that a defendant had, in general. a right to be present at his trial and a right to be represented but that those rights could be waived separately or together, wholly or in part, by the defendant himself. They might be wholly waived if knowing, or having the means of knowledge as to when and where his trial was to take place, he deliberately and voluntarily absented himself and/or withdrew instructions from those representing him. The trial judge had a discretion as to whether a trial should continue in the absence of the defendant. That discretion should be exercised with great care and it was only in rare or exceptional circumstances that it should be exercised in favour of a trial continuing.

The judge had regard to the fact that all evidence against the defendant Steen had been given and that Steen himself had already given evidence and that he was legally represented. The defendant Steen had absconded to the Philippines by obtaining a second passport The only risk was that the jury would reach an improper conclusion about the absence of the defendant and the prospect of a fair trial for the remaining defendants, Andrews and Alexander.

There was no extradition agreement between the United Kingdom and the Philippines. But Steen had entered the Philippines using an unlawfully retained passport and was deported back to the United Kingdom in time for the verdict. It is to be noted that the European Convention on Human Rights (ECHR) does not prevent States co-operating to obtain the deportation of fugitive offenders, provided that the co-operative procedures do not infringe any specific

---

141 [2001] Times, February 14.

rights protected by the Convention. Provided there was a legal basis for the arrest and deportation this is not contrary to Article 5 ECHR.[142]

Also, under Article 6 ECHR, the right to a fair trial in criminal proceedings, is the right to be present and to test evidence and to adduce evidence. This right was not violated because the defendant Steen had heard all the evidence, had given evidence and had been cross-examined. His barrister had cross-examined the 21 witnesses in the case. The defendant Steen had chosen to be absent at this stage and his interests were being protected by his legal representative.

The defendant was returned to the United Kingdom in time to hear his conviction in court and he therefore was not convicted in his absence so cannot seek leave to appeal on the grounds that his conviction was unsafe.

(b)—Extradition in Fraud Cases (Steen)
Human Rights of Extraditing a Person

The case of R v Steen and others[143] was an advanced fee fraud case brought jointly by the Crown Prosecution Service and the Serious Fraud Office. The defendants were charged in January 2000 and the case came to trial in January 2003, lasting until June 2003. This was an alleged fraud in which prospective borrowers were induced over three and a half years into paying an up-front fees in order to gain access to loans. In the course of this time, the defendants Alexander and Andrews received £1.5 million in administration fees and the defendant Steen received £2.5 million in due diligence fees from several hundred applicants. They were found guilty of conspiracy to defraud and Steen, Andrews and Alexander were given prison sentences of six, five and two years respectively.

In late May, during the trial but after the evidence against him had been heard in court, Steen absconded and fled to the Philippines, and a warrant was issued for his arrest. He was absent for most of the remainder of the hearing but was brought back to the court for the verdict. I will consider both the continuation of the trial in his absence and the manner by which he was brought back to the country and its implications in criminal proceedings.

The judge mentioned the case of R v Anthony William Jones[144] in deciding to continue the trial in Steen's absence. In the Jones case the court had ruled that a defendant had, in general, a right but not a duty to be present at his trial and a right to be represented. That those rights could be waived separately or together, wholly or in part, by the defendant himself. They might be wholly waived if knowing, or having the means of knowledge as to when and where his trial was to take place, he deliberately and voluntarily absented himself and/or withdrew instructions from those representing him. The trial judge had a discretion as to whether a trial should continue in the absence of the defendant. That discretion should be exercised with great care and it was only in rare or exceptional circumstances that it should be exercised in favour of a trial continuing.

The judge in Steen had regard to the fact that all evidence against the defendant Steen had been given and that Steen himself had already given evidence and that he was and continued to be legally represented. The defendant Steen had absconded to the Philippines by obtaining a second passport The only risks were that the jury might reach an improper conclusion about the absence of the defendant and the prospect of a fair trial for the remaining defendants, Andrews and Alexander.

There is no extradition agreement between the United Kingdom and the Philippines.

Extradition, which relies on the existence of a complex network of treaties and reciprocal agreements between States, must follow a series of rules:—

---

142 Vcalan v Turkey (Application 46221/99).

143 (2003) unreported

144 HL [2002] 2 WLR 524, [2002]2All ER 113, affirming the decisions in the CA (sub non R v Hayward, Jones and Purvis) and the court of first instance.

- there must be an identified person whose surrender is sought;

- the offence of which the accused is suspected must be within the terms of an existing treaty or reciprocal agreement between the two States in question;

- some offences are routinely excluded from the category of extraditable offences, for example, political, terrorist and religious offences; and

- the act which the suspect is accused of should be a criminal offence in both the relevant jurisdictions.

The Steen case is unlike the extradition of Vladimir Levin,[145] in that Levin was to be extradited from the UK to the USA, the procedure for this extradition being governed by the provisions of the Extradition Act 1870. It can be argued that Steen was extradited in a manner similar to that in the case of R v Horseferry Road Magistrate's Court, ex parte Bennett,[146] and, if so, the question to be considered is whether his extradition was illegal because it was not in accordance with any treaty.

The Bennett case reached the House of Lords on the question of whether the complicated, unorthodox and probably illegal method of extradition used should affect the outcome of his trial. The Court found that the trial was not affected but that the means of extradition was a serious abuse of power and should not go unchecked. Lord Griffiths stated that the courts should stop the trial of any defendant whose presence within the jurisdiction had been improperly obtained. He said "Extradition procedures are designed not only to ensure that criminals are returned from one country to another but also to protect the rights of those who are accused of crimes by the requesting country. Thus sufficient evidence has to be produced to show a prima facie case against the accused and the rule of speciality protects the accused from being tried for any crime other than that for which he was extradited. If a practice developed in which the police or prosecuting authorities of this country ignored extradition procedures and secured the return of an accused by mere request to police colleagues in another country they would be flouting the extradition procedures and depriving the accused of the safeguards built into the extradition process for his benefit. The courts of course have no direct power to apply direct discipline to the police or prosecuting authorities, but they can refuse to allow them to take advantage of abuse of power by regarding their behaviour as an abuse of process and thus preventing a prosecution".

Steen had entered the Philippines using an unlawfully retained passport, and the authorities in the Philippines co-operated voluntarily with the UK's request for his deportation back to the United Kingdom in time for the verdict. It is to be noted that the European Convention on Human Rights (ECHR) does not prevent States from co-operating to obtain the deportation of fugitive offenders, provided that the co-operative procedures do not infringe any specific rights protected by the Convention. If there was a legal basis for the arrest and deportation this is not contrary to Article 5 ECHR.[147]

Also, under Article 6 ECHR, the right to a fair trial in criminal proceedings, is the right to be present and to test evidence and to adduce evidence. This right was not violated because the defendant Steen had heard all the evidence, had given evidence and had been cross-examined. His barrister had cross-examined the 21 witnesses in the case. The defendant Steen had chosen to be absent at this stage and his interests were being protected by his legal representative. The defendant was returned to the United Kingdom in time to hear his conviction in court and he therefore was not found guilty and sentenced in his absence.

As the Steen case is not reported, it is speculative to suggest reasons for his conviction rather than release on the grounds of an unlawful extradition following Bennett. Possibly the distinction between Bennett and Steen is that Bennett had left the UK lawfully and the criminal proceedings started after he had left, whereas Steen left in breach

---

145 Re Levin (House of Lords), 19/6.97

146 [1994] 1 A.C. 42. The suspect was a national of New Zealand who had committed theft and fraud offences in the UK but was presently living in South Africa. The CPS decided not to use the Extradition Act 1989 but to wait until the South African government deported Bennett back to New Zealand and to arrest him en route and return him to the UK to stand trial.

147 Vcalan v Turkey (Application 46221/99).

of his bail conditions and on an unlawfully held passport and therefore the court in Steen decided that his conviction could properly proceed.

Cases referred to:

Vcalan v Turkey ECJ Application 46221/99

Re Levin House of Lords 19/9/97

R v Hayward, Jones, Purvis [2001] The Times. Feb 14.

R v Horseferry Road Magistrate's Court, ex parte Bennett [1994] 1 A.C. 42

R v Steen & ors [2003] unreported

(c)—Corporate Advances

Southwark Crown Court

Monday & Tuesday 12 & 13 May 2003.

TRANSCRIPT FOR CASE

T20010272   George Steen

David P Andrews

T20010250   Dennis R Alexander

This case started in January 2003 and will finish on 2nd June 2003.

There is $US 3 million out of Mr Steen control in various accounts in the Philippines. Steen and another were signatories. They could withdraw funds singly. There were banks accounts in the Philippines, Hungary and Jersey.

Mr Steen said he held the money in trust for the various applicants for business loans. The money was to cover due diligence work. Should anyone of the applicants wish to resurrect their case, that money would be used for another due diligence. Steen had a program called "money manager" which allowed him to work out how much money was unappropriated.

The Prosecution wants a print-out of Money Manager Program that shows the unappropriated amounts of money. This list is not in the possession of the police.

Steen asserted that he was able to allocate the money.

Defence barrister Mr Burkett QC: Steen has this list. He will distribute this list.

Prosecution : Have you written to all your clients to tell them that £x was still in the accounts? Go back to Tuesday. From January 1994 when you established this scheme "Corporate Advances". You had several hundred applicants. They were prepared to pay you at least for one due diligence programme. You said that every single applicant was unable to fulfil the criteria. There were two primary security provisions.

Each applicant was happy to give a "charge on land and buildings". But they also had to fulfil a "collateral bond requirement".

It follows that since the overlap period from January 1997, you were being sent the wrong sort of applicant.

Yet Steen received $US 1 million a year. There was cash-flow. That cash-flow went into an organisation which was essentially George Steen, Emma Steen and Marie the secretary.

Marie was paid £12,500 a year and less.

It follows that the vast bulk of the funds which came into Steen's control has been intended for Steen and his wife Emma. For example, the way you operated meant you were paid an income as a director of £40,000 a year from Philippines Finance, an unincorporated company. At the end of the day, you were getting drawings from Philippines Finance which drew income fees from Corporate Finance.

Of the $US 1 million a year, £12,500 went to Marie Peyton the secretary and the rest went to George and Emma Steen.

You had a good lifestyle. One third of the year you were abroad.

In 1994 you had nothing.

In 1999 you had $US 3 million in several bank accounts.

The programme wasn't designed to be a success, was it? You weren't looking for lots of successful applicants, were you?

Steen: There was a 2% fee with a successful applicant of which 1% was my fee, ½ % was for administration and ½ % for the funder.

Prosecutor: All the cases, and there were hundreds of them, were all failures. If they were weeded out by Corporate Advances not sending them to you, or if you yourself had weeded them out, you would not have earned a bean. Was that the only business programme you operated?

Steen: No, I had one in the Philippines . I sold it in 1999 for $US 3 million.

(Tuesday)

Prosecutor : Look at the definition of "collateral bond". The definition of the bond spelt out the consequences of the bond. The cost from the bank is 4% of the cost of due diligence. What about the Israeli Bond.? That was a junk bond, wasn't it?

Steen: No it was not a junk bond. It was 25% of the cost.

Prosecutor: The Israeli Bond is acceptable, is it?

40% of cost was what was said to be the cost of the Israeli Bond. This is according to Harvey. This was not "giving financial advice".

Was Harvey registered as a Financial Advisor? No.

But he was your agent, wasn't he? Yes? The Financial Services Act states that this is not "financial advice".

Steen: He sent the general letter out.

Prosecutor : The wrong sort of advice was given year after year. If Harvey had inserted three or four sentences, it would have weeded out the unsuccessful applicants from the beginning. This would have ensured that people understood what they were letting themselves in for.

They couldn't offer a "charge on land" nor could they sign a "collateral bond" because NONE of these applicants had 25 to 40% of the project or loan amount they required as free assets.

If they had been told on day 1—you will need 25 to 40% of free assets before you can acquire a loan of 100%, they would each and every one of them, have abandoned their application.

Steen: They all had an offer letter.

Prosecutor: We have that point. I am looking at, not 3 or 4 or 5 failures, but hundreds of failures.

Steen: I can't be specific. I asked Mr Andrews to give certification that he had given financial advice to applicants. This is one step I took.

Prosecutor: The Questions and Answers document you sent out. Why did you not explain about the 25 to 40% of free assets required re Peninsular Holdings?

Steen: In many instances, the questions and answers document was too generalised.

Prosecutor: If you had explained the 25 to 49% of free assets required in the Q & A document, this would have weeded out unsuitable applicants.

This was all you had to do. At the INITIAL phase, you could have spelt out the security implications. Your experience over years proved that not a single one was working.

Look at Bundle 1, page 26. Specific contractual documentation.

The first letter after receipt of advance money from Corporate Advances.

Look at this letter from George Steen.

Commercial Funding application.

Look at page 54—Document that accompanies the letter from George Steen. Look at first paragraph : "We have performed an initial review subject to a due diligence…..", ie, on what you have seen so far, you are prepared to continue. "The offer remains valid until 14th August. Failing that, I will close your file."

This is a warning and a time limit.

The small print of the offer letter states the same.

Why didn't you add the paragraph I suggested about the "collateral bond"?

You were putting pressure on people to sign, weren't you?

Steen: No. I think the word "bond" was made clear in the offer letter.

Prosecutor: Look at the case of Mr Sampson. Sampson failed the collateral test, didn't he?

Steen: We advise clients to seek independent legal advice.

Prosecutor: You did the first stage due diligence . This is the first of 3 stages. At this point you already had ½ the due diligence payment. Then Letter 2 was sent out. Letter 2 was written to dozens of applicants. They all failed. Did you not see that they were going to come to grief? Letter 2 invites the second tranche of Due Diligence payment. Mr Hardy then becomes involved—to get the collateral bond from the applicants. No-one ever got a collateral bond. You had 100% failure for 51/2 years! Why didn't you put a warning in your letter? Your business was founded on the premise that you would supply commercial loans, wasn't it?

Steen: I did stop the applications but then continued.

Prosecutor: Who did you discuss it with?

Steen: Andrew Scott.

Prosecutor: What was the nature of your discussion? Were you mindful of the money you were stacking up in Jersey and the Philippines?

Steen: No, because that was not my money.

Prosecutor: You then decided to send applicants a "specimen" letter. We will use blunt language. You can use blunt language, can't you?

Steen: Yes.

Prosecutor: The Due Diligence was in 3 stages. The first tranche was shortly after the Brighton meeting. Then you write a letter to the bank, a letter to the solicitor and a letter to the applicant.

Did you do a DUN & BRADSTREET check on every applicant? You have an account there, haven't you?

Steen: Yes.

Prosecutor: They keep a running account for you, don't they?

Steen: Yes.

Prosecutor: You have done as many checks on DUN & BRADSTREET since the trial started as you did during your business. Were you trying to dig up the dirt?

How much did you pay Mr Hardy?

Steen: $1000 per applicant.

Prosecutor: Mr Hardy became the interface to break the bad news that the securities the applicants were offering were inadequate. Hardy's task is to communicate with the applicant. Then after this stage, you would involve the ultimate lender.

Steen: Verification can be done by screen. BLOOMFIELDS can identify the bonds, etc.

Prosecutor: How can Mr Hardy tell you that he has done the verification?

Steen: Mr Hardy has connections with BLOOMFIELDS.

Prosecution: So Hardy tells you that bond is verified. You then submit it to the ultimate lender. You send the file with the business plan, draft, charge, etc plus a separate file of Hardy's with securities, insurances, etc. So you repackage it to be sent to the ultimate lender. At this stage you instruct a local agent to check out the business. BUT THIS IS WHOLLY THEORETICAL BECAUSE IT NEVER EVER HAPPENED, DID IT?

Do you then go on a plane to see the business?

Steen: Yes.

You spend weeks there, yes? It must take weeks from the time you hit the ultimate lender, then book time to go to Australia say, speak to accountants, do due diligence, it must take weeks.

After the commitment letter, do you put a provisional lender on a new file?

Look at the funding arrangements. You used to do domestic mortgages before, didn't you? Mortgages of between £8,000 and £20,000. That was peanuts compared to this. So you went into the commercial loans business. So where do you get the money from? How do you decide terms of business such as security and rate of interest?

In Panama you met Alan who introduced you to UPC, a pension organisation which needed to invest its money. UPC were interested. Similarly with Allied Bank but through their investors, ie their customers. There would have been contractual documents which any applicant would have to sign? There would have been a contractual document with UPC—their loan agreement. Similarly with Allied Bank's customers, there would have been contractual documents which any applicant would have to sign. There would have been a loan agreement with UPC, wouldn't there? Allied Bank's customers would have a contract with the individual investor and applicant. This was drawn up by a firm of lawyers in the Philippines. The lawyers wrote that UPC and Allied Bank would have no interest in your offer letter. Why?

Steen: There was a meeting to decide common documents because terms and conditions in the offer letter had been commonly agreed.

Prosecutor: How do you ensure that you would get your 11/2 %?

Steen: This would be drawn down from the loan. There is a 2% establishment fee in the commitment letter.

Prosecutor: But this is theoretical. It never happened. So how would you enforce this 1 ½ % if it wasn't paid, theoretically?

I suggest there would be a contract, an agency agreement or a brokerage agreement.

Steen: UPC document has such a provision in the letter.

Prosecutor: Where are the contractual documents between Peninsular Holdings, UPC and Allied Bank from 1993/4 to now???

Steen: They are in my office in the Philippines. The Police took them.

Prosecutor: How long will it take to get the documents here?

Steen: The documents are in the safe of Allied Bank.

Prosecutor: We want them here by tomorrow morning. I am putting you on notice. I want to see the contractual documents between Allied Bank and Philippines Holdings and UPC.

Steen: I tried to get the documents but I was not allowed to go.

Prosecutor: Emma your wife could have gone; she has her passport. What about your Commercial Director?

Steen: He is retired.

Prosecutor: You have two offices in the Philippines?

Steen: I have one office with the lawyers' office and one office at home. The documents are in the safe at home.

Prosecutor: What does the safe hold? A couple of lever arch files? Could Emma not have had access to that paperwork? Did it not occur to you?

Steen: No.

Prosecutor: Can your bank vault hold lever arch files?

Steen: Yes. Only I have access to the safe deposit box.

Prosecutor: Are you saying you could not have gone to a solicitor to let Emma have access?

I say that all that you are saying is a tissue of lies. You have no such documents. This is the 21st century. Documents can be moved round the world. You have strong connections in the Philippines. Did your secretary Marie never write to an external funder?

Steen: Marie has been to the Philippines. She knew.

Mr Burkett QC Defence Barrister: The Prosecution mentioned Maria's evidence. "He did have funding for applicants. He did not say where it was from". "He was connected to people in high places".

Therefore the position as put to the jury may not be wholly complete.

Judge : It is implicit in what she was saying that she was there.

Prosecutor: The defence clarified the statement of Maria's by reading it out. Maria's cross-examination re Steen's move to international finance rather than domestic finance.

Judge: My note is : "he was earning more, connected to people in high places".

Defence Mr Burkett QC: Marie said "he indicated that a source of funds was there".

Mr Leyton Prosecutor: There never was any correspondence held dealing with contractual relationship with you and ultimate lenders, was there?

Steen: There was correspondence with ultimate lenders.

Prosecutor: Are we likely to be hearing from Allied Bank, UPC, etc? Are you going to call any witnesses?

Steen: I will have to consider whether to call them.

I thought the police would have been able to get these documents.

Prosecutor: You got in touch with UPC. The possibility of funds comes before you establish business. Martha was the lawyer for UPC. She ended up as your lawyer and the Director of Philippines Holdings.

Look at the bundle, page 4 re contractual correspondence. Document 7759.

This is a letter you asked Martha to write. "Dear Mr Andrews (by this stage PHP was set up and she was director) We confirm that we have acted as corporate advisors to PHP. We continue to act to provide legal services…based on specific instructions received…. we confirm that funds are available to applicants….. Peninsular Holdings Panama.

(Screen—77690002).

"Please inform your lawyers that they may be permitted to copy our letter subject to the following conditions."

So Martha can confirm funds available solely as a result of a letter from your brother-in-law.

Corporate Advances finds applicants. You do get some rubbish. The purpose of employing Corporate Advances was to weed out this rubbish. So people had to put up money to Corporate Advances and confirm that they will fly to the UK with their business plans, etc. So Corporate Advances weed out applications. You get the first payment. Hardy comes in and gets the second payment. You then send file on to UPC, etc.

Did you retain any notes of your correspondence with Hardy or with UPC, etc?

Steen: Yes, they are in the Philippines; I was not allowed to go there.

Prosecutor: There is International Parcel Service, e-mail, etc. So you have no minutes of conversations about applicants?

Steen: These files are in the Philippines.

Prosecutor: You have no formal submission to UPC. All were failures but were discussed. The vast majority of your business was generated by Corporate Advances, wasn't it?

Steen: Yes.

Prosecutor: A large percent. So UPC did UPC and Allied Bank know that over 5 ½ years of business you were 100% unsuccessful? What about David Andrews? What views did Allied Bank have of David Andrews by December 1998?

Steen: No particular view.

Prosecutor: So for 5 years David Andrews did no business. They suggested to you that you should take on board more brokers. When you were giving your evidence you went on to talk of December 1998 when you paid for David Andrews to go to the Philippines?

Steen: The first trip of David Andrews to the Philippines was in 1994.

Prosecutor: But you said "my lenders had heard so much about him…." Why would they want to meet David Andrews who produced no business for 5 years? The truth was that this was a holiday. You were working really hard, were you? What files were you working on? All you did was write 3 standard letters to the solicitor, the accountant and the bank and the offer letter. What was the hard work you were doing?

Steen: Hardy was sending faxes to me, etc.

I had other business. A car rental to holiday makers and a music business.

Prosecutor: This was a jamboree, wasn't it? When you took Maria to various Xmas parties, it was just a party, wasn't it?

Steen: It was a large do—mainly social.

Prosecutor: You were a wealthy man in the Philippines, weren't you? The $1.5 million in the bank accounts. Shouldn't you move this money back to the UK to offer it back to the applicants? It is not your money. It is closer to the applicants than it is to you. What about you setting up a commercial loan system? You had new structures and a new scheme which needed corporate advisors to have thought it through. You said you spent 3 days with Hardy discussing what his job would be.

Steen: What we discussed was his job, letters, etc.

Prosecutor: When it is new you have to work out how it is going to operate. You would have to show him what was in the file. You would have to show him what were the things he needed to verify. Obviously he developed a system. By January 1997 he was sending out a series of letters.

Steen: What I wanted was for Hardy to provide assistance.

Prosecutor: Hardy developed a series of Q and A with standard answers. He has a fairly small part in the scheme. You must have done a similar thing with Corporate advances?

Steen: No because I was au fait with Corporate Advances.

Prosecutor: But this is a world apart. This is international finance.

Steen: As far as Applications Forms go, Corporate Advances modified one of the sentences.

Prosecutors: But we know how it works: Applications, solicitors, etc.

Steen: Other brokers were advertising by that time.

Prosecutor: You had adverts, letters inviting people over to the UK, etc.

Steen: I did not discuss inviting people to the UK. I didn't work that way with my other brokers.

Prosecutor: This is a new business. You go international. You discussed with Corporate Advances where in the world they were going to push the scheme. Where did it start?

Steen: Corporate Advances copied the model from International Business Organisation.

Prosecutor: You must have discussed with Corporate Advances the profile of the applicants. You must have said this is all going to rest on a charge on land and a collateral bond?

Steen: Yes.

Prosecutor: At the same time you were dealing with a new partnership?

Steen: There was no formal agreement.

Prosecutor: But you were partners with a new name? Here you were, two men starting an entirely new project. No longer doing domestic clients but multi-national clients. This is a huge change. You admit you needed to discuss the business?

Steen: We discussed the borrower and security conditions.

Prosecutor: You had not been using a collateral in your domestic business. This is a novel concept. You must have explained and discussed it with him?

Steen: The discussion only took a few minutes.

Mr. Leyton Prosecutor: All the more reason for you to sit down with people and discuss. You must have underlined to them that no-one is going to get a loan without a collateral bond—a free transferable collateral bond; that the sort of applicant you were looking for were ones with at least 25-40% unencumbered assets.

Steen : No.

Prosecutor: Why not?

Steen : It is emphasised in the offer letter.

Prosecutor: This entire scheme is posited on the collateral bond, isn't it?

Steen: No.

Prosecutor: The jury will judge. Can we go to the specimen letter—the standard correspondence letter (on page 2) sent out by Corporate Advances. One went to the broker; one to the applicant. "We are pleased to confirm that your application appears to meet with our current criteria...."

Were there letters not sent out?

Steen: I wasn't sure that these letters were sent out.

Prosecutors: You must have appreciated that they were sending out these letters.

Steen: No, I didn't know what was sent.

Prosecutor: Let's look at page 68. The letter here states "This is to Certify that D. Andrews is accredited as introducer to Panama business and is authorised in the conduct of business. Signed G. Steen".

You wouldn't have authorised him unless you knew how he did business, would you?

Steen: This was based on good experiences of Panama business.

Prosecutor: Look at Page 69, second paragraph. You frequently used two sentences which contained a definition of "assignable collateral bond". Where did that wording come from?

Steen: I can't answer that question.

Prosecutor: Did the three of you put your heads together to decide the meaning of "collateral bond"? Did you know exactly the ramifications of the meaning you gave to "collateral bond"?

Look at page 70: "The lender employs a specialist firm of management consultants to advise and assist where-ever possible." Could you say that Mr Hardy could advise and assist where-ever possible? Did you have any idea of the standard letters sent out by Corporate Advances?

Steen: I don't think so.

Prosecutor: Were you interested in what was being sent out?

Steen: I was aware.

Prosecutor: Did it ever concern you that Corporate Advances were sending such letters?

Did you ever sit down and analyse what these letters say after so many years of failure?

Steen: No.

Prosecutor: Look at page 20. This is the standard letter sent out before each admin. Fee is paid out. "On your full acceptance of the letter of offer...."

What does it suggest? It suggests that due diligence work will be finished before the standard commitment letter is sent. So this is a huge mistake and misrepresentation.

Steen: I would have certainly worded that differently. I was never shown that letter. I have never discussed that letter.

Prosecutor: You accept that there were hundreds of applications. People were upset. They complained. They wanted their loans. They wanted their money back. Some complaints went to you and some to Mr. Hardy. You replied that they cannot get their money back because they had breached their agreement. There were hundreds of upset people.

Look at page 32. This is another standard letter. "Please be advised that Corporate Advances is prepared to refund fee only under certain conditions....1........2......."

You must have discussed that sort of letter with Corporate advances?

Steen: I did not involve myself with any application fee. I didn't discuss it. I shouldn't have to explain letters that I played no part in writing.

Prosecutor: Corporate Advances has been working with only one commercial institution since January 1994. Is it true?

Steen : They are lying. Mr. Andrews was dealing with other people . They had other lenders such as Dubai Investments.

Prosecutor: That may be considered as "commercial secrets". Look at page 42. Standard letter……"…..that on completion, drawdown must be in US dollars.". Where did Andrews get that from?

Steen: I don't know. Early on when dealing with Panama, a draft had been sent for clearance and two months later it hadn't been cleared.

Prosecutor: So you did not sit down with Mr Hardy and Mr Andrews and decide that they will operate in US $? Did you not say, we are only using Chemical Bank and another? Is that not misrepresentation? There is one other standard letter to look at. "…on satisfactory completion of due diligence requirement…" There it is again. Due diligence means

Standard letter to a solicitor

Standard letter to the accountant

Standard letter to Dun & Bradstreet.

Look at page 77. Quotes of letter from yourself, quoted by Andrews in Corporate Advances standard letter.

The commonality with some of the applicants is that they come from overseas. But in over 5 ½ years they were scattered. Did you notice common factors in complaints?

Steen: There were complaints that Mr. Andrews said certain things at the Brighton meetings.

Prosecutor: There were people from the United States of America, Australia and New Zealand. That they would ever have had contact with each other would be bizarre. The common theme of complaint was "we didn't appreciate that the collateral bond did apply to us."

Steen: If ever an applicant complained to me, I took it seriously.

Prosecutor: Did you think the system was working?

Steen: There was nothing wrong with the programme. It was working.

Prosecutor: No. It was not working. There was 100% failure . There were allegations thrown up. There was the simplest possible way in ensuring that there could be no misunderstanding . You could simply have insisted that Corporate Advances put a few phrases in their standard letter explaining "collateral bond" and the ramifications of the collateral bond. Why didn't you insist that something was put to ensure that there would be no misunderstanding?

Steen: Whenever I received a complaint I took it to Corporate Advances. I was satisfied with their explanations.

Prosecutor Mr. Leyton: But it keeps on happening, year in, year out, doesn't it?

Steen: Not all the applicants were complaining about the collateral bond.

Prosecutor: You regard Corporate Advances as being "agent of the applicant". Which is why I asked about the "certificate". So, Corporate Advances was there to help the applicant, to smooth and do its best to ensure that the applicant got the loan. Were you aware that Corporate Advances used a standard letter? (document 33).

Steen: I knew there were standard letters.

Prosecutor: The applicant on receipt of that letter redirected their enquiries to you?

Steen: They had a system of numbering letters as like a Chinese restaurant's menu.

Prosecutor: Corporate Advances at the point of transaction would send out a HAND-WASHING letter. Of the 21 cases we heard as witnesses, the Applicant referred back to Corporate advances and the standard response was a number 33 letter, wasn't it?

Steen: I was not aware of that.

Prosecutor: The client then gets a HARDY letter. Mr Hardy then write a letter to Corporate Advances. Corporate Advances writes back to redirect their enquiries to you, Mr. Steen. You know that Corporate advances at this stage was at the stage of transaction of simply washing their hands of the client, don't you?

Did you go to Mr. Andrews saying, "Here I am, getting all these complaints. What are you doing about it?"

Steen: Yes, I wrote to Mr. Andrews but got no answers.

Prosecutor: Then why did you carry on doing business with them when they were doing this?

Steen: It was not my business.

Prosecutor: You could have stopped doing business with this outfit? You were still getting millions of dollars into your accounts and 95% to 98% of that came from business with Corporate Advances. There are only nine other cases that generated any fees to Peninsular Holdings between 1.1.96 and 3.6.99. (Coutts evidence). There was one in 1999, one in 1998 and seven in 1997 and the total income to Peninsular Holdings from these cases were £187,000, compared to $ 1 million from business with Corporate advances.

Steen: I am not entirely sure if this is accurate.

Prosecutor: There were a number of specific documents which Corporate advances sent out. There was the Question and Answer document sent to their applicants. Do you feel that those were full answers in that document? There is no reference to collateral bond in the Q and a document, is there? One of the first things the first standard letter talked about is that due diligence is to be completed in 14 to 21 days. Corporate Advances only refer cases to you. Do you consider this document, the first standard letter, an honest document?

Steen: It is not accurate.

Prosecutor: Question and Answer 5 in Q and A document, is that misrepresentation?

Steen: Yes, on Corporate Advances' part.

Prosecutor: Question 11. The whole scheme is posited on 60 to 75% of assets. In all cases US $. Is that true?

Steen: True.

Prosecutor: Question 17. What is repayment method? Collateral Bond only. Question 21. After commitment letter, what happens? Due diligence starts. Is that true? 30 days is completely optimistic, isn't it?

Steen: That has never been stated. It doesn't apply to Peninsular Holdings.

Prosecutor: Is that a misrepresentation?

Steen: Yes.

Prosecutor: You have never seen this document before?

Steen: I have seen this document before.

Prosecutor: Why didn't you put a stop to it?

Steen: It didn't relate to Peninsular Holdings.

Prosecutor: You could only have seen those documents if they were sent to people who dealt through you. Whether it is a general or a specific document, the moment it comes to you it becomes specific. It has intention to mislead.

Steen: It is a general document. Brokers commonly send out brochures.

Prosecutor: In the letter sent out inviting people to come for a meeting in the UK,; it contains the following:

- Loan amounts

- Interest rate

- Repayment details

- Funding

- Administration fee

- Bank guarantee for principal amount will NOT be required

- 3rd party guarantor will NOT be required.

What is missing?

The one thing that is important is not mentioned—collateral bond.

That is a total misrepresentation, isn't it?

Steen : Yes.

Prosecutor: Are you saying that in 5 ½ years you never appreciated that this document was saying "total misrepresentation" of the scheme? Clients would send this document to you at the time they were complaining.

Steen: Yes, clients did send me this document.

Prosecutor: So you were aware of the document that Corporate Advances was sending to applicants?

Steen: I accept that.

Prosecutor: That became part of the fraud you were operating?

Steen: I've never operated any fraud.

Prosecutor: Go to Mr. Samson's (an applicant's) correspondence.

Letter from Corporate Advances: "We have been in business since 1990". That is a lie, isn't it?

Steen: Yes. It should say 1994.

Prosecutor: Corporate Advances came into being in 1993.

Steen: I accept in principle what you say.

Prosecutor: "We confirm that we (Corporate Advances) have successfully completed 40 cases…" Is this correct?

Steen: No. It is a lie.

Prosecutor: Your letter to Mr Dooley (solicitor) on page 3. At the top of the page—"Mr. Andrews believes…that if the bank…. Then they would have considerable difficulty in maintaining their staff…".

So it was difficult, this fuss that Mr. Hardy had with the bank?

Steen: It was something to do with an escrow agreement.

Prosecutor: This is all to do with the new scheme, isn't it? Clients had complained. The banks got to hear about it. What you were being asked to do was to provide a letter to say that this was a bone fide operation with Mr. Andrews as broker. You knew that the Dooley letter was to be handed to Mr. Andrews that day to deal with the bank, didn't you?

Steen: Mr. Andrews' bank wanted confirmation that they had funds at their disposal.

Prosecutor: So the Dooley letter shows that you are a bone fide operation. So you knew that this comfort letter related to Corporate Advances. The problem arose because clients wanted to know if their deposits were protected via escrow account? The applicant Dooley handed over payment and he believed it was in an escrow account. This problem was clearly to do with the new commercial enterprise. Therefore clearly the evidence is that you are related to Corporate Advances. MINTER (another applicant) was a deal that was submitted, wasn't it?

Steen: Minter Construction Ltd. Was an off-the-shelf company I bought.

Prosecutor: This was an arms length transaction?

Philippines Finance—your old business—it was nothing to do with PHP?

Mr. Andrew Hathaway had applied for a loan through your dormant business Philippines Finance. Mr. Hathaway paid over the fees. He threatened to sue you. You decided to compromise by buying MINTER Construction Ltd for him. And to compromise the law suit, you arranged to lend MINTER CONSTRUCTION LTD $15,000 interest free to be paid back over 10 years. So it had nothing to do with PHP, and nothing to do with Corporate Advances? It was nothing to do with the new multi-million dollar loan business. Yet the DOOLEY letter went to Nat West Bank to show that Peninsular Holdings was bone fide?

Steen: It was a long time ago. I don't remember. The police raided the office in 1997 and took the file away.

Prosecutor: It was nothing to do with the Corporate Advances business, was it? So if it was sent to NAT WEST BANK, that in itself was a total misrepresentation. The £15,000 was not expressed in the letter to the bank. The bank would have suspected something if it had been mentioned.

You orchestrated the DOOLEY LETTER, didn't you?

Steen: Yes.

(Interruption by defence barrister about the Dooley file not raised in evidence. Judge said Steen can refresh his memory with the file during the 10 minute recess).

JUDGE: You and he are entitled to look at the file. But I don't think the details of the file are being actively pursued, subject to the normal restrictions).

Prosecutor Mr Leyton: Yes, I agree to a recess so that Mr. Steen can look at the file in case there is anything he wants to add to his previous answer.

Defence barrister: I would have sought to challenge the admissibility of the file. It has been put to the jury that Mr. Steen is dishonest. I want this to be inadmissible to the jury.

My learned friend interrupts the witness. I ask him not to interrupt the defendant.

The Prosecutor has challenged the Defendant to prove that 40% collateral bond.

If that exercise has been done, I want the Prosecutor to assure us that this exercise has been done.

Prosecutor: The 25% as is now asserted takes the prosecution totally by surprise. I am asking for him to produce this. This is something that the Defendant has asserted (25%) since he went into the witness box. It is not based on an analysis which the prosecution has carried out.

Judge: I want the Defendant to answer the question he is asked; on a few occasions I have had to ask him to do so.

RECESS.(25 minutes)

Prosecution: During 1994 it became apparent that the DOOLEY LETTER was being circulated. You protested at the circulation of that letter. It was a letter to assist in the relationship with the bank. This letter had nothing to do with the new commercial business. The $15,000 loan was arranged through a shell company which you bought to appease a complaining applicant. It had nothing to do with a multi-national company. The DOOLEY LETTER was a compromise arrangement which you came to with Mr. Hathaway. Yet Mr. Andrews was distributing this letter to applicants to this multi-national business. Yet you knew that one of your agents were distributing this letter. What did you think he was seeking to achieve?

Steen: To prove that he has secured finances.

Prosecutor: Look at the letter. So it is obvious to you that Mr. Andrews and Corporate Finances are distributing it to applicants to persuade the applicants that Corporate Advances had completed a loan application. Is this misleading?

Steen: Yes; at least.

Prosecutor: You knew that the moment it was in circulation it was a gross misrepresentation of the situation. The letter to Mr. Andrews said that the DOOLEYS are fed up with being pestered. It does not say that the letter is a misrepresentation. It is dishonest, isn't it?

Steen: No, it depends on what was in Mr. Andrews' mind at the time.

Prosecutor: The DOOLEY letter shows that a commercial loan transaction has been completed, an example of a multi-million dollar transaction, doesn't it?

Steen: Yes.

Prosecutor: We know that he can't have added a rider because if he said that it was just an ordinary $15,000 loan, it wouldn't have been much use. Mr. Steen, all the more reason to tell him that it was a misrepresentation if you behaved honestly, isn't it?

Steen: That is why I insisted it was withdrawn.

Prosecutor: But you had to undo the damage because dozens of people had read it?

Steen: I discussed the matter with Mr. Hardy and that is why I asked Mr. Andrews to stop circulating the letter.

Prosecutor: Now answer the question. DOOLEY & CO. have been inundated with enquiries. What did you do to ensure that that misrepresentation was stopped? You were thoroughly dishonest, weren't you?

Steen: No. I don't recall any applicants coming forward from that letter.

Prosecutor: The letter FROM Dooley states….."I still continue to receive a deluge of telephone calls…"

Wasn't this dishonest on your part?

Steen: No, I don't think it was.

Prosecutor: Look at page 30. This is a letter signed by yourself, Mr. Steen. It says…" send Dooley letter to clients only if absolutely necessary.

Steen: The main thrust of the letter was to show that a loan transaction had been completed.

Prosecutor: So the letter could be shown to a single client only if necessary?

Steen: I agree. But it wasn't a distortion that a loan was completed and it has funds to lend.

Prosecutor: Look at paragraph 1 of the DOOLEY letter. There was gross damage done to people who proceeded, wasn't there?

Steen: None of the people who made those telephone calls applied.

Prosecutor: Look at page 16. October 1998. This was a parallel scheme, wasn't it?

Steen: Yes.

Prosecutor: This was to do with Allied Banking Corp. This was not a loan to do with the scheme, was it?

Steen: Not to start with.

Prosecutor: A loan of $300,000 came out of an allied Banking Account. You were directly involved, weren't you?

Steen: Yes.

Prosecutor: The money was loaned to finish off the construction of the Golf Course at the Coral Reef Hotel. Did you have any interest in it?

Steen: No.

Prosecutor: This was a nine-month loan that you lent to Coral reef Hotel. Was it repaid? Was there a collateral bond?

Steen: Yes and No.

Prosecutor: Was there a collateral bond? Did you get your money back?

Steen: No.

Prosecutor: So Allied Banking had nothing to do with the type of business that you and your agents operated for 5 years? Yet a sanitised version of the Allied Banking loan was used to support the contention that you and Corporate Advances had succeeded in completing a loan?

Steen: Yes.

Prosecutor Matthew Layton (Clifford Chance): But if this letter was distributed by taking the Allied Bank heading off and the bank manager's signature off and taking the $ sign off and putting the Peso sign on, it would seem like a $10 million loan, wouldn't it? It would be a gross distortion, wouldn't it?

Steen: Yes.

Prosecutor: By October 1998 you were receiving all your business from Mr. Andrews at Corporate Advances. And here he is circulating the sanitised version of the Allied Banking letter!

Steen: I disagree.

Prosecution: I beg to differ. Look at Volume 3 page 3. This is a letter sent to Mr. White by a private investigation firm DOOLEY & CO. who were Peninsular Holdings solicitor–

"We know of at least 10 loans which have been completed from start to finish…."

This is a lie. You never completed a single loan, did you?

Steen: No.

Prosecutor: If you had been aware, what would you have done?

Steen: I would have gone crazy. I had never seen it before I was questioned in the police station. Unless Mr. Gray was referring to loans that Corporate advances had completed with other companies other than myself.

Prosecutor: What about the letter sent to Mr. White in Canada?

Steen: I have no knowledge of it.

Prosecutor: If you had knowledge of it?

Steen: I would have done something about it.

Prosecutor: It seems to have been specifically designed for Canada.

Steen: The first time I ever saw any one of Gray's letters was at the Police station. This prompted me to write to the SFO.

Prosecutor: If you had knowledge of it, it would be grossly dishonest, wouldn't it?

Steen: Yes.

Prosecutor: Corporate Advances was set up to arrange loans only through Peninsular Holdings in Panama. Within the set of correspondence were lots of letters. Indeed you have said you have seen whole files when some complaints are given. Look at document on page 16. It sets out the figures for repayment of the loan. You weren't doing repayment loans, were you?

Implying that repayment loans were available is misrepresentation, isn't it?

Steen: It did not refer to Peninsular Holdings.

Prosecutor: But it is so.

Steen: To send out an illustration that you are doing interest free loans and interest only loans is not a misrepresentation and is normal.

Prosecutor: One document that is missing is a table setting out the sliding scale of the due diligence scheme. The due diligence fee amount depended on the amount of the loan required. It would be a very simple way of calculating the fee relating the fee to the loan amount. For illustrative purposes this would have been god.

Steen: Mr. Andrews discussed it in Brighton.

Prosecutor: But this is after they paid £6,950, isn't it?

Steen: Yes.

Prosecutor: In this scheme you set up with Mr. Andrews and Mr. Alexander in 1993, did you advise the applicants that there would be a due diligence fee?

Steen: It never occurred to me to use a table.

Prosecutor: For some people the fee size came as a shock, didn't it? The applicants paid administration fees but never paid any due diligence fee. They ran aground.

Steen: Yes.

Prosecutor: To avoid the possibility of anyone not being able to afford the due diligence fee, it would have been sensible to tell them the scale of the fee.

Steen: It was not my place to tell them.

Prosecutor: If a few phrases as I suggested were ever used in the offer letter so that the offer letter was adapted to each individual requirement, would you agree with it?

Steen: No.

Prosecutor: Total Dishonesty is not a condition that will apply to you?

Steen: No.

Prosecutor: The collateral bond; that was totally dishonest. If it was said that due diligence was done by Coopers and Lybrand, that would be a lie?

Steen: Yes.

Prosecutor: Were there any Dorchester meetings?

Steen: Yes.

Prosecutor: These were around the time of the due diligence payment?

Steen: Yes.

Prosecutor: A long way away from the loan being drawn?

Steen: Yes.

Prosecutor: To suggest to anyone that the money would arrive before they got back to Australia would be a lie, wouldn't it?

Steen: Yes.

Prosecutor: So in 5 ½ years you never got a whiff of dishonesty?

Steen: Yes.

Prosecutor: At what point do you start thinking that suppose I believe the client rather than Mr. Andrews?

Steen: It was difficult to tell who to believe.

Prosecutor: How much longer were you going to go on with Corporate Advances?

Steen: I couldn't really say. The police informed me of Corporate Advances Ltd. Which had just been formed. But Corporate Advances Ltd. didn't go on. Our tempers had reached a climax.

Prosecutor: Because of course your income stream was remaining constant, wasn't it?

Steen: It wasn't income, it was money.

Prosecutor: Of course you had your MONEY MANAGER ACCOUNTING programme. When are you going to make a decision about the money in the bank accounts?

Steen: It will be done after the Philippines business is settled.

Prosecutor: what about the money from 1996? 7 ½ years ago. When are you going to decide whether you can keep it?

Steen : I am not in a position to answer that question.

Prosecutor: When will you pay back that money?

Steen: It depends on a case that may arise in the Philippines.

Prosecutor: Does that mean that you may be involved in a civil litigation?

Steen: Yes.

Prosecutor: Maria, your secretary, she had insight into the day-to-day activity at the Darlington office. She was there 11 months a year. You were there 7 months a year. She opened the post. She did what she was told. She didn't write the letters. She described you speaking regularly on the phone and at meetings with Mr. Andrews almost every day.

Steen: Yes.

Prosecutor: So you had almost daily contact with Mr. Andrews?

Steen: Regular contact.

Prosecutor: There were phone calls throughout the 5 ½ year period. But 98% of your business was done with Corporate Advances. There was a stream of new applicants and a stream of dissatisfied applicants?

Steen: Yes.

Prosecutor: Maria said that you and Mr. Andrews would discuss the clients happily but sometimes you would write letters to Mr. Andrews to please the file. If clients were complaining you would have to have correspondence to make the file look right. The applicants, she said, complained that Mr. Hardy said that certain securities did not have to be provided. PHB, she said, told clients that they had signed contracts so it did not matter what they were told. She said that your attitude was that it was the client's word against Mr. Andrews', was it so?

Steen: I am not responsible for what other people say.

Prosecutor: Unintentionally a client can come into contact with Mr. Hardy before the due diligence fee has been paid?

Judge: Remind Mr. Steen of such a client.

Prosecution: Ester Smallwood. The transaction comes to a halt if the client gets to Mr. Hardy before the due diligence fee is paid, doesn't it?

Steen: Yes.

Prosecution: Having realised that Mr. Hardy is totally non-negotiable, the client realises that they cannot go on.

Steen: I've not actually said this is the end of it, I talked of alternative arrangements.

Prosecution: Therefore the plan was, according to Marie, to avoid the applicant getting in touch with Mr. Hardy before they paid the due diligence fee. If you were behaving honestly, there would be no harm whatsoever in bringing Mr. Hardy in earlier, would there?

Steen: No.

Prosecutor: You could have sent these HARDY letters (without Hardy's name on them) to Corporate Advances. There would have been no harm whatsoever.

Steen: No. No harm.

Prosecutor: No harm to whom?

Steen: To the client.

Prosecutor: Absolutely. They would all have dropped out and you would not be sitting on an alleged conspiracy or on several million dollars?

Steen: No.

Prosecutor: Maria said that to make files right you would pretend to fax documents.

Steen: I tried to fax a letter and sometimes failed.

Prosecutor: You had a very average business from 1990 to 1993. You had a modest income and a modest turnover. Then you established this new scheme which was up and running by 1994. By 1996 there was a lot of money coming in, millions rather than thousands. You were running the show out of a modest office with Marie Peyton as your secretary and Emma your wife and Mr. Hardy, so overheads were low as a percentage of money coming in and Corporate Advances were getting more and more successful. So by 1997 your world would have been transformed?

Steen: Yes.

Prosecutor: By 1997 both businesses were founded on total failure and you bought a new office complete with a big boardroom?

Steen: Yes.

Prosecutor: You had a party, didn't you? This was a conspiracy with Mr. Andrews and Mr. Alexander, wasn't it?

Steen: I wouldn't call it that.

Prosecutor: They has a direct interest in every single dollar you got in due diligence fees, didn't they?

Steen: Yes.

Prosecutor: This new office building is a physical manifestation of the success of the whole new scheme, wasn't it?

Steen: Yes, but it was purchased at a low price.

Prosecutor: So you had a party to mark success and then you all went to a restaurant?

Steen: Yes.

Prosecutor: Did anyone at that meeting have any say on how miraculous it was that you were all making so much money on total failure for 3 ½ years?

Steen: No. I don't think we discussed business at all.

Prosecutor: But the sort of money you were all generating will enable you do pretty much what you wanted.

Judge: Before adjournment, we must clarify two things:

1. The Dooley letter had nothing to do with the scheme.

2. The Dooleys were inundated with telephone calls.

Monday 2nd June 2003.

SUMMING UP OF CORPORATE ADVANCES.

T20010250 Dennis Alexander, George Steen and David Andrews.

It was learnt that Mr George Steen has fled the UK and Europe and that although his passport was impounded by the police, he used a duplicate passport which he had in his possession. This happened on Saturday 24th May, 2003.

Directions by the Judge.

In the Lucas case, the jury can infer guilt by the defendant absconding. Arguments for and against telling the jury to infer that Steen is guilty. Discussing submissions.

Judge looks up Archbold Page 3197, "power to continue trial in absence". What is a proper conclusion for the jury to make about Steen's disappearance. Judge says that Steen's absence can contribute to the proof of guilt. Defendant's counsel wants to agree that he was sure that he has covered himself that he has tried the point of whether the jury should know about Steen's absence and the bought second passport. Steen's intention to leave had come into existence months before. The judge wants to avoid the jury being side-tracked from the evidence as to whether the defendant is guilty of conspiracy or not. Defendant's counsel wants the judge to direct the jury not to draw any inferences from Steen's absence. The case of Heywood on absence.

The Prosecutor gave out new copies of indictment, including a few more words.

Mr Layton Prosecutor said he does not intend to say anything about Mr. Steen's absence.

Members of the jury, don't try to understand everything but let the case come to you. In addressing you, I'll call the letters by shorthand, eg. The Number 33 letter. What is the case about? Alexander and Andrews and Steen have known each other since early 1990's. But by 1993-94 an entirely new business scheme was created. They were looking at an entirely different market—commercial loans measured in millions of dollars. The applicants were exclusively drawn from overseas. The two sources about the scheme are the contractual documents in volume 1 of the evidence and Mr. Steen's evidence about the early days and ho the scheme came into existence and about the 21 applications . There was a well organised system in place.

By 1996, Mr. Hardy had the best of two years experience. It was not a novel thing by 1996. Bear in mind the structure of the 3 organisations. They were 3 small, lean concerns.

This is not like a multi-million dollar corporation. A big organisation could never have a CEO who had hands-on information and direct contact with the applicants. These three must have known what was going on.

It's not that sort of thing.

In effect, there was a standard series of forms, documents, etc that went direct to the client and some of these documents passed to the other two organisations. Members of the Jury, the services of Mr. Hardy were in place and operating by 1996. What was Mr. Hardy's brief? It was screamingly obvious—to insist upon each applicant who reached him fulfilling each and every security measure. In particular, no applicant was to get a loan without putting up the collateral. Mr. Hardy's purpose was to make clear the ramification of the advance collateral bond. Funds were not to come out of the loan proceeds.

Look at the indictment.

It states that a conspiracy existed between 1.1.1996 and 16.6.1999 date of arrest. It is alleged that the 3 defendants conspired with Mr. Hardy to defraud applicants into paying advance fees, the defendants intending the applicants to be unsuccessful in obtaining each loan.

Given the experience of 2 years before the allegation of unlawful conduct followed by 3 ½ years more when no-one got a loan.

It is no defence that there was a possibility that someone might have got a loan. They defrauded—they operated a dishonest scheme.

There are occasions when there are perfectly legitimate schemes which become distorted. But this did not occur here.

The 3 ½ years is the bracket of time when they conspired . Members of the jury, the important word is "agreed".

Even if the defendant Steen on his own was the most dishonest person, what is alleged here is that they conspired. What is not in dispute is that the scheme that was administered over 5 ½ years was a total failure.

You may take the view that however disreputable the scheme was, there must have been an agreement. You must decide whether the defendant Steen had by 1st January 1996 had failed and then decided to defraud.

A tacit agreement to adapt the scheme in a way which turns it into a deceptive agreement. What he suggests after all that experience of two years, it was apparent to each defendant that it wasn't working for the applicants but it was working for the defendants. Look at the documents which help to determine the defendants attitude and knowledge. So you can establish what goes on during the period 1996 to 1999 to decide that the defendants attitude was fraudulent.

You cannot unlearn what you have learnt in the first two years.

It is a fact. This is the relevance of the first two years.

If you decide that two people have formed a fraudulent agreement, another person can join in at a later time and this is still a conspiracy. You can have a conspiracy where someone leaves before the end. Whether a conspiracy existed and whether another person joined in . If Mr. Alexander says that he was only an innocent book-keeper but that Mr. Steen and Mr. Andrews were in conspiracy, there is still a conspiracy.

All three were involved in failure for the first two years.

Why is failure obvious and yet each continued? Each of them had experience of failure but didn't resolve it. Where is any evidence of thought processes of them examining why there is a failure and reviewing the procedures? There was no change of the procedure. It was a conspiracy to behave fraudulently. There was no change as to types of applicants.

Suppose some of the applicants in the first two years had got loans?

They would have said it worked for two years and then it went wrong.

If after this time of hard experience they decided it couldn't work, there was a point where, maybe, an innocent business became a conspiracy.

If they were genuinely looking for loans for their applicants, they were not dishonest. However, you wouldn't on the evidence you heard suggest that Mr. Steen and Mr. Alexander were guilty but not Mr. Andrews because he was at the start of it. You heard evidence from 21 applicants. If you decided that the evidence they gave was unsatisfactory, then these 3 are innocent. The prosecution case does not stand or fall on each and every applicant but if the bulk were telling the truth, then you must convict the 3 defendants. But if all 21 applicants were deceived, effectively led into a trap, then that would establish fraudulent behaviour. But there were many many more applicants none of whom got a loan.

Start by taking an overview of the case. Use your common sense and experience of the world. Simply keep your feet on the ground. How in a nutshell do we put the case?

There were 2 lightweight operations: Alexander & Andrews and Steen & Hardy. Whatever view you take of Steen's ability to provide funds, after 2 years of failure, this must have told them that their good but dishonest living was sustainable and lucrative. That it was more lucrative to do this than provide real loans and only get a % commission.

They relied on the naivety of the applicants; the misrepresentation that took place was largely by omission.

For a more enquiring applicant, lies, direct lies, were told, oral lies rather than written lies.

This conspiracy was just a cynical disregard of the rights of applicants and turned a loser into a 'buyer beware'. We suggest you can infer dishonesty. It was a scheme which was abused by the defendants. If the size of the due diligence fee had always been made clear to the applicant, in tabulate form, that would have veered off a number of applicants. Had the cost of the assignable collateral bond been spelt out, such as, 40% of the loan we advance you must be put up front to us as a collated bond, this would have stopped many applicants from going on. The situation would have been that Corporate Advances and Peninsular Holdings would have been out of business. Their sole source of income was advanced fees. Mr. Steen gave evidence that considerable business was being done in the first two years. For Corporate Advances, it was the only source of income. So they would have gone out of business well before 1999.

Go to the financial schedules:

The financial flow-charts are 2 pages of documents at pages 9 and 10.

It is an overview of income from clients of Corporate Advances:

- £336,000 for 1996
- £400,000 for 1997
- £561,000 for 1998
- £226,000 for ½ of 1999 to date of arrest

This is a fairly smooth source of income. This is money from all applicants who are providing income to Corporate Advances.

A percentage share of due diligence goes to Peninsular Holdings

From calculating the income to Peninsular Holdings at £500 reading fee per applicant, it works out that the number of files read by Peninsular Holdings were as follows:

- 68 in 1996
- 66 in 1997
- 94 in 1998 and
- 35 in ½ of 1999 to date of arrest. = 266 files for which Steen got reading fees.

In 1996 Steen got $1 million.

Therefore Steen got paid

- $15,500 per file in 1996

- $16,500 per file in 1997

- $11,500 per file in 1998 for reading the files.

If these are fees for reading per file, we know that Corporate Advances is receiving administration fees.

Therefore in 1996 Corporate Advances had $5000 per application, $6000 per application in 1997, $6000 per application in 1998 and $6500 per application in 1999.

This is a constant and smooth flow of people who were providing income for these two organisations.

There were 4 Phases in the scheme:

Phase 1:

Lead-up to visit to UK; Q and A phase.

Phase 2:

Due Diligence Phase. Quite a few applicants fall by the wayside.

Phase 3:

Collateral Bond phase. All applicants fall at this point.

In the 21 cases we looked at, they all paid administration fees. Some never paid the due diligence fee. The final lot realise they couldn't make the collateral bond.

There was a sub-broker involved. Because the sub-broker was being honest, some applicants got to know of the collateral bond before they were meant to.

We suggest that the applicants got through Phases 1 & 2 through a series of misrepresentations.

The last Phase was the Complaints Phase. There was a complaints stage. They received stone-walling and aggression largely from Darlington. But the complainants are on the other side of the world. This scheme was open to abuse.

RECESS (10 minutes)

Complaint Phase

What was the effect of the failure on the client? They complained to CA & Peninsular. It works out that many paid admin fees and due diligence but none got the loan.

Not one got their money back. Not one got a loan. Each wrote at least 1 letter expressing unhappiness. That meant there were hundreds of complaints letters. Marie Peyton confirmed that there were dozens and dozens of complaints & requests for admin fees refunds to Ca also.

You heard the evidence of 21 applicants. We invite you to conclude that there must have been calls, faxes, letters of complaints. If you were a head teacher and a teacher was not getting any results you would begin to wonder. Marie was aware of what was happening about complaints. She said none of the letters ever was offered a refund. She said in relation to keeping the files in order sometimes George would receive letters of complaints and he would blame Andrews. Andrews didn't take any notice. When clients were offering securities, they were told by Hardy it was unacceptable, but Steen would say "It was the clients' word against ours". Hardy would come into the picture after due diligence was paid. When sometimes applicant got Hardy before due diligence was paid file stopped there. Marie Peyton did 90% of the paperwork up to the point when things could go wrong. Steen was absent 6 months a year. He didn't care—he just sent down an offer letter.

Eg we need to be more rigorous and weed out the unfeasible business plans.

Police statements—say very neat operations.

Central complaint of 21 applicants—you didn't tell me about the size of the collateral bond and the conditions.

Where is there any evidence that these 3 defendants discussed how to amend the scheme?

Eg. You own a path at the edge of a cliff. Someone falls off; someone else falls off; you would put up a fence; you would put up a warning.

Where is the warning in this scheme?

But pg 16 of standard terms shows how the payments work. Why didn't they put a table of collateral bond in relation to loan? Where is the letter from Peninsular to CA spelling out the request of the due diligence explanation to applicants?

Hardy said it will cost 40%.

He could have put that & a table in Q and a doc. Look at offer letter—extract of terms and conditions.

A bank guarantee is not required.

3rd party guarantor is not required.

But does not tell you what will be required.

Pg 26. Specimen of letter issued by Peninsular.

Letter attached to offer letter. Draws attention to time limit. Does not draw attention to collateral bond. Why not?

Because this scheme was a fraud. Income not derived from provision of loans by fees generated from applications. Where is evidence to help client get collateral bond? NONE.

Steen admitted collateral bond could have been less than 40%. Why did Steen not try to find a much cheaper bond? BBT co. established 15 moths before 1999 in Philippines. Steen said it was set up to get collateral bond . But it never operated. Pg 75. Why didn't Steen send a letter to NCA to say that you must tell applicants about due diligence fee?

3½ yrs CA received £1.5 million. Hand written bank reconciliations in Andrews home. Annual rent £4000. Income £1.5 million over 3 ½ yrs. Large tel bill and fax bill, advertisement, H & L, 2 small salaries, rest available to Alexander & Andrews.

Steen has $3 million sitting in bank accounts outside this jurisdiction, clear of all expenses, after he's paid Hardy and bought his new offices. How hard was the work Steen had to do?

Marie did 90 % of work. He just culls from his computer a series of well known phrases.

What were their attitudes after they collected the money? He hides behind Hardy who is paid $1000 per applicant to stop the clients. He used Dun & Bradstreet to dig up the dirt after the money is received. Why didn't he use Dun & Bradstreet search before he received the due diligence fee?

I will not work through the files.

What was the aim of the applicants? They wanted 100% loans. What sort of applicants wanted loans? Ones who couldn't get loans. If they had 40% collateral they would have got loans from their own banks. He encouraged applicants to up the loan applied for. The due diligence fee was scaled. It was unreasonable to ask for 1 or 2 million $. This made it easy for Hardy to turn down. Every single business plan did not indicate that had 40% collateral. The experience from 194 to 1996 would have shown them that client had to put up bond.

3 defendants:-

STEEN—he was in this business for 5 ½ yrs. He spoke to Andrews regularly. Did he ever have a line of finance available? Where is the correspondence? There is no paperwork, no evidence. He could have called Martha Mondrana his lawyer as witness. H could have asked the bank for copies. His explanation is that he is just a sub-broker. Where is there anything in the docs to indicate that after the had got past the Hardy bond, they would then be subjected to a due diligence by Steen on behalf of the ultimate lender? It is a total distraction. Where is the correspondence that he wrote to applicants to say that he had kept their due diligence fee in an escrow account? NONE. Andrews is the most unsuccessful broker in history with not 1 success in 5 ½ years. Steen was challenged about the 40% bond. Actually 40% was the highest amount. Look at DDS application when it got to bond stage.

40% collateral was for loans of 20 years

20% collateral bond was for loans of 10 years. Defence counsel talked of Prosecution's words "spoils of Steen & others"

Make sure that it is understood that spoils does not mean equal.

Steen was brought back by the Metropolitan Police to the United Kingdom on time to hear his sentence of six years imprisonment.

Issue 2—The New Extradition Treaty between UK and US

ENRON extradiction request for three bankers—the British Chapter

The UK 2003 Extradition Treaty and its usefulness in combating fraud—the case of US Department of Justice v Muldrew, Darby and Bermington.

A country can request that a UK citizen be extradited to that country to stand trial for fraud and other criminal matters as long as the alleged offence is a crime in both countries and carries a prison sentence of more than one year.

It is now well known that the US-UK Extradition Treaty which was drafted to modernise and streamline the 1972 Extradition Treaty has still to be ratified by the US.

This 2003 Treaty, if ratified as it stands will cause the United States to derogate its obligations under Article 9 of the International Convention on Civil and Political Rights (ICCPR) and set aside the UN Refugees Protocol, the UK having already done so since 1988, in line with Article 4 ICCPR which allows a state to derogate certain articles.

Since serious fraud is not synonymous with either terrorism or asylum, it follows that these derogations do NOT apply. Serious fraud is an extraditable offence under the 2003 US-UK Extradition Treaty because it is punishable by imprisonment or other form of detention for more than one year in both countries. In the UK, the offence of conspiracy to defraud is punishable by seven years imprisonment as a maximum sentence with no minimum stated sentence. A survey of the UK's Serious Fraud Office's trials over 5 years showed that the SFO used the charge of "conspiracy to defraud", a common law offence in 60% of its cases with 46% of defendants penalised with 1 or 2 year prison sentences.

On the other hand, the US treats conspiracy to defraud prescriptively U.S.C.S 1349 and S 1350. Section 902 of the Sarbanes-Oxley Act, codified at 18 U.S.C. S 1349, provides a new offence for attempts and conspiracies to commit fraud, including securities fraud. The Sarbanes-Oxley Act 2002 specifically contains an attempt to commit fraud which the old laws under Title 18, United States Code, did not contain, although under pre-existing law even an unsuccessful attempt to commit wire fraud was a crime. This offence carries a 20 year prison sentence and a fine of $5 million. We can see the huge disparity in punishment for the same crime.

But this new maximum penalty has been increased in the US from 5 year to 20 years because of the Enron fraud and is part of the statutory increases to the fines and terms of imprisonment for a variety of white-collar offences. This 20 year maximum prison sentence moreover, can be increased to 30years on sentence plus one million dollar fine if the conspiracy affects a financial institution[148] as the Nat. West

Bank is. An individual defrauded, the maximum sentence could be as much as 25 years plus a maximum fine. Furthermore, in the US criminal sentences are largely governed by the Sentencing Guidelines and prosecutors can simply include multiple counts in the indictment if the statutory maximum penalty falls below the potential sentencing guideline range. Moreover, as a result of the Sentencing Commission's amendments in 2001, (before the US-UK Treaty), the Guidelines' range for fraud offences involving large losses were already severe. In addition to these statutory increases in penalties, Sarbanes-Oxley Sections 805, 905 and 1104 directed the U.S. Sentencing Commission to review and amend the Sentencing Guidelines applicable to crimes involving securities, obstruction of justice offences, accounting fraud, and other related offences. In doing so, the Commission is instructed to ensure that the Guidelines reflect "the serious nature of the offences", the growing incidence of serious fraud offences, the "need to modify the sentencing guidelines and policy statements to deter, prevent and punish such offences" and the need for "aggressive and appropriate law enforcement action to prevent such offences".[149]

---

148 There are new guidelines for such serious fraud and now a Chief Finance Officer of a Fortune 500 company, say, could receive a prison sentence of 30 years to life, with no possibility of parole, even if this was a first offence.

149 See Sarbanes-Oxley Act 2002, ss 905 and 1104.

The case of <u>United States v Muldrew, Giles Robert Hugh Darby and David John Bermington,</u> conspiracy to defraud $7.3 million in transactions involving Enron Corp. has come to public notice because the three and fighting extradition to the US. The prosecution allege that, through a series of financial transactions, the three former bankers secretly invested in an Enron Special Purpose Entity (SPE), Southampton LP, and were able to siphon off $7.3 million that should have gone to their bank.

The SPE is of particular importance to this massive fraud of creative accounting. To look profitable Enron had to minimize losses and volatility, accelerate profits and keep as much debt off its Balance Sheet in order to keep a good credit rating. So SPE's were used to hedge certain investments. As an example, Enron would transfer its own stock to an SPE in exchange for a note or cash.[150] It directly and indirectly guaranteed the value of the SPE. The SPE would hedge the value of a particular investment on Enron's balance Sheet, using the transferred Enron stock as the principle source of payment.[151] Because of its historically rising stock price, Enron judged the risk that it would have to pay on its guarantees as remote. So when Enron's stock price fell unexpectedly, the SPE's value also fell, triggering the Enron guarantees, which further reduced stock price, which triggered additional Enron guarantees.[152] When Enron's investment and stock price both fell, the SPE would lack sufficient assets to perform its hedge. This caused the SPE's to breach the US' 3% independent equity requirement for non-consolidation, and so the SPE's debt became Enron's debt on its Balance Sheet. Mr Fastow usually was the SPE principal and when the SPE's thrived he received massive compensation,[153] mostly without Board approval. This was an ingenious fraud only because the value of Enron's stock became embedded in the value of the SPE; when stock prices rose, SPE's value rose but when the unexpected stock price collapse came; the guarantees were called in and could not be met. Such abuse of SPE's raised fundamental questions about the legitimacy of structured finance transactions, of which securitization transactions constitute the bulk. In a typical securitization transaction, a company transfers rights to payment from income-producing financial assets, such as accounts receivable, loans or lease rentals, to an SPE. The SPE in turn issues securities to capital market investors and uses the proceeds of the issuance to pay for the financial assets. The investors are repaid from collections of the financial assets. They buy securities based on their assessments of the value of the financial assets.[154]

In general, the global hedge fund industry is intensely secretive.[155] A recent survey of the industry revealed that the sector is rapidly expanding. It is estimated that there possibly may be 12000 hedge funds investing more than$7 trillion in the world's financial markets by 2008. Research has revealed that up to 1999, one could receive 30% returns, very lucrative indeed. Then most hedge funds tried to emulate the best and today, hedge funds' returns arte less than 2%.in this $1000 billion industry. .The Chairman of the US Federal Reserve describes hedge funds as the shock absorbers of the financial markets.[156] The corporate finance world is very complex and securitization is not normally a way for a company to obtain lower-cost financing through disintermediation. But securitization does avoid the mark-up charged by a middleman of funds and it enables a company to raise funds cheaply based on an allocation of risks that are assessed by parties having the most expertise. The difference between normal securitization and Enron's manipulation of SPEs is that Enron had high risk that stock prices could fall and that its asset values could fall

So the structured transactions have dubious economic value as in most securitization deals, the receivables are sold to SPEs with minimal recourse, so the SPE and its investor take the economic risks of collection and once the deal is closed nothing can happen to cause the risk allocation to be subsequently reversed.

The evidence requirements of Article 8 of the Treaty have been fulfilled because the allegations were made by guilty parties to the Enron fraud and the alleged transactions did take place. The dual criminality of the offence is positive as it is

150 Powers Report, page 13..

151 This hedging was used in virtually all Enron's SPE transactions.

152 Powers Report pages 41-2.

153 But even if he had board approval, performance-based compensation tied to a list of goals such as return on equity, cost of capital and so on, make the goals vulnerable to manipulation. Today the SEC has new rules on asset backed securities

154 Schwarcz. S. L, (1994), "The alchemy of asset securitization", Stanford Journal of Business and Finance.

155 Irving.R, (2004), "Hedge fund aspirations may have to be trimmed", Times Newspaper, 8th November, 2004.

156 Cole.R, (2004), "Transparency is needed for hedge funds", Times Newspaper, 10th November 2004.

punishable in both countries by at least 1 year imprisonment. It even qualifies for the requirements of the European Arrest Warrant as it provides a "description of the circumstances in which the offence was committed, including the time, place and degree of participation in the offence by the requested person". In any case, the European Arrest Warrant has been in force since January 2004. The UK government cannot refuse extradition because the death penalty does not apply to wire fraud. The UK cannot now derogate from the new extradition obligation because the event is not political, just criminal. The time that the charge has already stood is now 2 ½ years or 30 months (June 2002 to January 2005). The 3 former bankers can still be re-extradited to a third country, say in Europe. Also Switzerland has a Mutual Assistance Treaty with the US and any hidden monies can be found.

In theory, the UK's **Proceeds of Crimes Act** can be used to seize the disputed profits gained by the three British Bankers charged with US wire fraud because the profits relate directly to the offence charged. Section 88 provides that such monies be forfeited and dealt with in such a manner as the court deems fit. When the UK-US Extradition Treaty becomes law, that is, when the <u>1989 Extradition Act</u> or when it implements the EU Framework Decision on a European Arrest Warrant.

The 2003 Treaty however complies with the UK's Statute of limitations because limitations do not apply to criminal offences. The Extradition Treaty 2003 does not change the evidentiary requirements for extradition from the United Kingdom to the US but the requirements are lowered from a "prima facie" standard to a "probable cause" standard. Therefore there is nothing to stop the provisional arrest of the three men for extradition.

This is indeed a strange case as the three were formally charged by the U.S. Department of Justice with wire fraud in June 2002. The **UK-US Extradition Treaty** was ratified by the UK government in May 2003, signed by the U.S Attorney General on 31st March 2003, and implements the EU-US Treaty on extradition signed in Washington on 25th June 2003 and in force since January 2004.

The United Kingdom already had an arrangement for mutual assistance with United States in criminal matters. This was on entirely genera criminal matters and applied to assistance in respect of proceedings related to criminal matters, including any measure or step taken in connection with an investigation or the prosecution of criminal offences, including the freezing, seizure or forfeiture of the proceeds and instrumentalities of crime, and the imposition of fines related to a criminal prosecution.[157] This Treaty permitted oral requests later confirmed in writing.[158]

The three defendants appealed against the extradition. This appeal was not heard until 28 September 2004 (27 months after being charged). On 15th October, the English court recommended that the three be sent to Texas, US, for trial. Although the three argue for a UK trial, it is not a '*forum conviens*' for jurisdiction because all of the discoveries, the principle place of business, the other defendants, are in the US. Enron is a US company under US law.

To date many have pleaded guilty and the accountants Anderson gave $60 million as restitution, Citigroup bank gave $300 million and the Canadian Imperial Bank $80 million, totalling $440 million; they pleaded guilty and paid up and this surely must indicate the basis on which the 3 bankers should be extradited for fraud.

This article is in response to the Financial Times Magazine article (by Flintoff, "Extradition entreaty", of the 18th December 2004.) which entreated the reader to believe that these 3 men had human rights abuse issues. I believe not.

---

157 Article 19(3)(e) UK-US Full Mutual Assistance Treaty.
158 Article 4(1) UK-US Full Mutual Assistance Treaty.

Issue 3—Trans-National Organised Crime

Trafficking
The trafficking of women and children for prostitution; a proposed business solution to this trans-national organised crime

Abstract

This article looks at the crime of trafficking of women and children and the connected crime of money laundering. After explanation of the crime and background, it explores ways in which businesses do hide this illegal activity behind a legitimate business. It flags up some methods of discovering the activity, using standard fraud investigative methods. It explains the technical accounting transactions that hide such activity and discusses the UK's <u>Proceeds of Crimes Act</u> and how it will prosecute any trafficking crime. Recent research has shown that, despite journalistic reports such as the Economist's September 2004 article on pornography and trafficking which stated that there is an extremely small amount of trafficking crime in the UK, there is a large and growing problem of children trafficked to supply the pornography market and the clothing sweatshops and ethnic restaurants. Contrary to journalistic reports, the EU recently agreed that there is an alarming problem and have appointed a directorate to deal with trafficking especially of young children groomed for prostitution .The UK's new criminal agency Serious Organised Crime Agency (SOCA), has vowed this month to treat trafficking of women and children for prostitution as a very serious matter.

US intelligence estimates of trafficking of women and children for prostitution is that there are about two million women trans-nationally trafficked for prostitution. The US has many cases of child pornography; publishing child pornography and the trafficking that must be associated with the cyber-crime of illegal pornography. Australia is examined as a special case because Australia, more than the UK, has taken legal steps to curb trafficking; steps such as draconian immigration and nationality laws, there again targets the supply and results instead of the demand for prostitution. Australia has renowned academic knowledge experts on fraud and corruption and the writer illustrates that the solution is already there. Calculating that, using all secondary sources, the figure for child prostitution is about two million, there are about four million women and children trafficked each year for prostitution.

This article shows how little UK government cared for the problem. Whilst statistics on prostitution in the UK is all but absent, a good estimate can be made of sex trafficking to the UK. The article concludes by recommending business methods to indicate suspicious businesses connected to human trafficking for prostitution and recommending severe punishment corporate and individual, along with policy solutions to eradicate this disease or moral lapse increasing exponentially and in proportion to the civilised and sophisticated materialism of the West.

Introduction

Trafficking of women and children is part of organised criminal activity in which these women are transported from Africa, South America, Asia, Middle East and Eastern Europe to Western Europe[159] and North America[160] to be used as prostitutes and for child pornography and child prostitution, slave labour, automobiles couriers, body parts couriers, fauna and flora couriers, for stealing nuclear material, as drugs couriers, arms couriers, and even[161] to learn to pick-pocket in gangs This is all part of trans-national organised crime.[162] Facilitated through the rapid improvement in technology which criminals have exploited.

159 International Organisation for Migration, (2003), "Trafficking of women to Italy for Sexual Exploitation".
160 Centre for the Study of Intelligence, (2000), "International trafficking in Women to the United States: A contemporary manifestation of slavery and organised crime", Intelligence Monograph.
161 Mueller .G .W, (1998), "Transnational Crimes", Uncertainty Scenarios.
162. Mueller states that although definitions of what constitutes organised criminal activity vary from one country to another, the concept has gradually come to mean 'criminal activities extending into, and violating the laws of several countries'. Transnational crime

Where there used to be maritime piracy on the high seas, the trend today is rather for highly organised software piracy, part of the criminal process of producing paedophile and bestiality and perverse hard core pornography to supply the western appetite, this being a multi-billion pound pornography industry that generates huge profits. When these illicit and illegal profits are introduced into the formal economy, the conversion to legitimacy through the purchase of business properties, aeroplanes, stocks and shares and high living, is termed as 'money laundering'. Such money is also used to further develop the illegal businesses.

The women and children

Not all the women and children that are trafficked are caught and transported against their will. Some are women who pay the traffickers[163] to get them to western countries, thinking that they would have a better life, only to be forced into prostitution with no hope of reporting it, being illegal immigrants in the new countries. For commercial sex trade, women and children are trafficked from Africa, India, Pakistan, Russia, Kazakhstan, China, Middle East, Indonesia, Central America, Panama, Nicaragua, Honduras, Brazil, Thailand, Philippines, Japan, Ukraine, Eastern Europe and Dominican Republic.[164]

The women and children who are the supply side of many Western brothels and who act in hard-core, bestial and perverse pornography films and other material are trafficked to Western countries, namely the Netherlands, [165], Western Europe,[166] United States,[167] Greece, Spain, Switzerland, [168], Australia,[169] Germany,[170] Austria.[171]

It is as well to remember the eternal and universal plight[172] of women,[173] dealing with the supremacy of men,[174] to exploiting[175] the predatory sexual greed of men through the ages. From the recent stalking and killing of young girls by sexual criminals[176] for instant sexual gratification,[177] not dissimilar to the millions of instances of a lesser violence on women when

is different from international crimes (ie.crimes recognised as such by international law such as war crimes) and local crimes which can be influenced by factors beyond the boundaries of the affected jurisdiction, but which are limited to one jurisdiction.

163 Smith .P, '(1997), 'Human smuggling: Chinese migrant trafficking and the challenge to America's Immigrant tradition', Washington: Centre for Strategic and International Studies.

164 Redo .S, (1998), 'International Annals of Criminology', UN.

165 Source: Department of Correctional services, Ministry of Justice, Netherlands.

166 Economist, (1997), 19 April.

167 Winer. J, (1997), 'Alien smuggling elements of the problem and the US response', Transnational Organised Crime Journal, January 1997.

168 Robinson. C, (1994), The International Conference on Trans-national Migration in the East-Pacific Region: problems and prospects' ARCM, January 1994.

169 Pope. V, (1997), 'Trafficking in women', US News and World Report, 7 April, 1997.

170 Mugar, I, (1996), ' Trafficking in women for sexual exploitation', Geneva: International Organisation for migration, June 1996.

171 Mugar. I, (1996), 'Trafficking in women to Austria for sexual exploitation', Geneva: International Organisation for Migration, June, 1996.

172 Myres-Shirk.S, (2000), ' "To be fully human": U.S. protestant psychotherapeutic culture and the subversion of the domestic ideal, 1945-1965', Journal of Women's History (2000)1, 112-136.

173 See the website with links about human trafficking and slavery in China today; http://gvnet.com/humantrafficking/China.htm.

174 Neuhaus.J, (2000), 'the importance of being orgasmic: sexuality, gender and marital sex manuals in the United States, 1920-1963', Journal of the History of sexuality (2000)4, 447-473.

175 Ross.B.L, (2000), 'Bumping and grinding on the line: making nudity pay', Labour/Le Travail, (2000)46, 221-250. (Topic explained as the sexuality, labour and social class in the history of 20th century erotic entertainment).

176 Cole, S.A, (2000), 'From the sexual psychopath Statute to 'Megan's Law', psychiatric knowledge in the diagnosis, treatment, and adjudication of sex criminals in New Jersey, 1949-1999', Journal of the History of Medicine & Allied Sciences, 55(2000)3, 292-314.

177 Warren.J, (2000), 'New lands, old ties and prostitution: a voiceless voice', Journal of South East Asian Studies, 31(2000) 2, 396-404 [Review Article: Yamazaki Tomoko, Sandakan Brothel No.8 : An Episode in the History of Lower-Class Japanese Women, Armonk, London].

drunken men have raped wife, daughter, servant and stranger when inhibitons are unleashed, leading the circular devastation of unmarried mothers, unwanted[178] pregnancies, silence, fear, and social out-casting of the victim women[179] and offspring.[180] Even in modern times of liberal laws and legal equality, women still have the added burdens of co-ordinating families, childcare,[181] household management[182] as well as making a living[183] outside the domestic environment.

In the Western world, the sexual exploitation of children is much more covert because of moral and criminal distaste for this very serious criminal activity. Although the United States CIA has estimated the number of children trafficked to the US in 2003 as being only several thousands, estimates from studies done for UNICEF in 1997 revealed 300, 000 child prostitutes in the United States.

So it can be estimated that most of the child prostitutes in non—Western countries are servicing the demand for Western tourists who travel to the children's countries to indulge their criminality, making the 1997 estimate for total child prostitution some 2 million.

The United Nations estimated[184] that 1.2 million children[185] are trafficked each year.[186] This is not the total figure for all child prostitutes in the world as there are an extra estimated one million children in their own countries who are sexually exploited by tourists who travel to the children's countries for sex with children., making the probable number of these abused innocent minors about 2 million. Trafficking is part of Serious Organised Crimes and

---

178 Reagan.L.J, (2000), 'Crossing the border for abortions: California activists, Mexican clinics, and the creation of a feminist health agency in the 1960's', Feminist Studies, (2000) 2, 323-348. and also

McIntosh.T, (2000), '"An Abortionist City": maternal mortality, abortion and birth control in Sheffield, 1920-1940', Medical History (2000) 1, 75-96.

179 Garrett.P.M, (2000), 'The abnormal flight, the migration and repatriation of Irish unmarried mothers, 1922-1970's', Social History (2000)3, 330-343.

180 Levenstein.L, (2000), 'From innocent children to unwanted migrants and unwed mums: two charges in the public discourse on welfare in the United States, 1960-1961', Journal of Women's History, 11(2000) 4, 10-33.

181 Michel.S, (1999), 'Children's Interests/Mothers' Rights: The shaping of SAmerica's Child Care Policy', New Haven, Connecticut and also Valk.A.M, (2000), '"Mother Power": the movement for welfare rights in Washington, D.C, 1966-1972', Journal of Women's History, (2000)2, 104-126.

182 Ingra.A.R, (2000), 'Likely to become a public charge: deserted women and the family law of the poor in New York City, 1910-1936', Journal of Women's History, 11(2000)4, 58-81.

183 Heinicke.C.W, (2000), 'One step forward: African-American married women in the South, 1950-1960', Journal of Interdisciplinary History, 11(2000)1, 43-62.

184 The writer reasons that this UN figure is much lower by one million at least. If the UN figures for known child prostitution, not including figures for UK, Ireland, France, Germany, Italy, and the other developed affluent countries, then the UN's 1997 figures total 1, 651, 000 child prostitutes in Thailand, Philippines, India, Central America, US and Poland.

185 Reuters, (2004), 'Venezuela slams U.S over Human Trafficking sanctions', Top News, 13 September 2004. There is so much human trafficking from Venezuela that US President Bush has ordered a cut in US assistance for not doing enough to stop Venezuela's trafficking of women and children for sex.

Colombia has similar organised criminals who traffic drugs around the globe and who are so dangerous that they do not hesitate to kill to protect their criminal activities. See Brown. R, (2004), 'Death by deadline', Financial Times Supplement, 2 October, 2004.

186 Musacchio.V, (2004), 'Migration connected with trafficking and prostitution: An over-view.', German Law Journal Vol 5 No. 9. Musacchio states that the European Commission estimates that 120, 000 women and children are trafficked into Western Europe each year (a rather low estimate if the number of brothels in Western Europe is counted).

occurs for the purposes of prostitution,[187] Slave Labour,[188] the movement of drugs[189] and arms, and recently for the specific purpose of using children for thieving.[190]

That this trafficking of children is not a new problem is evidenced in the1997 Report on Transnational Chid Prostitution by the International Police' INTERPOL, which stated the incredible escalation of child prostitution over the last ten years is directly caused by the tourism trade. Child prostitution is the newest tourist attraction offered by developing countries. The parallel to this phenomenon in the Western countries is the explosion of a huge underground trade in child pornography in videos and magazines. Since laws against child prostitution are stringently enforced in most affluent countries, pornographic films and photographs often have their origin in countries where child prostitution has become a temporary escape from poverty for struggling rural people'.

International Conventions to combat trafficking

A significant number of organised criminal activities have caused authorities and non-governmental organisations to confer and create Conventions to persuade the world's countries to legislate and control such crimes. The 1949 Convention on the Suppression of Traffic of Persons and of the Exploitation of the Prostitution of Others is an indication of the serious situation even fifty years ago. The International Labour Organisation (ILO) pressed for the 1957 Abolition of Forced Labour Convention, an instrument which cover child prostitution as well as trafficked women in brothels. There was also the 1959 United Nations (UN) Declaration of the Rights of the Child.

The United Nations Convention of 1988 against Illicit Trafficking in Narcotic Drugs and Psychotropic Substances also covers money laundering and precursor chemicals and drugs. This 1988 UN Convention declares that these criminal activities

---

187 Reuters, (2004), 'Four commit suicide in Australia Child Porn Case', 2 October 2004.
    The FBI found thousands of audit trails of credit card transactions by men viewing child pornography from their computers around the world. Last week, the Australian police charged 400 men with keeping internet child pornography libraries, some of which had over 250, 000 images of child pornography, made in home studios.

188 Zia.F, (2004), 'The effectiveness of trade sanctions and ILO Convention 182 on the eradication of Child Labour in the United Kingdom and Pakistan', Paper (Do you wish to take 5? given at Annual Conference: Society of Legal Scholars, 22September 2004. The research shows that there are thousands of female children working in the sex industry, the clothing industry and the restaurant sector in the Midlands, in London and other areas of the United Kingdom. There are also thousands of foreign women working in the UK sex industry.
    The academic journals vigorously contradict the police's statements that 'trafficking is very rare' [Economist, 'It's a foreigner's game', 4 September, 2004. According to the Economist, the 'Poppy' project surveyed the UK sex industry. They said to the Economist, 'London's sex workforce is remarkably international. About a quarter of the women working in the four hundred and seventy British sex establishments turned out to be of Eastern European origin, the single largest group. Twelve percent of the women working in the UK sex industry are of East Asian or Western European origin, with other sizeable groups from Scandinavia and South America. Less than one fifth of the prostitutes were British'. The Economist article stated that 'such a rain-bow coloured workforce has given rise to the suspicion that many prostitutes are being imported as chattels. There have been incidents of women and children being trafficked into UK prostitution from Russia and the Balkans. The Economist stated that perhaps one reason why France and Sweden are closing commercial sex businesses may be because women and children are being trafficked to be exploited for commercial sex against their will.

189 Reuters, (2004), 'Columbian Drug Kingpin extradited to United States', 13 September, 2004. This extradited man was head of an organised trafficking organisation...

190 Damianova.J, (2004), ' In Western Europe, poor children kept as thieves', Reuters, 10 September, 2004.
    Children from Bulgaria, Moldova and Romania are smuggled into Western Europe and forced to act as thieves for the people smugglers. Austrian authorities estimate that up to 250, 000 children and teen-agers are sent out daily by organised criminal gangs to steal in the streets of Western Europe. The European police agency Europol say the problem is part of a wider pattern of human trafficking for the sex trade in Western Europe, for forced labour and crime.

need to be regulated, prohibited or criminalised and was followed quickly with the 1989 United Nations Convention on the Rights of the Child.

The UN continues orally fighting for the rights of the child even though the evidence of almost 2 million children in child prostitution does indicate that this rhetoric needs vigorous and simultaneous action to put an end to it. To list the UN's efforts, there was the 1991 'End Child Prostitution in Asian Tourism (ECPAT) a Non-governmental organisation which raised awareness of the crime. There followed the UN's 1992 'Programme of Action for the Prevention of the Sale of Children, Child Prostitution and Child Pornography'. Also, there was the 1996 'First World Congress against the Commercial Sexual Exploitation of Children'.

There is now a definition of the word 'trafficking'[191] and there is progress in that. The definition of trafficking in human beings in the United Nations Protocol to Prevent, Suppress and Punish Trafficking in Persons, especially Women and Children(2000) states:

'1. (a) 'Trafficking in persons' shall mean the recruitment, transportation, transfer, harbouring or receipt of persons, by means of threats or use of force or other forms of coercion, of abduction, of deception, of the abuse of power or of a position of vulnerability or of the giving or receiving of payments of benefits to achieve the consent of a person having control over another person, for the purposes of exploitation. Exploitation shall include, at a minimum, the exploitation of the prostitution of others or other forms of sexual exploitation, forced labour or services, slavery or practices similar to slavery, servitude or the removal of organs. The consent of the victim of trafficking in persons to the intended exploitation set forth in subparagraph (a) of this article shall be irrelevant where any of the means set forth in sub-paragraph (a) have been used.

(b) The recruitment, transportation, transfer, harbouring or receipt of a child for the purpose of exploitation shall be considered 'trafficking in persons' even if this does not involve any of the means set forth in sub-paragraph (a) of this article.

(c) 'Child' shall mean any person less than eighteen years of age.' In Fact, the term "trafficking" was not known in the United States, although since 1988, the US was using "aggravated felony" to mean "an offence relating to alien smuggling for which the term of imprisonment imposed is at least 5 years. By dwelling on the immigration side of people trafficking rather than the organised crime, the US has developed its immigration laws to the enactment of the United States Immigrant Responsibility Act of 1996 and the Anti-terrorism and Effective Death Penalty Act of 1996.[192]

How do Western countries react to this crime?

Germany's Committee on Equal Opportunities for Women and Men organised a colloquium in November 2002. And discussed trafficking of women and prostitution and studied the Dutch legalised prostitution industry as one direction they might take.

---

191 The Death Penalty is pronounced for an offence of failure to appear in court after conviction for people trafficking or alien smuggling.

192 The age of full adult responsibility differs in many countries. The minimum age of responsibility is as per this table:

Country	Full Adult	Minimum age
UK	18	10
France	19	13
Germany	19	14
Netherlands	18	12

Source: Newman.G, (1999), Oxford University Press

The Netherlands' solution to trafficking is to make prostitution a legal business activity. This means that prostitutes in that country must pay taxes and will be entitled to state benefits. It also means that mostly women legally domiciled there can work in the prostitution business, cutting the need for trafficking. This country research must be done to collect business data and discover exactly what proportion of its Gross Domestic Product is contributed by the sex sector.

The United States, in statistics estimated by government intelligence, state forty or fifty thousand women and children[193] were trafficked there for prostitution, notwithstanding that in 1997 the UNESCO figure was 300, 000 trafficked children to the US, the 1997 US illegal immigrants figure being 100, 000 from China alone, there seems to have been an astonishing fall in numbers in just six years.

The United States has decided to pass two recent laws, the United States Pledge Protection Act 2004 (to prosecute American citizens who travel abroad to procure sex with children) and the US Trafficking Victims Protection Act 2003 (to use new methods against those countries who do not discourage trafficking by withdrawing aid and other sanctions). Laudably, the US government has committed $50 million to support this programme (whether this aid has been deducted from another aid budget in unknown) This is a real monetary commitment to combat trafficking, but not so in the EU, where only vocal proclamations were made in the 2002 European Conference against Trafficking in Human Beings.[194] Similarly, UK laws and policy on pornography are inconsistent with the business truth, much like the UK duplicity about the perils of addiction to of gambling whilst simultaneously passing permissive and liberal laws permitting serious internet gambling habits.

The United Kingdom has never acknowledged "prostitution through trafficking .Rather, successive governments have seen the victims as illegal immigrant prostitutes, and sought to deport them. The situation has not been addressed and so there are no statistics on the subject, incomplete or estimated. That brothel keeping is included in the new Proceeds of Crimes Act and is defined as criminal conduct, is interesting. The UK will confiscate all earnings from such criminal activity, using the Assets Recovery Agency, it can therefore be reasoned that, instead of funding a project which will exclusively combat trafficking for prostitution, confiscated funds from prostitution will actually pay for the Assets Recovery Agency. But this is not the first time that the UK government has made overt condemnation of prostitution whilst ignoring the social and moral decay of British people who use trafficked prostitutes the demand for prostitution by foreign[195] women and children is there…The traffickers merely supply .Interestingly, the UK like the US, alleging no trafficking for prostitution their own countries, have both implemented draconian laws to tackle trafficking, which usually indicate a reaction to an enormous problem. at home As to the International Conventions, the UK was not a party to the Convention for the Suppression of the Traffic in Persons and of the Exploitation of the Prostitution of Others in 1949. The UK signed the UN Convention against Transnational Organised Crime, the Protocol to Prevent, Suppress and Punish Trafficking in Persons, Especially Women and Children, in 2000. There were Acts passed in 1898, 1908, 1912, 1922, and 1956 which attempted to curb prostitution, but never did they address trafficked prostitutes in particular. The UK Sexual Offences Act 2003 allows a maximum punishment of 14 years imprisonment for 'facilitating prostitution within the United Kingdom complete with legal definition of the word 'prostitute'.

UK legislation against trafficking is found in the Nationality, Immigration and Asylum Act 2002 and the Sexual Offences Act 2003. Section 145 of the Nationality, Immigration and Asylum Act 2002 covers the offences of arranging or facilitating the arrival, travel or departure of a person in the UK for the purpose of control over prostitution. Section 143 of this Act states that the penalty for this offence is a maximum of fourteen years imprisonment. The Sexual Offences Act 2003 deals with trafficking within and out of the UK for the purposes of sexual exploitation and

---

193 It is an enlightening fact that morally, the US regard gambling as wrong and with consistency, internet gambling is illegal in the US. The UK's moral tone against gambling, however, is completely dishonest as is illustrated by the UK's legal internet gambling, a stunning 65% of the global internet gambling., based on an analysis of the telecoms markets in 85 countries.

194 Similarly, UK laws and policy on pornography are probably inconsistent with the business truth, much like the UK pretence about the evils of gambling whilst simultaneously passing permissive and liberal laws permitting gambling with the further evidence of serious internet gambling habits.

195 United Nations Office of the High Commissioner for Human Rights, (2001), "The Race Dimensions of trafficking in persons", 11.7.2001.

the maximum sentence for such offences is also fourteen years. The Sexual Offences Act also has measures against buying the sexual services of a child, and causing, facilitating or controlling the commercial sexual exploitation of a child in prostitution or pornography. This Act came into force in May 2004.[196] .There is also the Criminal Justice Act 1987, section 2, which can be used by the Serious Fraud Office for compulsory questioning if trafficking involves serious financial fraud. Also, the Proceeds of Crime Act 2002 can be used to conduct financial investigations into suspected traffickers' financial affairs and to seize assets. Part VII of the POCA contains the money laundering offences. The definition of money laundering now extends to include proceeds of all crimes and section 329 states that the possession of criminal assets constitutes money laundering and there is the Extradition Act 2003 to return offenders. Yet the UK police in 2003 claimed that trafficking is very rare and that the majority of these women have come voluntarily to the UK to work as prostitutes.[197] It is this denial of the problem that causes the problem to be here after fifty years of combating this particular crime. The UK has four hundred and seventy 'brothels' in London alone and yet no-one addresses the real underlying organised trans-national crime. If migration to forced prostitution is merely the result of lack of prospects in the country of origin, unemployment and lack of education result in trafficked women and children, then those economic issues must be addressed. In 2003 the UK police made co-ordinated raids on several 'brothels' in the north of England, arrested the prostitutes and deported those with incorrect papers.

How can we track down and prosecute these traffickers? A possible way is by using common business methods of business investigation.

Practical steps to combat trafficking in the UK

The accountancy profession, especially, because of their recording and auditing functions, can help to detect trafficking by being vigilant on the Pay-As-You-Earn taxation side, spotting large tranches of very low-paid workers in the accounts records, spotting payments to lorry companies in a non-transport company's records,[198] spotting one-off payments to someone abroad, spotting mass purchase of cheap clothing and footwear, spotting money being deposited in many different branches of the company's bank, far away from the place of business, spotting sudden rises in income and spotting different modes of personal drawings.

What sort of accounts can reveal such organised crime? Any. From newsagents, tobacconists, doctors' accounts (sudden increase in patients), family firms with many low paid workers or much regular cash withdrawals, companies suddenly renting large cheap accommodation on the pretext of storage, sudden large purchases of cheap foodstuffs, clothing and footwear, sudden rises of income in any business from pornography retail outlets, massage parlours, market traders to new small subsidiaries abroad.

More Questions

How can such crimes be covered up in large companies' reports and access? It is well known that as companies grow larger, it becomes necessary to have several "books" instead of just one ledger and as companies grows even larger, these "books" are further sub-divided and one such "book" is the petty cash book. Whilst the petty cash account has advantages of handling and recording small cash payments by junior personnel and posting monthly entries to the main Profit and Loss account, it also has the disadvantage that the audit misses the significance of payments out of the petty cash

---

196 The first case of trafficking a child for prostitution in England was Attorney-General's Reference 6 of 2004, [2004] EWCA Crim 1275, in which the offender who was discovered to be in an organised international gang, was sentenced to prison for twenty three (23) years for kidnapping the child, living off immoral earnings and incitement to rape.

197 Economist, 'It's a foreigner's game', 4 September, 2004.

198 Lorries are frequently used as a method of mass transport by traffickers. There have been instances of many deaths whilst people are being trafficked. The most recent case was in Houston, Texas, USA, when 19 people died in a lorry full of 70 trafficked persons. After these deaths, two of the personnel
   Each faces 58 counts of harbouring and transporting illegal immigrants and if convicted, they could get up to life in prison sentences. See Lozano. J.A, (2004), "Deliberations resume in smuggling trial", Associated Press News Report, 20th December 2004.

account. This is where trafficking expenses might be legitimised through a large company's accounts. So a large well-known, decent, incorporated company may be involved in illegal activities such as trafficking for arms or drug courier purposes or for Value Added Tax frauds by using petty cash accounts. A well known example is of companies using people to but cigarettes and alcohol in Europe for personal use but in fact they are sub-dividing the transportation of corporate stock to avoid Value Added Tax.

Techniques of Data mining and accounting data-bases—useful for flagging up hidden trafficking.

For accountancy and management purposes, computer programmes are written to make it easy for data to be processed. For example, the accounting programme is written so that when an item is posted to an account, it may give you the running total to date, the account reference number and the budgeted figure for that expense. Such accounting software can be programmed to also include a flag-up of a creditor previously unknown to it. So if an engineering business starts to pay rent for premises elsewhere, it can be flagged up and checked. Like tackling other frauds, the accountancy software programme can be written to also flag up extra-ordinary items, for example, if there is a limit on how much stationery, say, can be bought from a certain supplier to a maximum of £200 per transaction, and the programme spots that the whole budget for the year has been spent in transactions of £200 in twelve transactions in January, it will flag that up. Money to facilitate trafficking can be hidden by such a means and the audit would not spot it unless the limit was broken or the total amount was much more than last year's figure.

Documentary Evidence

Another way that traffickers can use expense transactions is to create a highly paid fictitious person in the Payroll account in order to send steady large amounts of money to the trafficker's bank account to be used for his illegal purposes. Companies that end up in administration, though not traffickers, sometimes have similar types of fraud perpetrated in them. For instance, when the English company Finelist Group plc went into administration in October 2000, various huge payroll discrepancies were found, amounting to millions of pounds.[199] In general, personnel signs would be employee numbers and locations, categories of employees (full or part time), methods of compensation (eg, salaried, weekly, hourly, piece-work, overtime, holidays, bonuses, commission).

Finally, we can say that electronic documents can be forced to be disclosed such as e-mails, spreadsheets, presentations and word processing documents. Such electronic documents hold the key to tracing traffickers and since ninety seven percent[200] of all business document are electronic. The metadata which computers automatically create and store about each document and this can track the changes in a document, those who have had access to it or have changed it such as the cc on an email…

The Front Business? Questions that must be asked.

Are these regular for the type of business that this business purports to be? If a photography business is formed as a limited company and makes good net profits of over £100, 000 each year, you would expect that it has regular corporate clients, contract work and staff. If you find that this photography business is a one man company with a private aeroplane and that this company director then starts a second business which is a retail sex outlet, it might raise alarm bells that maybe this director is peddling more than photos, and if not, what type of photos is he producing and who audits his accounts, if indeed they are audited?. For indeed, even if this is a registered company, the rules are that an unqualified accountant, not an auditor, may prepare and submit accounts for small companies, those incorporated companies with a turnover up to 5.6 million pounds (see UK Statutory Instruments 2004, No.16, Companies Act 1985 which came into force in January 2004 and is know as the audit exemption threshold of 5.6 million pounds sterling) And such

---

199 See the Times, Friday 20th October 2000: "Accountants facing scrutiny over Fine-list" and Mail on Sunday, 22nd October 2000 "Black hole in car parts firm".

200 Lawson.M and Arazi.J, (2004), "Electronic disclosure", Mondaq Newsletter, 9.9.2004.

a preparer of accounts has no compliance accounting standards, no body to disqualify him. Could he be sued? The person perpetrating the illegal trafficking would not sue him. If they have a contract, it would be to fool financial bodies in order to facilitate money borrowing. An innocent preparer of such accounts for an illegal activity could not be sued by the lending bank for negligence under tort. If an accountant made an error in judgement and was ignorant of the real activity of such a business, then he could not be sued in negligence. In <u>Whitehouse v Jordan [1980] 1 All ER 650,</u> Lord Denning said that an error of judgement did not in fact constitutes negligence.

New Disclaimer by UK Accountants against negligence :

In January 2003, the Institute of Chartered Accountants in England and Wales issued a technical release, recommending auditors to include a disclaimer in their report and accounts: "This report is made solely to the issuer's members, as a body, in accordance with section 235, Companies Act 1985. Our audit work has been undertaken so that we might state to the issuer's members those matters we are required to state to them in an auditor's report and for no other purpose. To the fullest extent permitted by law, we do not accept or assume responsibility to anyone other than the issuer and the issuer's members as a body, for our audit work, for this report, or for the opinions we have formed." This recommendation appears to be a move towards the German contract law instead of the English tort law that auditors' liability at present come under. If damages caused by a wrong audit are recoverable under an implied contract between auditor and shareholder, the auditor is usually liable for simple negligence. There is general agreement that pure economic loss has to be compensated under contract law as the cost of protection is internalised in the contract. Auditors have recently lobbied the Department of Trade and Industry to amend section 310, Companies Act to allow auditors to negotiate a cap on their liability but the Office of Fair Trading Report of 5th August 2004 stated that a cap would not prevent the collapse of an accountancy firm and that, anyway, there is professional indemnity insurance and that accountants can form limited liability companies.

Example of Front Business: Photographic shop or Hard-core Pornography film studio?

If an auditor is not thoroughly familiar with the nature of the business, he cannot spot fronting arrangements that hide trafficking offences. This means that the auditor should really know the type of business he is auditing, the key business activities, the products, the service, the customers, the industry and the competitors. This is not as easy as it sounds because a company can have whatever name it chooses, apart from the prohibitions under the <u>Business Names Act 1985</u> sections 2 and 3, and Companies Act section 26. For example, the sex shop outlets which are on some UK High streets and are known as "Private" shops, are franchised from the American organisation which boasts in its annual report that it is "a purveyor of Hard Core Pornography". These Private shops, if formed as limited companies in the United Kingdom, can be registered at Companies House, Cardiff under a name other than "Private". Registered companies do not always declare their true business to Companies House. Also, there are broad categories for registration and there are no categories for sexual retail outlets, massage parlours, etc. Those will be registered under "other retail business" category and criminals can tick the wrong box because there is NO audit of the registration documents.

Commercial developments of companies can be tracked to disclose any illegal offences such as trafficking. These include change in activities, product history (for example, are they selling private hairdressing to hotel room occupants or are they selling sex? are they transmitting soft pornography films in night clubs as a service activity or are they filming paedophiles in action? Both activities would need projectors, film, storage premises, staff, but the latter would have purchase of equipment for perverse purposes, food items purchased clothes purchases, transport costs, aeroplane tickets, etc.)

The history of ownership/control and other significant events, for example major acquisition and disposals and major disputes can be the tell tale signs of other activities. The location of the business is important as is the description of properties occupied.

As in all things, preparation is the key to success. To stop trafficking in its steps, to catch traffickers in the early stages, to stop even the formation of such corporations, an accountant appointed to a new audit can pay particular considerations in a new engagement and must familiarise himself with the client's business, recording background information on the permanent notes file. He must obtain all necessary documents well in advance of the commencement of the first audit.

Profiling the trafficker; knowledge database that can be created and used by other countries

Profiling techniques can also be used to detect money laundering and thus trafficking. Bank statements of criminal suspects can be examined to identify cash deposits, unusual transactions, gross income, female dependant, nature of personal transactions, standard of living, taste in entertainment, internet transactions, transfers of moneys to large corporations, etc. The person can be checked against Companies' House records for director disqualification. An internet search might reveal some past criminality. His credit reference may be sought.

Conclusion

The writer leaves this concluding comment. Modern society has produced this peculiar variety of professional criminals. There are tremendous financial gains in the pornographic businesses. Even on a few products surveyed, it is clear that the margins are of the scale of nearly 900 percent and more.[201] The Annual Report of the 'Private' sex shop franchise business declares extremely healthy profits from this 'purveyor of hare-core pornography, as the report describes the business. Governments, despite their protestations, will do nothing to harm businesses; the health of the economy depends on businesses and the blur of the transition of trafficking to legal is very fuzzy. Many have been waiting for fifty years to stop the uncouth and savage act of sex exploitation. Now at last the European Commission have announced plans for a concerted effort against it and the newly formed United Kingdom Serious Offences and Crimes Agency

(SOCA) has announced its priority of combating trafficking for prostitution.

This report did not attempt to tackle the separate subject of child exploitation for computer pornography but plans to do so soon.

Cases

Attorney-General's Reference 6 of 2004 [EWCA] Crim 1275

Whitehouse v Jordan [1980] 1 All ER 650

Statutes and Conventions

Business Names Act 1985	UK
Companies Act 1985	UK
Criminal Justice Act 1987	UK
Extradition Act 2003	UK
ILO Convention 180	International
Immigrant Responsibility Act 1996	United States
Nationality, Immigration and Asylum Act 2000	UK

---

201 A simple survey of internet sex shops show prices of pornographic videos ranging from £25 to £75 in UK sex shops advertised on the internet. A video cassette would cost less than £1 to manufacture and so the margin from manufacturing the video cassette to sale of hard-core pornography to the public is 7, 500 a remarkable margin. Similar exercises can be done with all sex products and services to give a true accounting value to the sector in the UK, deducting expenses and allowing for contingency expenses of traffickers.

Proceeds of Crimes Act 2002	UK
Pledge Protection Act 2004	United States of America
Sexual Offences Act 2003	UK
Trafficking Victim's Protection Act	UK

United Nations Conventions

1949   Convention on the Suppression of Traffic of Persons and the Exploitation of the Prostitution.

1957   Abolition of Forced Labour Convention.

1959   United Nations Declaration of the Rights of Child,

1988   United Nations Convention against Illicit Trafficking in Narcotic Drugs and Psychotropic Substances

1992   Programme of Action for the Prevention of the Sale of Children, Child Prostitution and Child Pornography.

References

Brown. R, (2004), 'Death by Deadline', FT Magazine, 2October 2004.

Ebbe.O, (1989), 'Crime and delinquency in metropolitan Lagos: a study of crime and delinquency area theory', Social Forces.

Economist, (1997), 19 April.

Eluf. L .N, (1992) 'A new approach to law enforcement', New York: United Nations Development Fund for Women.

EU, (1996), 'Situation report on organised crime in the EU: 1995', Brussels: EU.

Farrington.D.P, (1996), 'Understanding and preventing youth crime', York: Joseph Rowntree Foundation.

Heise.L.L and Germain.A, (1994), 'Violence against women: the hidden health burden', Washington.D.C: World Bank.

House of Commons Hansard Written Answers, 15 November 2004.

Kerr.J, (1994), 'Calling for change: International strategies to end violence against women', The Hague: Development Co-operation, Information Department, Ministry of foreign Affairs.

Mueller.G.W.O, (1998), 'Trans-national crime; experiencing uncertainties', Uncertainties Scenarios.

Musacchio.V, (2004), 'Migration connected with trafficking in women and children', German Law Journal, Vol 5.No.9, September 2004.

Pope.V, (1997), 'Trafficking in women', US News and World Report, 7 April 1997.

Redo.S, (1998), 'International annals of criminology', UN.

Reuters (2004), 'Venezuela slams US over human trafficking sanctions', 13 September 2004.

Reuters (2004), 'Four commit suicide in Australia porn case', 2 October 2004.

Reuters (2004), 'Columbian drug king pin extradited to United States', 13 September 2004.

Reuters (2004), 'In Western Europe, Poor Children Kept as Thieves', 10 September, 2004.

Robinson. C, (1994), The international conference on transnational migration in the Asia-Pacific region: problems and prospects', January 1994.

Smith.P.J, 'Human suffering: Chinese migration trafficking and the challenge to America's immigrant tradition', Washington : Centre for Strategic and International Studies.

United Nations, (1995), 'Action against organised crime'.

Internet references:

Anti-Slavery International

http://www.antislavery.org/homepage/antislavery/trafficking.htm

Coalition Against Trafficking in Women.

http://www.catwinternational.org

US Department of State

Office to Monitor and Combat Trafficking in Persons.

http://www.state.gov/g/tip/

Issue 4—Financial Systems do not stop Fraud

UK Consolidated Financial Regulatory System

What fraud prevention factors are there in the UK financial regulatory consolidation; would the UK's model fit developing countries? No, be cause the UK, with £45 Billion fraud in 2003, 100% more than in 2002, is unsuitable as an example.

Abstract

The subject of centralisation of financial regulation has been studied for over a hundred years . The Paper examines the newly consolidated UK financial regulatory system and questions whether it can be successfully used as a model for developing countries. It concentrates on the banking system, this being the most important part in facilitating terrorism, money laundering, arms, drugs and people trafficking, the black economy and trans-national crime generally The analysis also looks at the US regulatory financial system, dozens of years old, which does not stem the flow of fraud. or regulatory non-compliance.

Introduction

In this work, the term developing country uses the meaning as in the World Bank's definition. and builds on the study of financial globalisation by Obstfeld and Taylor (1998),[202] Badwin and Martin (1999),[203] Bordo, Eichengreen and Irwin (1999),[204] Eichengreen and Sussman (2000).[205] There is a perception of increased financial globalisation which is correct, contrary to the writing of Frankel(2000).[206] Advances that are not comparable to decades ago[207] are the technological advances in financial services, electronic communication in the general public,the deregulation of financial systems and the diversity of new financial products. An objective often given for the need to globalise financial regulatory systems is the sharing of information to avoid risk problems such as an attack on a country's currency.[208]

UK regulatory personnel are moving from game-keeper to poacher as they change jobs to work elsewhere.[209] The true drive to better regulated markets is that developing countries wish for economic growth through more capital being available to them from developed countries, hugely assisted by high technology information systems that help to stop moral hazard and bed decisions, holding with Levine's theory (2001).

---

202 Obstfeld.M and Taylor.A.M, (1998), 'The defining moment:The Great Depression and the American Economy in the 20th Century', Chicago:Chicago University Press, 1998.

203 Baldwin and Martin studied globalisation and put the case for and against it.

204 Bordo.M,.D, Eichengreen.B and Irwin.D.A, (1999), 'Is globalisation today really different than Globalisation a hundred years ago?', Brookings Trade Policy Forum, 1999.

205 Eichengreen.B and Sussman.N, (2000), 'The Internationsl Monetary System in the long run', Washington:IMF.

206 Frankel.J, (2000), 'Globalisation of the Economy', Washington: Brookings Institution Press.

207 These facts are contrary to arguments put forward by Mussa(2000) in 'Factors driving global economic integration', Federal Reserve Bank of Kansas City . Mussa claimed that public policy was powerless in the face of advanced technology, this proving to be a fallacy when statistics reveal that it is the public that drive the demand for more advanced technology. Half the homes in developed countries have computers, shopping,banking, services and telephone systems are now mostly computerised and understood by most people. The SEC Annual Reports show the public conducting internet trading and in the case of the UK, 60% of global internet gambling in 2003 was transacted by UK residents from home computers.

208 Schmukler.S.L, (2003), 'Financial globalisation:Gain and pain for developing countries', p 28, World Bank.

209 The Times Newspapers in week ended 20th October ran articles about the swathes of staff from the Financial Services Authority who are leaving work in the non-regulatory sector.

Methodology

The work examines the new single Financial regulator of the United Kingdom, the Financial Services Authority. The US's single authority, the SEC was examined and five years' Annual Reports (1999 to 2003) were studied, compliance breaches recorded and analysed. Then sing the World Bank's 2003 database of financial systems of 130 countries, the common law developing countries and their facts were extracted and analysed. The banking systems with similar ownership patters to the UK's were then extracted and examined, including other relevant factors.

The most surprising finding is that the UK does not require capital adequacy levels from banks which open branches in the UK, unlike the rest of the EU that comply with the 1988 Basle Capital Adequacy Accord. Far from being a Model therefore, the UK financial regulatory system will be devastated when the 2004 Basle Accord is enforced in 2005, compelling the UK to require adequate capital from foreign banks with branches in London. Albeit speculation, but the 2004 Basle II Accord may be the catalyst that forces foreign banks to go to countries with actual legal competitive advantage, unless of course, the UK leaves the EU.

The UK Financial System

Since 1997, the UK has reformed its financial system by separating its banking supervision from the operation of monetary policy by creating the Financial Services Authority, a single regulator that covers banking, securities and insurance. This regulator is independent from the Bank of England and therefore independent from the government. The Bank of England has clear responsibility for operating monetary policy whilst the Financial Services Authority is responsible for financial services regulation. There is a Debt Management Office which is responsible for the government's debt management policy.

We will examine the FSA's results to see if it has achieved its goal of increased openness and transparency, price stability, long term policy predictability, translated into economies of scale, simplicity, prevention of regulatory arbitrage, accountability, reduced costs and improved policy co-ordination.

The Financial Services Authority

The FSA is a private company which discharges a public function and has regulatory powers through statute. It does not rely on government for its funding, but levies fees on the firms it regulates and uses this to cover its costs. It reports annually and must confer if it changes its fee structure. The FSA regulates banks, shares and insurance.

The FSA makes an annual report to the Treasury. The Treasury can initiate reviews of the FSA and so can the DTI. The FSA has a single enforcement regime applicable to all the firms and individuals it regulates. It has a risk-focussed, authorisation process applicable across all sectors. The FSA also supervises the London Clearing House and CREST, securities clearing and settlement systems

The UK's Debt Management Office (DMO)

The DMO is an executive agency of the Treasury. It is responsible for the government cash—flows and operates in line with the International Monetary Fund and the World Bank. The UK has a low level of government debt. The IMF regularly investigates countries financial systems for weaknesses and reports on its findings. In June 2003 the IMF reported in its Financial Stability Assessment Programme, that the UK's banks are well capitalised and profitable and have a low rate of non-performing loans. Although the IMF found that the UK has a high-quality accounting and disclosure regime., its insurance sector did not reach some internationally agreed framework with a great disparity between the insurance sector and the rest of the financial industry. Under the Financial Services and Markets Act 2000, it is now a criminal offence to conduct insurance business without authorisation by the FSA.

What constitutes a 'contract of insurance' is not defined by law although the FSA has put out guidelines to be enforced from 1st January 2005 when it takes over the supervision and regulation of the UK insurance sector.

Outside Forces

Apart from the IMF and the World Bank, there is the Basle 11 Capital Adequacy Revisions, the EU Risk-Based Capital Directive, the Solvency Directive and the Re-insurance Directive with which the UK must comply, the objectives of which are global economic stability and international security.

The European Union's efforts at regional security

The regional integration among the member states of the European Union(EU) can be viewed as the harmonisation of national laws. Beginning with Article 100 of the Treaty of Rome in 1958, Member States of the EU harmonised nearly 200 of their laws, regulations and administrative provisions in the areas of taxation, social policy, transportation, and the environment. An effort to assimilate as much legislation without each state losing its jurisdiction is a sort of national convergence by adopting similar legislation which is separately enforceable in each state. As much as 60% of member state legislation is derived from the EU and is directed mainly at trade and harmonising legislation is a way of achieving policy congruence without walking over national sovereignty.

The EU is highly integrated into the international financial system. It is this integration together with highly developed technological computerised systems that calls for even greater security from risks such as international crime, insider dealing, money laundering and other monetary frauds

There have been a series of Concordats of the Basle Committee on Banking Regulation and Supervisory Practices known as the Basle Committee. This is an informal consultative group under the auspices of the Bank for International Settlements at Basle, Switzerland., with representatives of the central banks of Belgium, Canada, France, Germany, UK, Italy as committee members. In 1992 there was the EU Directive 92/30,on the Supervision of Credit Institutions on a Consolidated Basis. The most recent harmonisation steps is the Basle Accord aimed at consolidation of the banking system through supervision, capital requirements, securitisation rules. The Basle Accord is a plan to recast some past EU Directives between 1993 and 2000 because it recognised a wider range of credit risks and seeks to put regulation in place by 31 December 2007 to mitigate these risks.

The most readily admitted risk to the EU financial system is acknowledged as the denationalisation of money which passes from one territory to another through banks' payment systems regulated by divergent national laws. Most European member states except the UK have laws which state that the point of transfer is the point when it reaches the recipient bank. There is no agreement moreover, of what law applies when different currencies are involved in a transaction.[210] Since there is no clear authority, transnational currency is unregulated internationally which have important implications for banking transactions but not for banking risks. The result of this transnational currency transaction only impacts on the parties in the transaction and it is for contract terms to foresee and install appropriate jurisdiction and currency clauses.

---

210 For instance, in the case law <u>Libyan Arab Foreign Bank v Bankers Trust Co. [1989]</u>. In 1986 the US attempted the freeze Libya's asset because of suspected terrorist activities. Some of the money was US $ held in the London branch of Bankers Trust., a foreign branch of an American Bank. The US President ordered the Bankers Trust to transfer the $130 million to America. The Bankers Trust refused and the case went to court. It was held by Justice Evans that the deposited money was subject to English law.

Contrary to this decision is the decision in a later case <u>Wells Fargo Ltd v Citibank [1991]</u>, in which the New York law was applicable to a Eurocurrency transaction because the transfer location was New York.

But in the case of Wells Fargo (Asia) Ltd v Citibank, the court found that New York law would be applicable.

Surveys

Surveys of banking news and regulatory literature show that the most important risk in banking is imprudent lending[211] especially credit risk and security risk, even in the modern electronic age.[212] The collapse of one large bank due to no liquidity can have major repercussions in the international financial system. It is the illiquidity that is the risk and the electronic speed of news, transactions and market trading only increase the danger of financial instability transmitted instantly and globally. This was recognised by the First Basle Accord in 1983, reacting to the 1975 failure of the Bankhaus Herstatt and the failure of Banco Ambrosiano in 1982. The Committee on Banking Regulations and Supervisory Practices issued a Revised Basle Concordant on Principles for the Supervision of Banks' Foreign Establishments, International Legal Materials. There followed the 1988 Basle Capital Adequacy Accord[213] in an attempt to protect the EU against risks from American under-capitalised banks.[214] [215] Following the UK's Bank of Credit and Commerce International (BCCI) collapse,[216] the Minimum Standards for the Supervision of International Banking Groups and their Cross-Border Establishments was put in force in 1992.

Minimum Standards of 1988 Basle Capital Adequacy Accord

The Minimum Standards were that all international banks and banking groups should be supervised by a home country regulator; there should be prior consent from the host country and from the group's home country before creating a cross-border bank; supervisory authorities should be able to investigate and collate information about the bank; and the home country authority can impose restrictive measures consistent with these minimum standards before such a cross border bank can be established.

By 1995 75% of the Euro-markets consisted of US dollars and competition among member states increased creating arbitrage and laxity in regulatory systems. Indeed, the available global portfolio has 80% invested in the US, UK, France, Germany, Canada, Hong Kong, Switzerland and the Netherlands, making a study of EU and US banking regulations essential to combating money laundering. Since most of global money passes through these developed countries, it is logical to expect that it is in these countries that significant fraud will occur and therefore it is these countries that need stringent implementation of anti-fraud systems, not the small developing countries.

A comparison of one of these systems, the UK's, with developing common law countries might reveal why fraud is increasing despite good regulatory systems, what aspects of regulatory systems are actually working and should be implemented in developing countries, what intangible processes do work and so should be implemented and whether unrecorded and undiscovered factors play a role in the exponential increase in financial fraud .

The 2004 Basle II Capital Adequacy Accord

A new regime replaced the 1988 Basle Capital Adequacy Accord in June 2004 and has 31 December 2007 as the due implementation date. The Basle II was necessary because there are still significant issues in the EU banking system, these

211 Access to funding is a critical business need of any company. It is also central to any fraudulent scheme.

212 For example, The Economist, (1993), 'New tricks to learn: survey of international banking', 10April, 1993, p.14.

213 The Basle Capital Adequacy Accord had the goals of requiring banks to maintain higher levels of capital reserves through the maintenance of capital-to-asset ratios that are risk-based and to establish a level playing field so that a bank based in one country will not receive a competitive advantage by enjoying lower capital adequacy standard than a bank located in another country. Capital reserves are a means to minimise credit risks of banks, ensuring their safety and soundness.

214 In 1988 the Euromarkets comprised US$ 4 trillion., three times the US domestic deposit market.

215 The US Savings and Loans Industry was deregulated in the 1980's and entered into speculative trading in land and development deals resulting in institution failures and a severe crisis in the US banking industry mainly caused by excessive lending.

216 BCCI had engaged in fraud and other illegal activities It escaped supervision because of its complex corporate structure in Luxembourg, Cayman Islands, UK, US and elsewhere. It had fraudulent book-keeping and entered fictitious loans of US$ 1.3 billion. It did not record US$ 600 million of deposits; it conducted money laundering in Florida and secretly controlled 4 US banks; in total it accumulated liabilities of US$ 10.64 billion while retaining only US$1.1 billion assets.

being intra-group exposures, supervision, scope of consolidation, supervisory co-operation and credit risk mitigation. The 2004 Basle II replaces the 1988 Capital Accord and its corresponding EU directives on capital adequacy. The capital adequacy rules of 1988 have been proved to be ineffective and the new capital adequacy will involve more sophisticated, risk-sensitive calculation of capital requirements, a choice in ratings indicators, basic, standardised and advanced measurements, a new specific component for operational risk, a new framework for securitisation and broader, more sophisticated recognition of credit risk mitigation. It also includes changes to the trading book regime. The directive to implement the Basle II has three levels, 160 Articles open to amendment only be legislation, 14 Annexes open to amendment only by the European Banking Committee and an ongoing scrutiny by the Committee of European Banking Supervision.

The United Kingdom's breach of the Basle Capital Adequacy Accord

For the UK, the Basle II Accord will bring huge differences in its intra-group exposures which, at present, attaches zero % risk to intra-group transactions, ignoring even the 1988 Basle Accord on capital adequacy!! There will be extreme consequences for the UK when it is forced to implement capital adequacy regime The 2004 Basle II Accord has only few exemptions to capital adequacy for intra-group concerns, as per the 2000/12/EC/Article 80,7. These exemptions are only for a type of firm within the same consolidation, within the same risk management, in the same member state. Some UK banks have Channel Island subsidiaries which will have to comply. Because supervisory review will be of a firm's whole risk profile, it will represent one supervisory review for the whole of the EU and since current practice varies in different member states, it will produce in time a consistent regulatory system applicable across the EU, similar to the federal banking supervision by the US's SEC agency. It will apply to every single banking entity in the EU.

It will force the newly consolidated regulatory agencies of member states to regularise their systems and work together because there must be prior consultation of other supervisors.

Credit risk mitigation in the EU

To mitigate credit risk, the 2004 Basle II Accord will accept a wider category of collateral than at present. It will require that companies' accounts have off-Balance Sheet netting and will examine guarantees and credit derivatives. Once a company chooses its approach to credit risk, it must use that method consistently. The legal aspects of EU banks' credit risk mitigation will be that documentation must be binding on all parties and legally enforceable in all relevant jurisdictions. A bank must conduct sufficient legal review to verify satisfaction of this test and have a well founded legal basis for concluding that it is satisfied. The bank will have to undertake further review to ensure continuing enforceability. The bank will have to comply with any filing or registration requirements and have a right to realise assets promptly. The opinion as the credit risk mitigation must include opinion from an external solicitor.

How will credit risk mitigation be monitored?

The legal issues with regard to credit risk mitigation include identification of relevant jurisdictions—what is the governing law of agreement?; which is the jurisdiction of incorporation?; which is the jurisdiction of any branch?; are there any EU counter-parties?; which is the relevant jurisdiction for collateral?; what are the conflicts rules in respect of these jurisdictions?; where are the physical collateral such as gold or commodities located?; where is the financial intermediary located?; who will monitor implementations?.

The legal problems in implementing credit risk mitigation are that a bank must ensure that derivative falls within the eligible category, it must review its terms of compliance which must be direct, clearly defined, with no permission of unilateral cancellation; it must specify minimum credit events and have a robust basis of valuation of cash settlement.

The main forces that drive the harmonisation of banking regulation

Fraud, money laundering and corruption and the information technology revolution may be the other major drivers in harmonisation

How do money launderers use the banking and non banking systems?

The techniques of money laundering can be put into three categories, namely banking, non-banking institutions and non-financial businesses. Obvious money laundering through the banking system can be seen in large deposits and transfers, false name accounts, electronic structured transactions, shell and front companies for layering transactions, use of lawyers, accountants, and trustees to pass money by, collection accounts, compliant banks, loan back arrangements, telegraphic transfers, bank drafts, money orders, cash withdrawals, travellers cheques and internet banking.

Non bank financial institutions used in money laundering are bureau de change, money remittance services or giro houses, underground banking, foreign exchange transactions, single premium insurance products and postal services. Non financial businesses used for money laundering are professional facilitators, secretarial companies, real businesses, commercial trade transactions through free trade zones, internet casinos, real estate companies, cross border purchase of precious metals and use of warrants in the metal markets.

The black economy is estimated at 7% of Gross Domestic Product; in the UK, 9% of GDP in the USA, 10% in Germany, 25% in Italy, Spain and Greece, 50% in Russia and Central and Eastern Europe, a very serious problem.[217] Money laundering is also due to drug trafficking, human trafficking, terrorism,[218] infringement of trademarks and copyrights, trafficking in human body parts, illegal gambling, piracy, marine thefts and marine pollution and much else. The seriousness of the problem is reflected in the formation of the international organisation, Financial Action Task Force(FATF) to combat it.

Money laundering is the concealment of the beneficial ownership of funds. In today's electronic banking systems it is very difficult to contain original information once money travels electronically from country to country. The only way to read the source of the illegal proceeds is at the stage when it is first introduced into the banking system. This requires national laws to criminalise money laundering. This in fact privatises the function of policing the illegal proceeds. Governments' domestic laws therefore force citizens to act as police without payment and with threat of punishment for not doing so, much like the UK collects its Value Added Tax at present.

Money laundering was being combated since the 1988 United Nations (Vienna) Convention Against Illicit Traffic in Narcotic Drugs and Psychotropic Substances, ratified by nearly 100 countries, including the EU. That same year the Basle Committee on Banking Regulations and Supervisory Practices issued a statement of principles titled "Know your customers".

An examination of the US fifty year federal regulatory system

The US was the first to enact strict money laundering legislation in the Money Laundering Act 1986. Even before 1986, all US financial institutions were required to file a currency transaction report, enforced by the US 1970 Bank Secrecy Act. And US banks were required to report suspicions to the government, unlike in the UK where to breach such confidentiality was illegal. It is not until the 2004 Basle II Accord that the UK has been forced to incorporate into its legislation compulsory tipping off by employees to the government, to be enforced by December 2006.

But the US, although implementing their Bank Secrecy Act since 1970, still suffers from huge money laundering problems which led to the enactment of the 2003 Patriot Act in an attempt to ensure national financial and other security, with renewed vigorous enforcement such as the $50 million fine imposed on AmSouth Bank in October 2004. An

---

217 UN Global Crime figures,2003.

218 Borchersen-Keto.S, (2004), 'Terrorist groups using cash couriers to move money', Washington: Compliance Headquarters, September 2004. The writer reported that the US Secret Service had recently investigated counterfeit bank notes in Korea and found evidence of a going concern business with sophisticates technical equipment.

analysis of the US Securities Enforcement Commission (SEC) Reports reveal that the SEC regularly makes serious enforcement orders in investigating and supervising its financial institutions, the necessity for the Commission being apparently imperative.

SEC REPORTS (1999 to 2003)—Referrals to Division of Enforcement

	1999	2000	2001	2002	2003
self-regulatory organisations	1	0	0	0	0
broker-dealers	131	123	112	76	92
investment advisors	56	54	54	48	55
investment companies	19	18	8	14	14
transfer agents	15	11	12	7	9
insurance companies	1	0	0	0	0

There were also 1473 broker dealers with less serious deficiencies in 1999 to 2002, 3976 investment advisors with other deficiencies, 703 investment companies with other deficiencies and 1038 transfer agents with other deficiencies in the 4 years from 1999 to 2002, a serious problem when it is considered that the US has had the SEC regulating finance since 1936.It is noted that even today, very few US firms have formal whistle-blowing systems in place.

Serious money laundering and fraud in US banks today

The money laundering criminals are so hard to deter that the US formed a Financial Crimes Enforcement Network (FinCEN) in 2003. Like a recurrence of the Savings and Loans collapse in the 1980s, the SEC has recently investigated a trillion dollar mortgage institution Fanny Mae which guarantees one quarter of all residential mortgages in the states of the US. Fanny Mae was found to have engaged in hedge betting, accounting manipulation and systems deficiencies. So even with a record of fifty years of SEC regulation, a serious collapse of a mortgage institution is happening again in the US.

On 25 October 2004, the US regulators imposed a fifty million dollar fine on AmSouth Bank in Birmingham, Alabama.for not reporting money laundering activities.[219] Deficiencies in the bank's compliance programme led to failure to comply with the suspicious activity reporting requirements. A clear deficit in the "know your customer" policy is apparent in this case. The senior attorney of Bankers Systems Inc said in the article, *'Know your customers.[220] In order to know when a report might be triggered, you must know who your customers are, the type of activity to expect from them and where the funds to open accounts come from. In AmSouth Bank, there were numerous instances where accounts were opened without this type of knowledge. With high-risk customers, you must perform due diligence and investigate the company's background. You must also ask about the source of funds used to open the account and monitor account activity. Had AmSouth done this, they would have spotted the red flags triggering a report. Even if they are dead, report. The fact that the subject is dead does not negate your responsibility to file a report. Again, the government uses the report to investigate the patterns of crime and related illegal activities. The fact that one party to a particular transaction dies does not mean a criminal investigation is necessarily over....'*

219 Burt.S, (2004), 'Regulators impose $50 million BSA Penalty', Bankers Systems Inc:26 October, 2004.
220 This term "Know your customers" is a term

Further US legislation to curb money laundering and fraud

US banks are under the legislation of the Bank Secrecy Act whose central purpose is to safeguard the US financial system from the abuses of money laundering, terrorist financing and other illicit finance. The US Bank Secrecy Act ensures that financial institutions create policies, programs and procedures and systems that will help protect themselves from financial crime and by making information available to the government through required record-keeping and reporting. The Act has criminal provisions that are reserved for persons who commit the most serious crimes of wilfully, intentionally violate the provision of the Act. Other than this, it carries a civil enforcement penalty. Recent large scale penalties have driven US banks to begin to file reports defensively and to clog the system with such defensive reports.[221]

The UK will soon implement the EU Market Abuse Directive which will compel whistle-blowing of irregularities by employees. However, unlike the US Bank Secrecy Act, there is no criminal sanction provided for any person who deliberately manipulates the market, only civil fines. Lloyd reinsurers, a syndicate that was previously unregulated, will now be subject to the requirement for authorisation for their risks on their behalf.

Factors in the UK Financial Regulatory System

(a) The UK's Consolidated Financial Regulator, the Financial Services Authority (FSA) is an independent limited company.

Financial sector supervision is more rigorous than other regulated sectors because they manage the health of the banks, preserve the stability of the financial system, protect consumers, and prevent market collapse. Weak supervision, ineffective regulation and political interference have been stated as factors for financial collapse by finance writers. Some examples of countries which faced collapse due to these factors are Korea, Indonesia, Japan and Venezuela[222]

Contrary to such countries, those with independent regulators have wide autonomy in setting rules and regulations in order to achieve their goals. Supervisory integrity is crucial to regulation and in some countries legal protection is offered to supervisors.

Budget independence is also crucial if supervisors must be free from political pressures and must be able to build up funds. The UK is one step ahead in that the UK's FSA also has independence from its central bank, the Bank of England. There must be no conflict of interest. The key to effective independence is accountability and the FSA is in an ideal position for this because it is an independent limited company and must submit its accounts to the Treasury. and filed accounts at Companies House. Like all other such limited companies the FSA will have to provide a clear public statement of its objectives. In cases of emergency the override mechanisms must be stated clearly.

(b) The UK is a liberalised economy with mature financial markets

The liberalisation of capital markets in the UK has been extensive and has taken place over a long period of time. Exchange controls were abolished in 197 and direct controls dismantled soon after that. Indirect controls on bank lending were removed, and bank reserves were no longer required. Controls on mortgages and consumer credit were relaxed. The securities market was deregulated.

From the 1980's there was a shift away from self-regulation in the banking and securities sectors towards statutory regulation. There was the Financial Services Act 1986. The banking sector was supervised by the Bank of England. There was already statutory regulation of the insurance and building society sectors before 1979. Since the 1980's when home ownership became widespread, financial scandals impacted directly on the consumer and there was a public call for reform of self-regulation.

221 Fox.W.J, (2004), 'Mony Laundering Speech', Virginia: ABA 2004 Money Laundering Enforcement Conference.
222 Quintin.M, (2004), 'Should financial sector regulators be independent?', Int. Monetary Fund.

Since 1997, the Bank of England is responsible for regulating monetary policy and the new Financial Services Authority (FSA) is responsible for financial services regulation. A Debt Management Service is responsible for the UK Government's debt management policy.

The UK had weak monetary and financial policy up to the year 1997 and was ineffective in financial regulation. So a new economic framework was established.

It is hoped that a consolidated financial regulator will bring economies of scale, simplicity, prevention of regulatory arbitrage, accountability and administrative co-ordination. There is no mention of fraud, even though fraud has been rising each year and was estimated at £40 billion in 2003.

To achieve these aims the single regulator was created to be independent, incorporated and self funding. The 2000 Financial Services and Markets Act which came into force in November 2001 gave the FSA powers to sanction, regulate, fine and investigate ; the Treasury conducts independent performance reviews of the FSA,there is a Financial Services Practitioner Panel and a Consumer Panel, and a Complaints Commissioner. The FSA has uniform investigatory processes for all sections it supervises. The UK was the first country to be assessed against the OECD Money Laundering Code in 2003 The only shortfall found was in the insurance industry.

(c) The UK Markets Abuse Act 2005 will make whistle blowing by employees compulsory. This is taking heed of many analyses and studies which reveal that it is not the regulatory systems but whistle blowing that is the most used means of discovering corporate fraud.

	Source of discovery of fraud
tip from employee	26.3%
accidental discovery	18.8%
internal audit	18.6%
internal control system	15.4%
External audit	11.5
tip from customer	8.6%
anonymous tip	6.2%
tip from vendor	5.1%
notification by law enforcement agency	1.7%

Source: CSPNET(2003), Fraud Discovery Institute, Los Angeles, US.

(d) The UK already has witness protection measures in place in its legal system.

There are also new protection measures in place for victims of traffickers. Section 51 of the Criminal Justice and Public Order Act 1994 created two new offences of intimidating a witness and harming or threatening to harm a witness.

(e) the UK has informally put in place the OECD Corporate Governance Rules

Corporate governance best practice is self-regulated in the UK. An industry-wide Working Party was set up to improve the reporting of Corporate and Social Responsibility and Corporate Governance and concluded that there is a need for a more efficient and open approach to the means of reporting such information between listed companies. Since

September 2004, there is a new Corporate Responsibility Exchange (CRE), an online disclosure tool for listed companies to report voluntarily.[223]

The UK breaches the Basle Capital Adequacy Accord

The UK authorities do not apply any capital requirements whatsoever for foreign bank branches. At present, if a major international bank like the Citibank London is involved in a particular transaction, the UK authorities expect that the deal will be supported by the entire capital of Citibank and not just by the capital of its London branch. If a poor country's branch wants to set up in London, the UK usually requires that they also set up a subsidiary before the UK grants the licence. But according to the Basle Concordant, host authorities are responsible for foreign bank establishments in their territory Basle Core Principle 23 stipulates that banking supervision must practice global consolidated supervision. over their internationally active banking organisations, monitoring and applying prudent norms to all business conducted worldwide.

A home country supervisory authority must safeguard the domestic financial system by preventing under-supervised foreign banking establishments in its jurisdiction. The UK must have figures for the percentage of its bank assets that are foreign owned although it chose not to reveal this figure, even though this information should be shared, although the UK did decide in February 2004 to sign a Memoranda of Understanding (MOU—a statement of co-operation between banking supervisors) with Korea.

This may be one reason why there are so many foreign banks in the UK, contrary to the situation in other EU member states who do comply with the Basle Concordant. This can be seen as a blatant breach by the UK of the Basle Accord which must not continue if the UK is to meet the requirements of the new Basle Capital Accord II in 2005. The capital consequences for all foreign banks with branches in London are extreme.

The Developing Countries Financial Situation

How far away are the developing countries from financial regulatory consolidation with regard to banking? All these countries have a single bank regulator ., being the country's Central Bank, except India and the Maldives which have an independent supervisory agency .(Appendix 1) Total bank assets represented as a percentage of Gross Domestic Product is a good measure of the size of a country's banking industry and Malaysia, Malta, New Zealand and Vanuatu have bank-based financial systems..(Appendix 2)

Government owned bank assets in developing countries

As to government ownership of bank assets, Botswana, Cyprus, Gambia, Malaysia, New Zealand, Samoa, Seychelles, Singapore, Solomon Islands, South Africa, Tonga, Trinidad and Tobago have very little or zero government ownership like the UK. As to foreign owned bank assets, Botswana, Gambia, New Zealand, Samoa, Solomon Islands and Tonga have practically out-sourced their banking industry whilst Bangladesh, Cyprus, Guyana, India, Malawi, Nigeria, Seychelles, Slovenia, South Africa, and Trinidad and Tobago have very low figures. Only 12% of developing countries make their regulators legally liable for their actions; 25% of countries have a deposit insurance scheme. Depositors in the remaining 75% of countries with no deposit insurance must carry out their own monitoring of these banks. Further studies on foreign bank presence in developing countries reveal that they represented 18% of the total number of banks in those countries.[224] Some countries apply stringent capital requirement for foreign bank branches. But the UK, which did not divulge this figure to the World Bank, is neutral about the way foreign banks operate in London.

---

223 International Corporate Governance, September 2004, Issue 131, p 2.

224 Classens.S and Lee.J.K, (2002), 'Foreign Banks in Low Income Countries:Recent developments', World Bank.

Funding of Capital for developing countries with branches in the West

One serious issue for developing countries with bank branches in the Western countries, less risky countries with lower capital requirements in the Basle II, is the problem of funding the capital required.

Cost to developing countries of supervising branches of international banks

The converse of this is that Bank supervisors in the developing countries must find the resources to regulate those branches of large international banks in their territory. How will countries such as Botswana, The Gambia, Samoa, Solomon Islands and Tonga afford expensive supervision of the foreign banks which make up their banking industry? Large international banks with branches in developing countries usually have very expensive centralised computerised systems and therefore supervisors in these developing countries will be forced to buy expensive computerised systems to enable them to carry out their supervisory and monitoring duties.

The impact of Foreign banks ownership of bank assets in developing countries

Another issue is that such countries as Botswana, The Gambia, Samoa, Solomon Islands and Tonga can easily follow Argentina's collapsing banking system largely owned by foreign banks,[225] which can be extremely damaging to these countries.[226]

In any case, the IMF empirical studies in 2000 convince that growth or volatility depend on the business soundness of a bank and not on its ownership.[227]

Conclusion—UK as model

Gambia, Malta, Samoa, Solomon Islands and Tonga are all developing countries with single banking regulators and 'common law' legal systems. and no or extremely small amount of bank assets owned by the government. The UK has a 'common law' legal system, a single banking regulator and no banking assets owned by the government. Can the UK financial regulatory system be a model for these countries? Let us look at the factors (year 2003) to see—

---

225 Argentina's real predicament is contrary to the theory of Levine (1999)who argued that greater foreign bank participation was a stabiliser against crisis in a poor country . See Song.I, (2004), 'Foreign Bank Supervision and Challenges to Emerging Market Supervisors', p 32, IMF.

226 Bank of England, (2002), Financial Stability Review', London: Bank of England

227 IMF, (2000), 'The role of foreign banks in emerging markets', IMF.

Banking system	UK	Gambia	Malta	Samoa	Solomon	Tonga
Deregulated	yes	yes	not yet	not yet	no	not yet
single regulator	yes	yes	yes	yes	yes	Yes
accountable to	FSA	govt	govt	Bank	govt	Govt
Fraud (of top 100 countries)	(3rd)-£40 billion-	no	No	no	no	No
Fraud per capita(of top 100 countries)	(2nd)£40 billion	no	No	no	no	No
Regulator self-funding?	yes	no	No	yes	no	No
Corporate Governance?	voluntary	no	No	yes	no	No
Capital Requirements	none	no	not yet	no	no	No
Share info	no	no	not yet	no	no	No
High Tech?	yes	yes	yes	no	no	No
Afford supervisory costs?	yes	no	No	no	no	No
Govt corruption (of 100)	no	40th	No	no	no	No
Embezzlements (of top 50)	no	no	No	no	no	No
Inflation	2.3%	4.6%	2.4%	4.1%	7.6%	4.7%
Black Economy	12.6%	no	No	no	no	No
Other	fraud	unempl.	division	storms	ethnic violence	Sound

Sources: UN Crime Trends; OECD Data; World Bank & IMF Data; Journals.

The Table shows that the UK is not of model material, mainly because it the third most fraudulent country, also apparent because of its recognised informal or black economy As related previously, the UK does not require capital adequacy from banks whose branches are in its territory. For a developing country, Tonga is trying very hard and has made commendable steps towards liberalising its market. Solomon Islands can be seen to be at risk of political instability if its ethnic violence erupts, just as Samoa's devastating storms can cause economic instability. Gambia's government corruption can be seen as a risk factor together with its high unemployment caused by the forced nationalisation of its main agricultural crop, peanuts. All of the developing countries have sound levels of low inflation, no black economy, no fraud, and none can afford the cost of supervision, computerised systems for supervision or funding to meet capital requirements for their branches in other countries They all have created an institutional setting and financial infrastructure for effective market functioning and if their Central Banks were to be self-funding and independent, they could be said to be creating robust systems that will grow and survive.. Whether the UK's billion pound fraud is due to its liberalised market is for another study.

Bibliography to the "UK Financial System"

Angel.J, (1998), 'Consolidation in the Global equity market: an historical perspective', Georgetown University Paper 19.2.98.

Bacon.C.F, (2004), 'The Due.com group of companies. United States: Next generation due diligence', Internet Legal article: Mondaq.com 1st October 2004.

Barnett.M, (2004), 'Covering his Fanny', US News and World Report.

Barth.J.R and Levine.R, (2001), 'The regulation and supervision of banks', World Bank.

Bradley.C, (1999), 'Transatlantic misunderstandings: Corporate law and society', University of Miami Law Review Vol 55 269-314.

Burt.S, (2004), 'Regulators impose $50 million dollar BSA Penalty', Bankers Systems Inc.

CPASNET, (2003), 'Fraud discovery', Los Angeles, July 2003.

Deloitte Touche Tohmatsu, (2001), 'Futuristic presentation of the Balance Sheet of an insurance group under Future IAS', Deloitte Touche Tomatsu.

DeLong.B, (2004), 'Should we still support untrammelled international capital mobility? Or are capital controls less evil than we once believed?', Berkleey:The Economist's Voice Vol 1

Dwyer.O and Borrus.A, (2004), 'Fannie Mae:What's the damage?', New York: Business Week.

Europa, (2004), 'Guidelines for Phare Programme implementation in candidate countries for the period 200-2006 in application of Article 8 of regulation 3906/89', EU website.

Fox.W.J, (2004), 'Address to the 2004 Money Laundering Enforcement Seminar'.FinCEN.

Freshfields Solicitors,(2004), 'IAS: why it matters to borrowers and their banks', London: Freshfields Bruckhaus Deringer, unpublished seminar Paper 14th Oct.2004.

Halliday.T, (2004), 'Global lawmaking and market-building', Law and Society Vol 38, 213-220.

International Monetary Fund, 2003-4 Country Reports.

Johnson.L, (2004), 'UK:Financial Services & Insurance—Insurance Regulation', London:Pinsents.

Lyman.D, (1999), 'Money Laundering', Thailand: Tilleke & Gibbins

Lucy.J, (2004), 'Market demutualisation and privatisation: The Australian experience', Paper 20.5.2004 Internation Organisation of Securities Commission.

Mehmet.G and Xavier.C, (2004), 'Country institutional differences and multinational advantage in banking', University of Minnesota School of Management.

Norton.J.J, (1998), 'Financial sector reform and international financial crises: the Legal challenges', Essays in International Finance & Economic Law No.16 1998.

Quintyn.M and Taylor.M.W, (2004), 'Should financial sector regulators be independent?' IMF.

Sadurski.W, (2004), 'The impact of the EU Enlargement upon democracy in the New Market States of Central & Eastern Europe', Europ. Law Journal Vol 10, 371-401.

Schmukler.S.L., (2003), 'Financial globalisation: gain and pain for developing countries', World Bank.

Securities Exchange Commission, (1999 to 2004), 'Annual Reports', SEC.

Stuetzle.W and Hamre.J, (2003), 'Transatlantic responses to global challenges: The way forward', Transatlantic Strategy Group on Security and on Economics, Finance and Trade.

Weiner.J, (1999), 'Globalisation and the harmonisation of law', London:Pinter Press.

THE UK CONSOLIDATED FINANCIAL REGULATION MODEL

2003- IMF assessment- "UK now has well-functioning safety net, systemic liquidity, system-level surveillance, insolvency arrangements, high-quality accounting & disclosure regime."		
2000- Financial Services and Markets Act FSA can create and enforce detailed rules without Parliamentary approval.	United Kingdom (only govt rule—UK Govt will only borrow to invest. Public sector NET DEBT to be less than 40% of GDP.)	Financial Services Authority— a private limited company with regulatory powers conferred by statute supervision of banks, insurance and money market institutions
UK Treasury - supervision of FSA		Annual Reports filed like any limited company
1986 Financial Services Act—	Govt. regulation of banks, securities, insurance, building societies	Bank of England
1979-Exchange Controls abolished.	MORTGAGES & CONSUMER CREDIT	self-regulation

Source: UK Report on Observances and Codes, IMF, March 2003.

COMMON LAW COUNTRIES—BANKING REGULATORY SYSTEMS

Country	Bank Regulator	Single?	Accountable to?
Bangladesh	Central Bank	yes	Government
Botswana	Central Bank	yes	Government
Cyprus	Central Bank	yes	Bank Board & Government
Gambia, The	Central Bank	yes	Government
Ghana	Central Bank	yes	Bank Governor

Guyana	Central Bank	yes	Government
*India	Board of Financial Supervision (BFS)	yes	Reserve Bank of India
Jamaica	Central Bank	yes	Government
Kenya	Central Bank	yes	Government
Lesotho	Central Bank	yes	Bank Board
Malawi	Reserve Bank	yes	Government
Malaysia	Central Bank	yes	Government
*Maldives	Maldives Monetary Authority	yes	MMA Board
Malta	Central Bank	yes	Government
Mauritius	Central Bank	yes	Bank Board
Namibia	Central Bank	yes	Government
New Zealand	Reserve Bank	yes	Government
Nigeria	Central Bank	yes	Government
Samoa (Western)	Central Bank	yes	Bank Governor
Seychelles	Central Bank	yes	Bank Governor & Board
Singapore	Central Bank	yes	Bank Governor & Board
Slovenia	Central Bank	yes	Government
Solomon Islands	Central Bank	yes	Government
South Africa	Registrar of Banks	yes	Bank Governor & Government
Sri Lanka	Central Bank	yes	Bank Governor & Government
St Kitts	East Caribbean Central Bank	yes	Monetary Council

Tonga	Reserve Bank	yes	Government
Trinidad & Tobago	Central Bank	yes	Government
Vanuatu	Reserve Bank	yes	Government
Zambia	Central Bank	yes	Government
*United Kingdom	Financial Services Authority (FSA)	depends	Government
*United States	Comptroller of Currency	depends	Government

Source: Extracted from World Bank Database of Country Replies to a questionnaire—year 2000

STATISTICAL INFORMATION—BANKING IN COMMON LAW COUNTRIES

Country	Total Bank Assets per GDP(%)	% of Total Bank Assets Govt. Owned	% of Total Bank Assets Foreign Owned	Supervisors liability?	Deposit Insurance Scheme?	Enforcement Regulation Mandatory?
*Australia	?	0	17	no	no	no
Bangladesh	?	70	6	no	yes	no
Botswana	29	2	98	no	no	yes
*Canada	154	0	100	no	yes	no
Cyprus	76	3	11	no	yes	yes
Gambia	40	0	76	yes	no	no
Ghana	19	38	54	no	no	yes
Guyana	?	19	16	yes	no	yes
*India	48	80	0	no	yes	no
Jamaica	74	56	44	no	yes	yes
Kenya	56	?	?	no	yes	yes
Lesotho	?	51	49	yes	no	yes
Malawi	?	49	8	no	no	yes
Malaysia	166	0	18	no	no	yes
*Maldives	?	75	25	?	no	yes
Malta	291	0	49	yes	no	yes

Mauritius	96	0	26	yes	no	yes
Namibia	?	?	?	no	no	yes
New Zealand	154	0	99	no	no	no
Nigeria	28	13	0	no	yes	yes
Samoa	?	0	93	?	no	yes
Seychelles	?	0	0	no	no	yes
Singapore	?	0	50	no	no	?
Slovenia	66	40	5	no	no	yes
Solomon	?	10	90	?	no	no
S Africa	90	0	5	no	no	no
Sri Lanka	?	55	?	no	no	yes
St .Kitts	?	?	?	?	?	no
Tonga	52	0	100	no	no	yes
Trinidad &Tobago	?	15	8	yes	yes	yes
Vanuatu	126	10	25	no	no	yes
Zambia	?	23	64	no	no	yes
*United Kingdom	311	0	?	no	yes	no
United States	66	0	5	no	yes	no

Source: Extracted from World Bank Database Built on Country Replies to Questionnaire—

Issue 5—American Illegal Securitisation—Banking in the Unregulated Mortgage Market

American Mortgages (Fannie Mae)

TITLE: 'FANNIE MAE—a United States government sponsored enterprise and a complex securitized bank enjoying non-regulation."

ABSTRACT

Fannie Mae is a government sponsored enterprise created by the US Congress to increase liquidity in primary and secondary mortgage markets as well as to supply low-cost capital for housing loans. Quietly over a few decades, it transformed itself into a high risk group which refinances securitisation transactions but which sits unregulated in the banking sector, one of the most regulated industries in the world.

Lawsuits filed against Fanny Mae in 2004 were the first indication outside the corporation that there was financial fraud and deceit operating at Fanny Mae, known before 2004 as 'a paragon of strong corporate governance' Like many whistle-blowers before them, these shareholders heralded the exposure of this 'megalith monster", reminding us of Enron, Worldcom, Savings and Loans, Microsoft, Tyco, General Electric, Adelphia, Global Crossing, Healthsouth, the New York Stock Exchange, and Medicaid .The global financial system is again compromised.

INTRODUCTION

Fanny Mae is a publicly held company, the biggest corporation in the United States' $7 TRILLION mortgage investment market and hold one quarter of this secondary mortgage market for US home loans .It is the second—largest issuer of debt in the US after the federal government. which guarantees Fannie Mae to a total of $2 trillion.

RECENTLY DISCOVERED IRREGULARITIES

The corporation is alleged to have held back expenses at year end in order to keep profits steady as per forecasted figures and so achieve bonus compensation targets. It has manipulated its earnings per share ratio[228] since 1998. This was so that it could maintain stable earnings at the expense of accurate financial disclosure. It employed an improper reserve in accounting for the amortisation of deferred price adjustments under GAAP Accounting Rules and tolerated related internal control deficiencies. As far back as 1966, studies by Brief[229] demonstrated that cheating on the earnings ratio was a bad influence on resource allocation, prices and output, the business cycle and economic growth in general.

This false accounting manipulated those investors who simply trusted and market by taking the earnings ratio as the main decision factor of sound investment, investing in Fannie Mae.

---

228 Earnings per share is found by dividing profit attributable to the ordinary shareholders by the number of ordinary shares in issue and the price/earnings ratio, the more important ratio, is calculated by dividing the share price by the earnings per share. This relates the company performance to external perception. Generally a high price/earnings ratiois a good indicator of market support . For companies quoted in the financial press as Fannie Mae often is, it is essential that the price/earnings ratio is consistent and comparable and any area that determines profit will have an effect on this ratio. That is why Fannie Mae decided to treat certain operative expenses in certain ways—to keep the p/e ratio "smooth". Alexander. D, (2000), 'Financial Reporting', London: Chapman & Hall.

The accounting technique of 'earnings smoothing' is common to many serious financial frauds. It was used at Microsoft systems Inc, Waste Management Inc, Enron Inc. It involves inflation of earnings per share, the key being that debt was under-reported and operating costs were also under-reported.

229 Brief. R, (1966), 'The origin and evolution of nineteenth century asset accounting'. Butterworths.

PAST MORTGAGE COLLAPSES—THE SAVING AND BANKS DISASTER

It must be remembered that there was a mortgage market scandal in the US .; the Savings and Loans debacle[230] which caused billions of dollars of bank losses in 1989 Savings and Loans were small time money lending co-operatives which grew in poor communities and gathered deposits from people in the neighbourhood by paying interest on savings and lending the money to other neighbours who wanted to borrow money to buy homes. With government permission, this grew, but with rising inflation and fraud, deposits were spent and loans were taken out to pay loans until the system crashed and depositors lost their money when US federal debt rose to $2000 billion .

THE PRESENT MORTGAGE ISSUE

Now only 15 years later, it is happening again in the mortgage market. From a deficit of 542 billion US dollars in 2003, the US had a retained mortgage portfolio of $1000 billion plus debts to EU and Asian banks of $800 billion and a sharp increase of hedge funds to US $ 40 billion. The US also has $ 210 billion in credit card loans.[231] With US business mostly equity based, compared to the equity and fixed income business base of Europe, there is not much competition between banks.(See Table 1 for net capital flows)

Table 1-UNITED STATES CAPITAL FLOWS 2001 to 2003

Direct Investment Billion $	Year 2001	2002	2003
Inward	152	40	82
Outward	minus 120	minus138	minus155
Net	32	minus98	minus73
Portfolio Investment Private Sector:			
Inward	399	388	379
Outward	minus 85	minus 16	minus64
Net	315	404	314
Foreign Official sector's assets in US	50	95	208
Net Foreign Liabilities of US Banks	minus17	minus70	minus70
All Other Flows	81	58	60
Total Flows, net	416	528	579
Net capital transfers	minus22	minus 47	minus37
Current A/C balance(deficit)	minus394	minus481	minus542

Source: Bureau of Economic Analysis, (2004),US.

230 O'Shea.J, (1991), 'The DAISY CHAIN—the sensational and true story of the greatest banking scam ever—the Savings and Loans scandal', London: Simon & Schuster.

231 Bank of England, (2004), 'The Financial Stability Conjecture and Outlook Report', p.28.

Fanny Mae's present financial fraud is not an exception to the rule in the mortgage market in the US. The Federal Bureau of Investigation (FBI) reports in 2004 state that the whole US mortgage market is fraudulent.[232] The FBI have investigated hundreds of mortgage frauds[233] recently covering billions of US dollars which are defrauded, causing billions of dollars of losses to financial institutions. Such mortgage fraud is occurring in Charlotte, Washington, New York, Georgia, Missouri, California, Nevada and many other states and is therefore widespread.[234]

FANNIE MAE'S FRAUD AND FINANCIAL IRREGULARITIES

(1) It put the US Federal Government at risk.

The first impact is the potential loss to the US federal government which guarantees Fannie Mae up to $2 trillion, whilst Fannie Mae itself guarantees the payments of $1.9 trillion of mortgage-backed securities.[235] The US government already owes other debt totalling 7.1 trillion dollars to Japan, China, Saudi Arabia, including 80 billion dollars to France, Germany and Russia. Regulatory investigations and litigation, a steady amount yearly as per the SEC yearly enforcement actions (Table 3), is costly. For instance, Worldcom's fraud litigation cost the taxpayer almost US $3,000 million to the year 2002, Enron's about 60 million US dollars, conflict of interest and other cases over US $1025 million.[236]

(2) It put the Global Financial Markets at risk.

This could impact on the US dollar which could be devalued and since 66% of US assets are owned by foreign domiciles, devaluation might follow if such owners cease to invest in the US assets and this will cause an erosion of the US market. But, peculiarly, although the US financial situation is aberrant compared with Europe including the UK, its stock market performance is very similar to that of the UK and Europe[237] (see Table 2 below) This may be because the US has one trillion dollars invested in the UK and European banks whilst 50% of the UK's assets are invested in the US, smoothing out the market performances.

---

232 Fleishman. S, (2004), 'Mortgage fraud concerns FBI', Washington Post, 18 September 2004.

233 US examples of mortgage fraud are (1) buying a house with a large mortgage at a greatly increased price from a partner, selling it back to him quickly for its real market price and leaving a large mortgage unpaid; (2) fictitious credit histories in order to obtain large mortgage; (3) forged loan documents; (4) mortgage foreclosure methods used to buy property in order to conceal the true buyer's name.

234 Frieden. T, (2004), 'FBI warns of mortgage fraud 'epidemic'. Seeks to head off 'next S & L crisis', Washington :CNN Law Centre. By 2004 all these states which suffered mortgage fraud had enacted new and amended legislation to stop anti-predatory lending home loan practices.

235 Mortgage-backed securities offer investors the chance to enhance their overall yield their fixed-income portfolios with securities that are government guaranteed like Fannie Mae's or that carry an AAA rating.

236 Source: Bank of England, (2004), ;Financial Stability Review', June 2004., p 56.

237 Kaplan. S. N and Bengt. H, (2004), 'Report on the State of U.S. Corporate Governance 2004 ', AEI-Brookings, University of Chicago:Joint Centre for Regulatory Studies, Publication 04-02, p1. The report states that currency movements affects market returns and attempts to attribute the US 's similar performance to corporate governance which it claims is better than other nation's corporate governance. Other factors are publicly avaliable information about executive pay, and country productivity.

Table 2 COMPARISON OF STOCK MARKET RETURNS US,UK,FRANCE and GERMANY

	'85	'87	'89	'91	'93	'03
US	31.7%	5.2%	31.%	30.%	10.%	12.%
UK	53%	35.1%	21.%	16%	24.%	12.%
FR	83.2%	-13.4%	36.%	18.%	21.%	12.%
Gm	136.5%	-34.3%	47.%	8.8%	36.%	8.5%

Source: Stock Markets Historic Data

(3) Unqualified Accounting Statements of the Auditor misled the market.

In clear violation of Accounting Standards, the auditors of Fannie Mae, issued an unqualified audit certificate.[238] The 2002 Sarbanes Oxley Act made drastic changes to corporate governance The Chief Executive Officer must certify that each periodic financial report. fully complies with the requirements of sections 13(a) and 15(a) of the Exchange Act and that the information in the report is fair and true in all material respects, of the financial conditions and results of the company. There are now criminal sanctions for signing a false report.. Violation of section 302 carries civil penalties to the Chief Executive Officer and violations to section 906, certifying accounts knowing it to be false, subjects him to a fine of up to one million US dollars or imprisonment for up to ten years, or both.[239] If the CEO or CFO wilfully makes such a certification, the penalties increase to a maximum fine of US $ 5 million and twenty years imprisonment. And in addition to the penalties for false certifications, the Act establishes new criminal offences, including destruction, alteration or falsification of records in connection with federal investigations and bankruptcies proceedings, conspiracy, or attempt to commit securities fraud; and retaliation against whistleblowers It also increases criminal penalties for securities, mail and wire fraud, the violations of the Exchange Act and the Employee Retirement Income Security Act. There are new sentencing guidelines for corporate crime, effective as of November 2003. The Sentencing Guidelines apply a chart that uses two variables—the crime's offence level and the offender's criminal history, to determine the length of prison sentence. In a complex accounting fraud which causes millions of dollars in losses to banks and others, a chief financial officer can face thirty (30) years in prison. An examination of levels of federal securities fraud class action litigation from 1992 to October 2004 show that the average number of securities fraud lawsuits for this period was 222.cases This indicates the seriousness with which the SEC views fraud and with the 30-year prison sentence available, should be a sober check on illegal intentions.

(4) Insufficient Regulation for a multi-trillion dollar organisation tarnishes the reputation of the US financial market.

It is surprising that a business with mortgaged assets valued at three trillion dollars was regulated by a minor body, the Office of Federal Housing Enterprise Oversight (OFHEO) and supervised by the Secretary of Housing and Urban Development and not directly by the Securities Exchange Commission.

---

238 Financial Statements that are unqualified are normally relied on as showing a true and fair view of the financial position, performance and changes in financial position of an enterprise.

239 Robinson . J. K., Lashway,.S.T, (2003), ' The Sarbanes=Oxley Act of 2002: A brief Summary of the New Professional Responsibility Obligations for Security Obligations for Securities Attorneys, New Criminal Provisions, and Reforms to the Sentencing Guidelines', American Bar Association Section in Litigation, Spring 2003.

Because Fannie Mae's Regulator is the OFHEO which is not a financial regulator but a housing regulator, the fraud continued for years. This has similarities with other large frauds such as the Enron fraud. Enron had very little regulation and lobbied government for even less regulation at a time when the SEC was proposing stricter controls on corporate 'conflict of interest'

(5) Illegal, unlicensed, securitisation of debts.

Just as Enron quietly expanded its illegal internet futures trading under its energy regulator instead of under strict futures trading financial regulators. (Because of its futures trading over the internet, it should have had the same level of regulation as the Chicago Board of Trade or the New York Mercantile Exchange.) Fannie Mae quietly stayed with the Housing Supervisor and grew into a massive trillion dollar bank-like business using the legal loophole that it was not a bank but a 'thrift'

Table 3 Enforcement actions of the SEC : 1999 to 2003

	1999	2000	2001	2002	2003
self-regulatory organisations	1	0	0	0	0
broker-dealers	131	123	112	76	92
investment advisors	56	54	54	48	55
investment companies	19	18	8	14	14
transfer agents	15	11	12	7	9
insurance companies	1	0	0	0	0
Federal securities class action fraud litigation	203	215	493	268	216

Table compiled by author: Sources: Securities Exchange Commission—Annual Reports 1999, 2000, 2001, 2002, 2003; Stanford Law School Clearinghouse Data; American Bar Association—Committee on Criminal Litigation.

(6) Gross Capital Inadequacies

Gross Capital inadequacies have been hidden by a complex use of Special Purpose Entities to hedge certain Fannie Mae investments. Basically Fannie Mae had no assets to speak of that could possibly represent its debts. To speak colloquially, Fannie Mae took loans out to buy property and took more loans out to pay those loan payments and took further loans out to make those payments, etc. Their fancy names are hedge betting, derivatives, securitization, options, etc. This is also the method used by Enron. No one would have found out about Enron's fraud if stock had continued to rise, and they would have continued to tell lies in the accounts for ever. The trick here is that Enron sold assets at a profit to non-consolidated Special Purpose Entities and recognised these profits in its financial statements.. It sold itself to itself for a profit and put the profit on the Balance Sheet, making it look even wealthier when in fact it was bankrupt many times over. Similarly, .Fannie Mae guarantees its own loans. If house prices in the US start falling, Fannie Mae will suffer great losses on top of the drop in asset value due to inflating its past 5 years earnings per share. But the global economists know that Fannie has government guarantee. The situation has caused a spread of banking panics in many countries as people wonder if the federal government will bail Fannie Mae out. The federal government has decided that it will not be allowed to collapse.

ADDRESSING THE LEGAL ISSUES—CLOSING THE GAPS?
Market Response

The Federal Reserve's response to Fannie Mae's false accounting and fraud was to refuse to promise to buy back open purchases of dated paper such as 10-year T Notes and the European Central Bank took all Fanny Mae debt from its reserve base. Fannie Mae's own Regulator, the Office of Federal Housing Enterprise Oversight has demanded that Fannie Mae must, from now maintain 30% more capital than current rules stipulate. The OFHEO also demanded changes to the contracts of the CEO and the MD so that they would only be able to draw on their stock options and salary before September 2004, as per SEC rules. Asia has encouraged trade by offering rate swap contracts and low rates to corporate borrowers. Fannie Mae's stock price has decreased from $128 before this news to $70.10 on 6th November 2004[240] when Fanny Mae redeemed $350 million securities and the dollar fell.

HOW 'THRIFT' INSTITUTIONS ESCAPES BANKING REGULATION BUT BECAME SECURITIZED GROUPS

The financial services corporation, Fannie Mae, is unregulated and is heavily involved in unregulated cross-border securitisation to the sum of trillions of US dollars. It is not classed as a state bank and "it has been getting away with murder". A state bank is defined in the United States Charter 1813 as organised and operated under state law. A savings association, like Fannie Mae, savings and loans association or thrift institution is not a state bank.

Such Thrift institutions are only regulated by the US Treasury's Office of Thrift Supervision for consumer credit issues, a lenient and softer supervisor than the US banking supervisor. These 'thrifts' escaped through this loophole and over the years have steadily engaged in the financial services market, tax and estate planning, securities, custodial matters, trust transactions artificially allocated, low quality or high risk assets, money laundering, black economy, drugs trafficking, generating capital through stock purchase loans overseas, terrorism, organised crime, subjective underwriting criteria.

In the mid 1980's the US discovered it had massive fraud in these savings and loans institutions which resulted in hundreds of billions of dollars of losses. Until this time, the 'thrift' industry consisted of mutual entities, like the UK's mutual building societies. Thousands of these entities were put into receivership and thus put up for sale and new owners, foreign and US, were given incentives to buy the bankrupt thrifts, with the state promising the new owners non-supervision, carrying forward of losses acquired for tax relief, concessions to be unregulated and to engage in any lawful activity.

Later, these so-called 'thrift' companies were acquired by other financial non-bank organisations which made use of the regulatory slack to operate insurance companies, securities, savings accounts, loans, credit cards and mortgage loans, until the US Gramm-Leach-Bliley Act 1999 which stopped commercial companies from holding 'thrifts'. This law was not retrospective and so such 'thrifts' formed before 1999, were allowed to continue in business. This is how Fannie Mae came to use bond futures, derivatives, hedging and corporate swaps.

---

240 Quote.com, (2004), 'Fannie Mae Redemption', 2 November 2004, Washington:: Quote.com.

STATE LEGISLATION TO PREVENT PREDATORY MORTGAGE LENDING

And when Fannie Mae's illegal securitisation came to light in 2003, it triggered a US consumer lending alert by the federal government., quickly followed by changes in legislation in various states.

There is the amendment to the New Jersey Home Ownership Security Act 2002 in November 2003 A new section 279 amended the Act to eliminate 'covered loans' and to prohibit 'loan flipping', a fraud. The section also excluded escrows to pay for future taxes and insurance.[241]

The state of Massachusetts also enacted legislation as a direct result of Fannie Mae fraud, namely, the Massachusetts Predatory Home Loan Practices Act 2003, to be applied to all loans closed on or after 7 November, 2004. The Act includes a prepayment penalty incurred in the refinancing of a loan and the Act stops the previous unfair terms of misleading advertising, unreasonable terms, fees and charges on all home mortgage loans. It also makes 'loan flipping' illegal and prohibits the financing of credit insurance, with compulsory mandatory reporting of payment history. The Act permits a court to rescind or bar a lender from collecting on a home mortgage loan contract that violates the law. The Act prohibits the following terms and practices—no lending without home counselling; no lending without regard to repayment ability; limit on financing points and fees; limit on payment to contractors; no recommending default on existing debt; no evading the Act; no prepayment penalties; no increased default interest rate; no balloon payments; no call provision; no negative amortisation; no modification of deferral fees; no advance payments; no mandatory arbitration clauses. New York also has similar new legislation.

The state of Maine now has new mortgage legislation Maine Truth in Lending Act 2004 with anti-predatory lending provisions. The state of Nebraska also reacted to the Fannie Mae fraud and made amendments to its Nebraska Mortgage Bankers Registration and Licensing Act. Since January 2004, Oklahoma has in force a new anti-predatory lending law, the Oklahoma Anti-Predatory Lending Law, while New Jersey also made amendments to its New Jersey Home Ownership Security Act.

NEW SEC REGULATION FOR FANNIE MAE

The SEC also, has now advised such non-publicly held subsidiaries of bank holdings, that in spite of being independent, they should, but not must, comply with section 301 and have an audit committee. Also, the SEC is now in discussions to bring new disclosure requirements for ASSET-BACKED SECURITIES (ASB'S) for the asset-backed market.

NEW LAW RELATING TO OVERSEAS FINANCIAL BANKING BUSINESS

Now the connection with the EU Basel Capital Accord, EU Market Abuse Directive, EU Prospectus Directive,[242] money laundering and new US federal

Regulation is absent for Thrift Cross-Border activities which include all manner of financial activities transferred to foreign countries. This poses high risk for such countries' markets, even though foreign banks' jurisdictions are governed by the International Money Laundering Abatement and Financial Anti-Terrorism Act 2001. Already, some of the US savings and loans holding companies have European operations and are already protected under the Gramm-Leach-Bliley Act 1999, because they were formed before 1999 and the Act is not retrospective.

These 'thrifts' engage in offering clearing-house services through a foreign agency office, including global custody, settlement, securities lending, paying agent and CEDEL depository services; investing in foreign currency-dominated certificates of deposit and foreign debt instruments and providing foreign currency exchange forward contracts to commercial borrowers; foreign currency exchange services; making loans on the security of foreign real estate; re-insur-

---

241 Thacher Proffitt & Wood LLP, (2004), 'Consumer Lending Alert', June 2004.
242 Revell. S, Jones. T, Kalderon. M, (2004), 'The Prospectus Directive and its implementation in the UK', London: Freshfields Bruckhaus Deringer, October 2004.

ance activities, provide internal asset-management services to reduce tax, and establishing foreign real estate investment trusts!

These thrifts are currently not subject to federal financial services regulation other than the 'thrift' regulator. The US with the Basel Committee, have developed specific rules for these 'thrifts' in the EU, such as the Joint Agency Statement on Parallel Banking Organisations ('thrifts') and the Office of Thrift Supervision (OTS) now has a role as a consolidated financial services regulator under European Union Directive 2002/87.[243] The United States now has joint legislation with the European Union, partly governing the EU banking sector..[244] The Bank of England Financial Stability Report 2004 reveals that the US accounts for the largest single country exposure of UK—owned banks. It is planned that the US will impose a similar weighted capital requirements from European owned banking institutions which are operating in the US.

US 'thrifts' have, over many years, let into the global financial system trillions of dollars of unregulated financial products, most of which can be summarised as 'junk bonds'. The EU and the US now wish to call an amnesty on and start afresh with new regulations to be applied only to new products. This is the crux of the European Union's Basel II Accord and the United States's Depository Institution Management Interlock Act 2000 (DIMIA). Cross-border financial interaction with some form of security via capital requirements for all banks and non-bank institutions is now in place.

COMPROMISES MADE TO THE USE OF INTERNATIONAL ACCOUNTING STANDARDS

The EU has agreed to allow the US banks (and all other parties) to use their present accounting standards but restate the accounts to statements EQUIVALENT to the International Accounting Statements.

No definition of the word "equivalent" has been given. It was the use of GAAP Accounting standards which Fannie Mae used to manipulate its operating costs, profit and earnings per share for at least five years.

THE US ACCOUNTING STANDARDS BOARD

The Powers Report which was commissioned. soon after the Enron collapse, reported that Price Water-house Accountants had breached SEC requirements in giving a true and fait opinion on the exchange of Enron shares for the Special Purpose Entity's "put note"; had failed to treat the Special Purpose Entities as Enron assets and had treated a third-party debt as equity; had made insufficient and opaque disclosures to the SEC; had condoned the use of derivatives for hedging risk; had condoned disproportionate employee bonuses which had not gone through the proper procedure of Board approval and had left untangled the complicated incomprehensible financial transactions or securitisation and most alarmingly, had failed to see anything wrong in Enron's two year period of internet futures trading in volumes equivalent to the trading of a small Stock Exchange, without SEC approval or licence.

The SEC is considering whether to compel companies to make their earnings ratio public, filing their earnings information to include a side-by-side reconciliation of the announced earnings to GAAP Accounting Rules, along with a plain—English narrative description of any differences. to earnings calculation using International Accounting Standards.[245]

---

243 Croke. J .J and Manbeck. P. C, (2004), 'Revisions to Proposed Basel Capital Adequacy Framework', The Banking Law Journal, New York: A. S.P ratt & Sons.

244 There is at present $1 trillion in the EU banking sector.

245 PR NewsWire, (2004), ;Mutual Fund Industry urges Accounting and Auditing Reform', 9 July 2004.

SECURITIZATION DEBT AS USED BY FANNIE MAE

Securitisation debt has a lower interest-rate cost(see Table 4 below) than say, corporate debt Securitized capital market debt is called "Commercial Paper". The Table below shows the short term attractiveness of securitisation compared to Ordinary bank rate; the small reductions in bank rates make for very substantial cash-flow differences when the securitisation involves billions of US dollars and is one method of providing liquidity for companies not in a position to borrow, so preventing bankruptcy, although a company should be prudent enough not to take the high risks that securitisation entail.[246]

Table 4—Securitized and ordinary commercial bank rates

Year	2000	2001	2002	2003
Commercial Paper—1 month	6.2%	3.8%	1.7%	1.0%
Commercial Paper—2 months	6.3%	3.7%	1.8%	1.6%
Commercial Paper—3 months	6.3%	3.6%	1.7%	1.7%
Prime Bank Rate	9.2%	6.9%	4.7%	4.0%

Source: Bloomberg.com.

The US securitisation industry deals in trillions of dollars of securitisation each year, a very lucrative industry. The US Federal government has implemented the Sarbanes—Oxley Act 2002 demands transparency in the financial reports and could literally wipe out the securitisation industry, causing several states to enact laws that permit 'true sale' treatment without regard to the substance of the transaction.[247]

When US banks show signs of deep financial trouble, they can be bankrupted, a practice alien to Europe The Federal Deposit Insurance Corporation (FIDC) is authorised to conserve the debtors' bank balance. But the FIDC's power does not extend to assets which are no longer owned by the bank, i.e. securitized debt

US CORPORATE GOVERNANCE CHANGES THAT DID NOT PROTECT AGAINST FRAUD

It is a telling fact that in the history of US corporate governance, rewards by way of shares was not usual,; the usual method of calculating management reward was the use of accounting ratios as indicators of performance and earnings per share was the chosen ratio, this same earnings ratio which was manipulated by Fannie Mae.

After the OECD Corporate Governance Rules were published in 1998, corporate governance Codes of Conduct[248] were operated and share incentive schemes for employees and for the Management Board became popular and institutional

---

246 Schwarcz. S, (2004), 'Securitisation post-Enron', Vol 25.No.5, Yeshiva :Cardozo Law Review

247 Delaware was the only US state to brazenly enact the Delaware Asset-Backed Securities Facilitation Act 2002, give Delaware the right to determine what constitutes a true sale in a securitisation transaction. The Act states that "any financial assets purported, in the transaction documents, to be transferred in a securitisation transaction "shall be deemed to no longer be the property, assets or rights of the transferor."

248 These included—
   a) A nominating committee and not the CEO must select the Board members;

investors grew. US corporate executives[249] enjoy higher salaries and bonus share options than executives in other countries, There is shareholder primacy[250] as there is in Europe although it is institutional shareholders who have increased share ownership from 30 to 50% from 1980 to 1996 at the expense of individual share ownership which has decreased from 70% in 1970 to 48% in 1994.[251] These institutional shareholders are by definition financially astute and should have challenged Fannie Mae's management where there was an accounting issue.[252]

THE SECURITIES EXCHANGE COMMISSION—FEDERAL REGULATOR

There was much conflict of interest in the Enron financial fraud and there is at Fannie Mae, conflict of interest because the directors of the Board have been involved in approving all of the securitisation deals, which are so complex, that it is questionable whether they understood securitisation.[253] More importantly, the 2002 Sarbanes-Oxley Act was the reaction the recent serious financial frauds and it mandated some corporate governance changes for listed companies. CEO and CFO's must return to the company any profits if they sell their their shares within 1 year of the Financial Reports. There is more insider trading regulation and better accounts transparency because now, off-Balance Sheet transactions and Special Purpose Entities must be reported. The audit committee has more power, responsibility and independence to monitor the Board with criminal sanction for misreporting. Outside accountants and lawyers are required to calculate the asset register The SEC also set out for NYSE and NASDAQ, similar corporate governance rules to the Cadbury Code used by LSE listed companies.[254] The voluntary code recommends at least 3 non-executive directors and one non-executive Chairperson for each company Board. But the SEC was not the regulator for Fannie Mae, so these rules did not apply.

CONCLUSION

Fannie Mae highlights the vast multi-trillion dollar unregulated US financial market which has also permeated across borders. It has been play-acting as the paragon of good corporate management, whilst in fact it led the US insurance market in inflating prices, conflict of interest, bid rigging, a complacent regulator, and insufficient capital/liquidity plan, manipulation of its earnings ratio to lend an air of liquidity and soundness, and poor audit and internal controls. Fannie

---

b)   Annual CEO reviews;

c)   non-executive directors

249 Hall. B and Leibman. J, (1998), 'Are CEO's really paid like bureaucrats?', Quarterly Journal of Economics, 112, No.3, p 653-691. In their study, they found that average pay tripled from 1980 to 1994. In a later study by Hall and Murphy, (Hall.B and Murphy.K, (2002), 'Stock options for undiversified executives', Journal of Accounting and Economics, 3,42.), said that the trend continueduntil 2001.

250 Perry. T and Zenner.M, 'CEO compensationin the 19990's:Shareholder alignment or shareholder expropriation?', Wake Forest Law Review.

251 Gompers.P and Metrick. A, (2001), 'Institutional investors and equity prices', Quarterly Journal of Economics. The study interestingly reveals that executive shareholders only own 2% of shares of a company. This dismisses arguments about executive power and indicates a fair reward.

252 The SEC rules, revised in 1992, give shareholders the power to communicate with management teams when and how they wish, provided that the SEC is informed also.

253 There has been a sharp increase in credit exposure from hedge funds, the leveraged loan market and spreads this recent quarter. Of the whole world total of leveraged loans, the US is and has always been the biggest issuer, nearly 280 billion dollars of three hundred billion dollars this year. High yield bond issuance was also very active and the interest rate market was very volatile.

254 The Cadbury Code, used by London listed companies apparently results in increased turnover of CEO's due to the presence of non-executive directors on the Board, rather than from separate CEO and Chairperson., (another Cadbury Code recommendation).. This was the result of the study—Dahya.J and Travlos. N, (2002), 'The Cadbury Committee, Corporate Performance, and Top Management Turnover', Journal of Finance, Vol 57, p 461-483.

Mae engaged in high risk synthetic securitisation, the use of credit risk mitigation techniques, that is, collateral, guarantees and credit derivatives, for hedging the underlying exposure without collateral.

The result of this alarmingly massive financial fraud is that many states of the US speedily enacted new legislation against anti-predatory money lending. Recently Germany amended its Mortgage Bank Act to protect the Pfandbrief holder's rights in case of an issuer's insolvency; since Germany has 70% of the European covered bond market and some of the market share of US Treasury and Agency Paper which the Asian Central Banks no longer wanted .

In deceit, Fannie Mae misused structured finance vehicles, designed to lower financing costs and spread investment risk, to carry out sham transactions and mislead investors, analysts and regulators about their true financial condition.

STATUTES AND CONVENTIONS

Anti-Predatory Lending Act 2004 (Oklahoma)

Asset-backed Securities Facilitation Act 2002 (Delaware)

Basel Capital Accord (European Union)

Depository Institution Management Interlock Act 2000 (US)

Graham-Leach-Bliley Act 1999 (US)

Home Ownership Security Act 2003 (New Jersey)

International Money Laundering Abatement and Financial Anti-Terrorism Act 2001 (US)

Market Abuse Directive (EU)

Mortgage Bank Act 2004 (Germany)

Mortgage Bankers Registration and Licensing Act 2004 (Nebraska)

OECD Corporate Governance Convention 1998.

Predatory Home Loan Practices Act 2003 (Massachusetts)

Prospectus Directive (EU)

Sarbanes-Oxley Act 2002 (US)

Truth in Lending Act 2004 (Maine)

BIBLIOGRAPHY

Alexander. D, (2000), 'Financial Reporting', London: Chapman & Hall.

Bank of England, (2004), 'The Financial Stability Conjecture and Outlook Report', p.28, June 2004.

Basel Committee on Banking Supervision, (2004), 'International Convergence of Capital Management and Capital Standards: A Revised Framework', p 1-7, 11-15, June 2004.

Bloomberg.com, (2004), Market Data.

Croke. J. J and Manbeck. P .C, (2004), 'Revisions to Proposed Capital Adequacy Framework', The Banking Law Journal, New York: A. S. Pratt & sons.

Dahya. J and Travlos. N, (2002), 'The Cadbury Committee, Corporate Performance and Top Management Turnover', Vol 57, p 461-483, Journal of Finance.

Davies. P and Behrens.J, (2004), 'Commercial bankers see the bright side of Basel II', American Banker, 28 April 2004.

Economist, (2004), 'Basel Lite', 3 July 2004.

Economist, (2004), 'Now for the hard part', 15 May 2004.

Economist, (2003), 'Safety First: How to handle bank regulation', 3 May 2003.

Fleishman. S, (2004), 'Mortgage fraud concerns FBI', Washington Post, 18 September 2004.

Freiden. T, (2004), 'FBI warns of mortgage fraud 'epidemic': Seeks to head off "next Savings and Loans crisis"', Washington: CNN Law Centre.

Gompers. P and Metrick. A, (2001), 'Institutional investors and equity prices', Quarterly Journal of Economics.

Hall. B and Leibman. J, (1998), 'Are C.E.O 's really paid like bureaucrats?', 112, No.3, p 653-691, Quarterly Journal of Economics.

Hall. B and Murphy. K, (2002), 'Stock Options for un-diversified executives', 3, 42, Journal of Accounting and Economics.

Institutional Investor, '(2003), 'Basel Under Threat', July 2003.

Iwata.E, (2004), 'Celebrated CEO faces crisis', USA Today, 6th October 2004.

Kaplan. S.N and Bengt. H, (2004), 'Report on the state of US Corporate Governance 2004', AEI-Brookings, University of Chicago: Joint Centre for Regulatory Studies, Publication 04-02, pi.

O' Shea. J, (1991), 'The Daisy Chain—the sensational and true story of the greatest banking scam ever—the Savings and Loans scandal', London: Simon & Schuster.

Paletta. D, (2004), 'Can Basel fix home-host problems?', American Banker, 30 June 2004.

Paletta. D, *2004), 'Basel II Nears Endgame: Outlining the next moves', American Banker, 28 April 2004.

Perry. T and Zenner. M, (2000), 'CEO compensation in the 1990's':Shareholder alignment or shareholder expropriation?', Wake Forest Law Review.

PR Newswire, (2004), 'Mutual Fund Industry urges Accounting and Auditing Reform', 9 July 2004.

Quote.com, (2004), 'Fannie Mae Redemption', 2 November 2004.

Revell. S, Jones. T, Kalderon. M, (2004), 'The Prospectus Directive and its implementation in the UK', Seminar, London: Freshfields Bruckhaus Deringer, October 2004.

Robinson. J. K and Lashway. S. T, (2003), 'The Sarbanes-Oxley Act of 2002: A brief summary of the new Professional Responsibility Obligations for Security Attorneys; New Criminal Provisions and Reforms to the Sentencing Guidelines', American Bar Association Section in Litigation, Spring 2003.

Santo. J. A.C, (2000), 'Bank Capital Regulation on Contemporary Banking Theory: A Review of the Literature', p 1-24,Bank for International Settlements, September 2000.

Schwarcz. S, (2004), 'Securitization post-Enron', Vol 25.No.5, Yeshiva: Carduzo Law Review.

Securities Exchange Commission, (2003), Annual Report.

Securities Exchange Commission, (2002), Annual Report.

Securities Exchange Report, (2001), Annual Report.

Securities Exchange Commission, (1999), Annual Report.

Simmons. L and Ryan. E. M, (2003), 'Post-Reform Act Securities Lawsuits', Cornerstone Research, New York: Cornerstone.

Stanford Law School, (2004), 'Clearing House Data', Securities Research Section.

Thacher, Proffitt & Wood LLP, (2004), 'Consumer Lending Alert', Newsletter, June 2004.

Willie. J. (2004), 'Japan, then Argentina, no muddle', Hat Trick Newsletter

Issue 6—Immoral Markets

Carbon Credits Market

The Carbon Credit Markets—Western Financial Opportunity Born out of Potential Global Crisis due to Centuries of Western Pollution

Abstract

Early studies in the 1980's of the transboundary or regional impact of air pollution has given way to the realization that the threat is now global in scale. Evidence emerged linking the release of chlorofluorocarbons, halons and other chlorine based substances with the gradual destruction of the planet Earth's ozone layer. This layer located in the stratosphere but still well within the earth's atmosphere, is important because it filters sunlight and protects the earth from ultraviolet radiation. Loss of this atmosphere shield would have serious implications for human health, agriculture and fisheries productivity over a long period, and could leave future generations a legacy of irreversible harm. The major risk is from CO2 emissions which are linked with patterns of energy consumption in the developed industrial world.

This Paper describes the route of international agreements, regional regulations and country statutes passed since then to stem the degree of pollution, on pain of penalties and describes how the same western industrialised countries which caused the pollution are now set to reap vast financial and economic benefits from their own offences by creating a market for the pollutants and trading their excess pollutants for cash-poor and undeveloped countries levels of under—pollution, thus keeping the levels of pollutants at the same high levels by continuing to pollute whilst restraining under-developed countries from advancing because they have sold their right to industrialisation to the already industrialised countries.

The Paper concludes by envisaging the environmental, legal and economic scenario decades from now and questions whether this securitization of western pollution is fair on the rest of the world.

Introduction

The twenty six elements of the United Nations environmental programme were established in 1972 at the Stockholm environmental matters Conference on Human Environment, to promote international co-operation and to recommend policies to co-ordinate environmental programmes alongside other UN Agencies such as the International Marine Organisation, International Labour Organisation, International Oceanographic Commission, International Atomic Energy Agency and the International Monetary Fund.

The main effect of the environmental programme is to prevent, reduce and control environmental harm through monitoring of countries' activities so that there is sovereignty over natural resources and non-pollution and protection from hazardous waste of international water courses as this affects air pollution, vegetation and habitation.

The European Union

The EU with its twenty five member states has ratified environmental treaties and because it can issue regulations to its member states has passed the 1986 Unified European Act and the 1992 European Union Convention to ensure that its member states have defined environmental objectives to preserve, protect and improve the quality of its environment through tax and development measures.

In 1993 the EU passed the Regulation EEC/93/1836 which was an environmental management and auditing scheme for European industry, compelling member states to use the best technology available in order to cut pollution. The Council Directive 75/436 Euratom, imposed on the steel industry the international system of "polluter pays" and a regulator of the environmental finances called Financial Instrument for Environment, LIFE, which was formed by EEC/92/1973 to control pollution from motor vehicles, lead, industrial plants, waste incinerators, and air quality assessment and management. There are to date over 1000 pieces of domestic legislation in the world and these mention climate change as a motivation to enforce environmental laws internationally and domestically.

The Kyoto Protocol to the Climate Convention was adopted in 1997 and made binding obligations to reduce emissions of greenhouse gases. Under this Protocol, developed countries agreed to reduce emissions to 5.2% below the 1990 levels in the period from 2008 to 2012. United States of America has refused to agree to the ratification of the Kyoto Protocol and denies the problem with the ozone layer.

Directive 2000/25/EC in 2000 was to prohibit gas and pollution emissions by motor engines, reporting on sulphur content by 2003.

But the 2003 reports were not sent in by France, Belgium, Austria, Italy in 2003 and the European Commission issued them a written warning. In 2004, Directive 2004/35/EC laid down environmental liabilities for any pollution caused.

Other countries and CO2 emissions

In the United States, more than half the power companies are expecting penalties for mandatory limits on CO_2 emissions whilst Canada admits to an increasing proportion of pollution by over 2 percent a year and the Swiss have proposed a tax on CO_2 emissions in their country.

Of the ten new EU member states, Slovenia does not have government issued policies on the environment; neither does Romania, Latvia, Estonia, Bulgaria, Cyprus, Poland and Malta, there being very little regulatory infrastructure in these poorer member states despite lavish EU aid of billions of Euros to bring them to an acceptable level in readiness to join the EU.

The Proposed Emissions Trading Plan

In 2000 the United Kingdom issued a consultation paper to the European Commission proposing a swap market for divesting a country of its over-pollution as per its permitted quota by paying an under-developed poor country which does not use much of its own pollution quota to put on its records the over-polluting country's excess pollution. So this market will allow emitters to trade carbon allowances on the open market, like a commodity. It is calculated that emission trading will add flexibility in terms of when and where emission reductions are to take place. So emitters face large abatement costs and some countries may prefer to buy additional allowances from the market if prices are lower than the costs of implementing in-house measures. At the same time, countries with industrial plants which have low abatement costs can try to beat their own emission targets and sell off their surplus allowances at a profit. So polluting the under-developed countries will continue by the industrialised countries who buy their additional allowances by securitization.[255] The polluter continues to pollute and harm the polluted by a legal financial device because the atmosphere is not a distinct category.

---

255 In a typical securitization transaction, the company originating or sponsoring the transaction sells rights to payment from income-producing financial assets, such as pollution credits as in this case, to a special purpose entity which in turn transfers such rights to a second such entity which issues securities to capital market investors (organised markets and exchanges) and uses those proceeds to pay the originator. The investors in the securities are repaid from collections of the financial assets. They therefore buy the securities based on their assessments of the values of the financial assets. Some people (see Janger. E. J. (2002), 'Muddy rules for securitization', Journal of Corporate and Financial Law, 301-306.) regard securitization as reflecting the uncompensated risks onto third parties, taking advantage of these third parties.

256 This can be viewed as a regional reaction to this environmental threat. Agreement that the global community is gradually recognising the essential threats to planet Earth, posed by increasing destruction of the environment, global warming, water pollution, and groundwater pollution, is undisputed. But the promulgation by the west that there is a relationship with under-development and

Since some European countries including the UK have started to implement emission trading programs to be ahead of other countries,[256] it is imperative that all countries are helped to bring them up to readiness so that when trading begins the poor countries with strong trading power in carbon credits have the financial infrastructure to get their true worth to those polluting industrialised countries who need to trade. There are issues with carbon trading that are unresolved. The proponents of carbon trading say that such markets will help to monitor emissions and cost the reduction of emissions, whilst opponents say that rich countries that have polluted the planet are purchasing the right to pollute by buying emission allowances.[257] Even the Eastern European countries that have joined the EU in May 2004, refurbishing their steel plants with £millions PHARE[258] aid, have the same emission limits set in 1990 by the Kyoto agreements. Their new steel plants will emit less CO_2 and so they will be able to trade their surplus. It has been argued that such countries will be the cause of even greater CO_2 emissions as they offer their excess allowances for sale to such large consumers as the USA.[259]

So what are the unresolved issues with regard to these carbon trading markets? They are—

1. Limits have not been agreed to.

2. The sources of emissions traded have not been agreed—eg. should emissions from nuclear energy, hydropower, steel plants, be allowed to be traded?

3. How will the emissions stated by polluting countries be verified? What standardised model of measurement will be used?

4. Will there be taxation on each transaction? Will there be a limit to the size of each transaction?

5. Who will book-keep the levels of carbon traded to the carbon-credit countries? Who will certify these amounts?

6. Statistics reveal that even in 1850, 80% of CO_2 emissions resulted from the North. Why is this continued overuse of the planet being allowed? Why is this inequity been consolidated into legislation? Why has the Western world agreed to continue the industrialisation of their countries at the expense of the undeveloped countries which will be forced to remain undeveloped?

7. What aspects of this carbon trading are being addressed by companies Corporate Governance Rules? Corporate responsibility in such carbon trading companies must demonstrate how they are managing risks and maintaining control. One of the most critical areas in these businesses is that of Information Technology and the measurement and control of IT processes and procedures., presenting timely and accurate reports to supervisory bodies A most

---

global destruction is fiercely disputed. The writer disagrees with the perceptions put forward in the article Delbruck. J, (1993), 'Globalisation of law, politics and markets—implications for domestic law: A European Perspective', Indiana Journal of Global Legal Studies, Volume 1, Issue 1, Fall 1993.

257 Equity Watch, '(2001), 'Carbon on sale', Centre for Science and Environment.

258 In readiness to join the EU in May 2004, the PHARE programme provided funds to build institutions and gave Romania 140 Million Euros a year from 1990 to 2000. The ISPA aid programme provided investment of 270 Million Euros to Romania alone for environmental and transport infrastructure for the 10 joining member states., to be spent between the years 2000 to 2006. Romania receives 153 Million Euros per year for development, a total of 257 Million Euros of aid until the year 2006.

259 Retallack. S, (2001), 'The Kyoto Loopholes', Third world Network, March 2001.; See also The Centre for Science and Environment's criticisms; see also the criticisms of The Corporate Europe Observatory, their statement on the issue being.."Many corporate ventures that might become eligible for emission credits—nuclear power plants, so-called 'clean coal' plants as well as industrial agriculture and large-scale tree plantations (including genetically engineered varieties)—have extremely serious negative social and environmental impacts. Investments in 'carbon sinks' (such as large-scale tree plantations) in the South would result in land being used at the expense of local people, accelerate deforestation, deplete water resources and increase poverty. Entitling the North to buy cheap emission credits from the South, through projects of an often exploitative nature, constitutes 'carbon colonialism'. Industrialised countries and their corporations will harvest the 'low-hanging fruit' (the cheapest credits), saddling Southern countries with only expensive options for any future reduction commitments they might be required to make".

necessary corporate governance tool in such companies would be a corporate governance stock index which can aid global confidence; such an index would help investors by simply indicating how good the corporate governance of the company is as a score. The UK, for instance, initiated Greenhouse Gas Emissions Trading Scheme (ETS) in 2000, which allows UK companies that exceed their targets for energy reduction to 'bank' credits for the reduction in carbon dioxide emissions that result, these credits having a monetary value BASED ON DEMAND[260] and which traded can be profited from.

8. There have been no Corporate Governance Rules agreed for energy trading UK companies, nor is there an open register of such companies.

9. There is no agreed fines and other penalty system[261] in place for such companies. There is no environmental certified audit of such companies.

10. There is no UK legislation relating either to excessive emissions or to limits on trading or to pricing brackets to avoid unfair competition and exploitation. The UK has not produced a Model for measuring emissions nor an audit system for certifying emission trade transactions, not any Accounting Standards to reveal these transactions.

11. There have been no regulatory systems set up to monitor uniformly the state of the technology used to in process controls, no government incentive by way of extra tax allowances for capital spending .on computer control systems for metal production processes.

12. The Kyoto Protocol, ratified by the majority of countries except the biggest polluter United States of America, lists six greenhouse gases, being carbon dioxide, methane, nitrous oxide, perflourocarbons, halocarbons and sulphur hexaflouride, which all have a CO2-e value as follows:

Greenhouse Gases	CO2—e value (in tonnes)
Carbon Dioxide	1
Methane	21
Perfluorocarbons	6590-9200 (varies by 39%)
Halocarbons	140-11700 (varies by 8200%)
Sulphur Hexafluoride	23900

Source: Rio de Janeiro earth summit Report (1992)

---

260 This method can be seen to be high-handed since it stresses the superiority of the free market economy and particularly the Anglo-Saxon model over any other economic or societal model. It represents the stateless society administered by laws of the market as per Milton Freidman's 'Capitalism and Freedom' (1962) when clearly this is of global concern and should be decided among nations including those not enamoured of liberalism.

261 For instance, in the case of marine pollution, US statute prescribes criminal penalties and fines of up to $25,000 a day for each day of violation, with half the fine given as a reward to the whistle-blower if violation reported by a whistle-blower. This is the discretion about fines to be imposed through domestic enforcement as per the **United Nations MARPOL Convention.** Yet the US, Norway, Bahamas and Panama have been found to be the worst offenders of applicable environmental marine laws. (see Dehner. J. S.,(1995), 'Vessel-source pollution and public vessels: sovereign immunity v compliance. Implications for International Environmental Law', Environmental Law Journal, Fall 1995.

It is obvious that the varying value of perfloucarbons by 39% and of Halocarbons by 82 time the amount that could be stated, calls for an audit of these values and certification every time these values are recorded, if the figures and carbon credits traded are not to be deemed a nonsense. There is no such provision, nor is these any acknowledgement of the apparent problem this can cause. Other calculating issues are for example, in respect of aluminium production, when two units of aluminia plus three units of carbon produce four units of aluminium plus three units of CO_2 emissions. Aluminium, used in car production, has a long life in which the reprocessing produces less carbon dioxide and companies that recycle aluminium must calculate the CO_2 emissions differently.[262]

13. The trade of greenhouse emissions in exchange for money has already begun[263] and not only does it trade in power stations emissions, factory emissions, steel manufacturing, aluminium manufacturing, it also deals with aviation emissions,[264]

These are just some of the issues that have not even been acknowledged and that remain un-addressed by the UK Initiative on carbon trade markets, begun in the year 2000.[265]

The Global Atmosphere

The atmosphere consists of fluctuating air-mass and it cannot be equated with airspace which, above land, is simply a spatial dimension subject to the sovereignty of the adjacent country. The overlap with territorial sovereignty means that the atmosphere cannot be treated as an area with common property. It is beyond the jurisdiction of any state. It cannot be compared with the high seas. It is a shared resource. Its control and regulation was stated in the Geneva Convention on Long-Range Transboundary Air Pollution of 1979. It is not clear how exactly the audit of CO_2 emissions will take place and there is bound to be litigation about it.

In case of fraud by way of false statements as to carbon credits or carbon emissions, the dispute would be a criminal matter. Would proceedings be granted in the place where the fraud was discovered[266] or the country which is alleged to have

---

262 Report on Greenhouse emission challenges, New Zealand Aluminium Smelters Ltd., April 2004.

263 It is booming business as 2,100,000 tons of carbon dioxide were sold in October 2004 at a price of between E 8.65 to E 8.75 per ton of carbon dioxide., a total sale of E11.31 Million euros or about £7.92 MILLION . The commission on £7, 920,000. must be high and there must be commission to be made on every transaction, a lucrative market indeed. We do not what percentage of the E 8.7 per ton of carbon dioxide the developing countries are paid, but like the charity trade in which the worldwide charity Oxfam deals and declares that 85 pence in every sterling pound currency donated is spent in administration, it would not be surprising if the developing countries are getting the equivalent, ie £1.2 million going to the developing countries and £6,720,000 to the carbon traders.

264 Carbon Finance, (2004), Newsletter, Issue 11, October 2004.; the International Civil Aviation Organisation produces guidelines for the sale of aviation emissions—this sale will start from the year 2008.

265 The UK carbon markets initiative which began in 2000 has not been thorough in its inception. It has failed to address the primary issue of which type of process a country would choose to use, whether it would continue with old, polluting equipment in metal production or whether it would calculate a cost/benefit analysis of paying for new clean equipment and save on emissions or pay to trade its emissions in the carbon markets planned. For itself, it is obvious that the UK has not addressed this problem . The UK has a disjointed set of planned programmes to install a mixture of more nuclear power stations, wind farms, and contracted-in coal and raw materials for its metal production, rather than use its planned carbon market as per its own initiative. See articles by Jameson. A, (2004), 'Clean-coal technology could cut CO_2 bill by £3 Billion.', The Times Newspapers, p36, 22 November 2004. UK's ageing power stations can be replaced with new clean coal-technology power stations that will cut greenhouse emissions.

266 As in the case of Molins plc v GD S p A, [2000] All ER (D) 107, reversed, .in which there was a written agreement to be construed and interpreted under English law, yet GD issued proceedings in Italy about the payment of royalties . Since the Italian court was 'first seized' of the action, under article 21 of the Convention on Jurisdiction and the Enforcement of Judgements in Civil and Commercial Matters 1968, (The Brussels Convention), the English court was obliged to stay the proceedings, had the plaintiff been properly served with notice, but since notice was served by fax which was not acceptable, the English court was allowed to proceed.

committed fraud? Could such decisions be made beforehand by agreement; could it be settled by arbitration, even though it is criminal because it would also constitute breach of contract? What would be the penalties? Will penalties, if monetary, be passed back to consumers in increased prices? Would there be an emergency action if a country had grossly exaggerated false statements, to the extent of putting the world at risk? What would be the penalty? And what of the human rights of that country's citizens?

The only case about atmospheric pollution is the 1939 Trial Smelter arbitration case[267] in which a Canadian smelter[268] caused damage as far away as seven miles into Washington, United States. The Trial Smelter case is the precedent that states can litigate against each other to prevent damage and environmental injury for which they are responsible. After the Trial Smelter case, there was more diligent regulation of smelters in Canada, ordered by the court and compensation paid also. The burden of unavoidable harm will still lie with the suffering party. At present Germany has such an excess of pollution in carbons that to get rid of the excess pollution it has, it would need to sell its greenhouse pollution at a cost to Germany of $1.22 BILLION United States dollars, working back to approximately 1,220,000,000 tons of EXCESS carbon dioxide pollution to be gotten rid of before the end of this year, according to the carbon trading rules. Germany does not have 1.62 Billion Euros spare cash to sell off its present excess pollution, even if there were enough countries willing to buy it; therefore Germany has been trying to persuade on a change of rules in order to carry forward its excess pollution for the year, much like a book-keeping account does.. Similarly France has excess carbon pollution, Carbon Trading on the Chicago Stock Exchange this year shoed a sale price of a ton of carbon dioxide pollution to be Euro 0.94 per ton of pollution to the present Euro 8.7 per ton of pollution, a price increase of 925 percent in ten months. America treats its excess carbon pollution, ranging into trillion tons of carbon dioxide pollution, as nonsense and has tried to have the case against it dismissed in court. Australia's carbon dioxide EXCESS emissions today are valued at US dollars 1.15 BILLION and Australia will have to borrow $US 1.15 Billion to pay to get rid of its excess carbon pollution by December,; it plans to borrow the money and pay it back over the next 20 years. This is the present seriousness of the financial and pollution precariousness in the western world.

Terrorism by Sabotage and no Global Jurisdiction

With respect to crime, be it financial fraud relating to the planned carbon pollution trading or acts of terrorism,[269] there are no international conventions on jurisdiction. There is however, a regional treaty between some Latin American

---

267 Trail Smelter Arbitration, 33 Ajil, [1939], 182.
   The Consolidated Mining and Smelting Company Limited of Canada operated a zinc and lead smelter along the Colombia river at Trail, British Columbia, about 10 miles north of Washington's border. Between 1925 and 1935 the US Federal government complained about its sulphur dioxide emissions, failed to agree at two arbitration hearings and finally the US sued Canada for damage to land and failure of crops. The US was awarded $428,179.51 in damages and costs and a mandate to the Canadian company to maintain equipment to measure wind velocity, direction, turbulence, atmospheric pressure, barometric pressure and sulphur dioxide concentrations at Trail, which the court ordered to be no more than a certain level. This case was the catalyst for the US/Canadian air pollution treaties.
   Since then, there have been 3 similar cases, one in Arizona (see article Audubon, 'Smoking smelter shuts in Arizona', p 147, March 1987), one in Washington(see article in International Wildlife Journal,(1984), 'Anti-pollution costs cited in closing of Tacoma smelter', September/October 1984.) and one in Mexico(see article Business Week, 'A Mexican smelter has the Southwest all fired up', 22 July 1985.).

268 Smelters of the old-fashioned kind are still producing today, especially in the Eastern European countries. For example, in Slovakia, smelters which produced smoke and dust and grit have only recently been replaced with gas boilers due to the PHARE aid programme to bring the new EU member states up to EU environmental standards.

269 Terrorism is a real threat to global security and environmental safety, more so now than ever. With the suicide bombing of the World Trade Centre with a live projectile by way of a full aeroplane aimed at a building, it is not inconceivable that terrorists, devastated and frustrated might try to annihilate the whole world by disrupting the electronics of a nuclear power station or several large metal producing smelters, causing a sudden increase in pollution as never experienced before. The International Law Commission has defined terrorism to include:

countries, the Bustament Code, attached to the Havana Convention on Private International Law in force since 1935 between Brazil, Bolivia, Costa Rica, Cuba, Dominican Republic, El Salvador, Guatemala, Haiti, Honduras, Nicaragua, Panama, Peru and Venezuela. The EU has the 1968 Convention on Jurisdiction and the Enforcement of Judgements in Civil and Commercial Matters but no convention on criminal matters, although there is legal assistance in criminal matters. As far as the United Kingdom is concerned all crime is local as per the common law rule and any extraterritorial crime will rely on extradition laws, UK prosecutors retaining absolute discretion[270] whether to prosecute or not. A Commonwealth Scheme for Mutual Assistance in Criminal Matters exists and was ratified in 1986 by 29 Commonwealth countries. However the Commonwealth Scheme has no guaranteed reciprocity.[271]

Then there is corruption,[272] lack of professionalism and conflict of interest; but the most daunting task is the matter of regulating[273] and auditing the pollution levels of every country to ensure uniformity and equality. For financial investigations, a Memorandum of Authority is often used, these having set principles that state that the country will give the requesting country assistance even if the MOU violates the requested country's laws; in strictest confidentiality; agreeing between the countries how they would gather the information requested; with the right to refuse to assist a country in the public interest of the requested country; and able to punish persons in their country who refuse to comply with the request.

And this is the knob of the problem. Will all countries be treated equal? Will a poor country with high carbon credit[274] be given a fair value for that carbon credit or will that credit be discounted because that country is undeveloped? The legislation on carbon credits must be applied equally Dworkin argues that the measure of equality is the treatment of all people as free and equal human beings. A further condition of Dworkin's equality would be that attitudes towards risk-taking and preferences for material resources be evenly distributed throughout the world's population. For it is wrong that an unclothed and hungry uneducated person should die so that a fat, healthy, educated, materially wealthy person should live, and if one must die so that the other may live, then it is the one with the abundance of experiences, fulfilment and usage of the planet's resources who should expire to allow the other some of what was always his due but

---

"(1) Any act causing death or grievous bodily harm or loss of liberty to a Head of State, persons exercising the prerogatives of the Head of State, the spouse of such persons or persons charged with holding public office;

(ii)   Acts calculated to destroy or damage public property or property devoted to a public purpose;

(iii) Any act likely to imperil lives through the creation of a public danger;

(iv) The manufacture, obtaining of arms, explosives or harmful substances with a view to committing a terrorist act.."

The UK Terrorism Act 2000 provides its own definition of 'terrorism'. which terms 'country' and 'government' as any country or any government, taking on the mantle of responsibility for the world.

270 The vesting of broad discretionary powers in all public officials leads to the possibility of dictatorship. Vague statutes lead to immoral behaviour where people will pick and choose the laws they want to enforce and the people against whom they wish to enforce them.

271 See Robinson.P.L, (1984), 'The commonwealth scheme relating to the rendition of fugitive offenders: a critical appraisal of some essential elements', International Comparative Law Quarterly Journal, Volume 33, pages 617-624.

272 The Gini and Power Distance Index for Countries by level of corruption state the ten most corrupt countries as Columbia, Pakistan, Mexico, India, Venuezuela, Philippines, Thailand, Turkey, Argentina and Brazil, whilst they state that the ten least corrupt countries are Denmark, Finland, Sweden, New Zealand, Canada, Netherlands, Norway, Australia, Singapore and Switzerland in that order.
Karstedt. S, (1997), 'Inequality, power and morality', Australian Institute of Criminology Paper.

273 This specialised field mainly has a "Memorandum of Understanding" (MOU) to rely on. The Memorandum of Understanding to Establish Mutually Accepted Means for Improving International Law Enforcement Cooperation, 1983, can consist of just diplomatic notes on related matters. The UK's Financial Services Authority has a wide range of MOU's with authorities in many countries. Since 1991 countries that agree to use MOU's have adopted a set of Principles of MOU's.

274 That there is much global poverty today is beyond dispute. The World Bank's Report on poverty states that there are 1.1 Billion persons living on less than $1 a day and with reduced life expectancy of 46 years, when western industrialised countries have populations with life expectancy increasing to over 70 years. Poor people are those in East Asia and Pacific China, Latin America and Caribbean, South Asia, Sub-Saharan Africa.

denied him until now. The American Declaration of the Rights and Duties of Man state at Article 28 that "the rights of man are limited by the rights of others, by the security of all, and by the just demands of the general welfare and the advancement of democracy". Theoretically, there is no derogation, restriction or limitation available from this article and a person has the inherent right to enjoy and utilise fully and freely their national wealth and resources.

If we consider that health is the factor which is to be protected with the ozone layer, then all people are important and equal and their carbon credits must be equally valuable. The trading of carbon credits in markets at the price according to demand is the using of wealth maximisation as a normative ideal in the insurance of a social good, the ozone layer.

As far as human rights to the environment goes, there have been cases in 1994[275] and 1998[276] that make it quite clear that Article 8 provides a solid basis for claiming adequate environmental protection. The human rights by way of political rights can be affected. The Rio de Janeiro Declaration on Environment and Development includes principle 10 which states that "environmental issues are best handled with the participation of all concerned citizens, at the relevant level". So right to private life, right to property and right to political participation into areas that affect environmental protection can all be protected under the right to a fair trial.

Conclusion

There is much controversy on greenhouse emissions and the strategy planned to reduce these as outlines above. The market size needs to be determined and the market power also. Governments must be proactive and monitor any mergers in this market of carbon trading. There must be limits put on consolidation in this market to avoid monopoly and anti-competitive activity.

This very important market must start on a level playing field and consideration must be put on aiding poor countries to set up the required regulatory financial systems to facilitate carbon trading; international accounting standards are needed to treat such transactions uniformly in company reports and accounts, corporate governance rules on ethical transactions need to be formulated, capital requirements in place if securitization is to be used in this market, and a global reaching supervisory body set up with monitoring and enforcement personnel, independent from each country's financial supervisory agency, separate to the World Trade Organisation and its non-compulsory and retaliatory sanctions. All this would require enormous resources, which could be met by the polluting countries urgently needing such a market.

Statutes and Conventions:

American Declaration on the Rights and Duties of Man 1795

Convention on Jurisdiction and the Enforcement of Judgements in Civil and Commercial Matters 1968 (Brussels Convention)

European Union Convention 1992

EU Regulation EEC/93/1836

---

275 Lopez-Ostra v Spain, (1995) 20 EHRR 277-300, was a case in which the ECHR declared that Spain had violated the right to environmental protection when it failed to prevent environmental damage caused by a waste-treatment plant built near the applicant's home. The government failed to implement regulations and procedures. Awarding her damages and mandating the scale-down of the plant, the court said that *"severe environmental pollution may affect individuals' well-being and prevent them from enjoying their homes in such a way as to affect their private and family life adversely, without, however, seriously damaging their health"*.

276 In the case Guerra v Italy, (116/1996/735/932), 19 February 1998, the court held that the toxic emissions of a chemical factory in an Italian town was a violation of Article 8 on respect for private and family life which a public authority is obliged to observe. Severe environmental pollution may affect individuals' well-being and prevent them from enjoying their homes in such a way as to affect their private and family life adversely, the court said.

EU Directive 75/436 Euratom

EU Directive 2000/25/EC

EU Directive 2004/35/EC

EEC 92/197

Geneva Convention on Long-Range Trans-boundary Air Pollution 1979

Havana Convention on Private International Law1935

Kyoto Protocol   1997

MARPOL Convention 1995

Unified European Act 1986

United Kingdom Terrorism Act 2000

Case-law

Guerra v Italy (116/1996/735/932) 19 Feb 1998

Lopez—Ostra v Spain [1995] 20 EHRR

Molins plc v GD SpA [2000] All ER (D)

Trail Smelter Arbitration, 33 Ajil, [1939], 182.

Bibliography

Alston. P, (1999), 'The EU and Human Rights', Oxford University Press.

Birnie. P, and Boyle.A.W, (1992), 'International law and the environment', Clarendon Press, Oxford.

Business Week, (1985), 'A Mexican smelter has the southwest all fired up', page 70, 22 July 1985.

Carbon Finance, (2004), 'Newsletter', Issue 11, October 2004.

Carter. B.E and Trimble. P.R, (1991), 'International Law', Little, Brown and Co, Boston.

Corporate Europe Observatory, (2001), 'Saving the Kyoto Protocol means ending the market mania', July 2001.

Dehner. J . S, (1995), 'Vessel-Source Pollution and Public Vessels: Sovereign Immunity v Compliance. Implications for International Environmental Law', Environmental Law Review, fall 1995.

Delbruck. J, (1993), 'Globalisation of law, politics and markets—implications for domestic law : A European perspective', Indiana Journal of Global Legal Studies, Volume 1, Issue 1, Fall 1993.

European Commission, (2004), 'Country Report: Environmental Law', REC.

EU Business, (1998), Council—Environment', Council Press Release 453, 20/21 December 1998.

Fairlamb. D, (2003), 'The smog trade', Business Week, 14 July 2003.

Freidman. M., (1962), 'Capitalism and Freedom', University of Chicago Press.

Guest. S, (1997), 'Ronald Dworkin:Profiles in legal theory', 2nd ed., Edinburgh University Press.

International Wildlife, (1984), 'Anti-pollution costs cited in closing of Tacoma smelter', volume 14, page 29, September/October 1984.

Jamieson. K. M, (1994), 'The organisation of corporate crime—dynamics of anti-trust violation', Sage Publications.

Inciardi. J. A and Siegal. H. A.,(1977), 'Crime: Emerging Issues', praeger Publishers.

Karayiannoupoulos. F. A. (2004), 'International Environmental Law', Community Plant Variety Office, Greece.

Karstedt. S, (1997), 'Inequality, power and morality', Paper presented at the Australian Institute of Criminology.

Kramer. L. (1993), 'Environmental protection and Article 30 EEC', Common Market Law Review, Vol 30, 111-143.

Newsweek, (2004), 'Sequestration', 4 September 2004.

New Zealand Aluminium Smelters Co Ltd, 'Greenhouse gas emissions', April 2004.

Purdy.R. and Macrory. R., (2003), 'Geological carbon sequestration:critical legal issues', Tyndall Centre Working Paper, No.45 January 2003.

Rakowski. E, (1991), 'Equal Justice', Clarendon Press, Oxford.

Smith. A., (1779), 'The theory of Moral Sentiments', Edinburgh Press.

Smith. A., (1776), 'An Inquiry Into the Nature and Causes of the Wealth of Nations', Edinburgh Press.

Tees Valley Joint Strategy Unit, (2004), 'Air pollution', Newsletter April/May 2004.

World Bank, (2004), 'World development Indicators 2004'—Statistical Report., The World Bank Group.

Issue 7—Terrorism and Sabotage

An Examinatisn of the Formerly Largely Unregulated Global Charity Sector and the Impact of Anti-Money Laundering and Anti-Terrorism Legislation

"A REVIEW OF NOT-FOR-PROFIT ORGANISATIONS, THEIR GIVING, AND THE NEW MONEY LAUNDERING, ANTI-TERRORISM AND ASSET FREEZING LEGISLATION IMPLEMENTED IN THE US, CANADA, UK, FRANCE AND GERMANY"

This Paper took its title from the assumption that,. Since the banking industry was already secure before the Money Laundering Regulations and the Charity Industry was not, money laundering would be found in the charity industry if it were to be found. So the writer gauged the laundering law implementation costs o against any laundering found in the charity industry and also in the banking industry. None was found and so the writer concluded that over five hundred billion dollars was spent on needless implementation of money laundering law.

Abstract

An examination of the implementation of money laundering laws in UK, US, Canada, France and Germany after 2001 .appears to have succeeded only in psychologically allaying popular fear by visible actions that appear to be combating terrorism. This review shows the difference in attitudes between the different states in their approach to charities. Germany and France not creating special legislation for charities with extremely generous tax breaks, whilst the federal United States stepped up its Inland Revenue Investigations as a monitoring method. The United Kingdom has only just introduced a new Charities law and recent money laundering legislation .Overall, all these countries spent many times more United states dollars per capital on anti-terrorism laws than they gave to charity.

The writer concludes that, even if this emergency and undemocratic law-making was the incorrect route to take, it might be argued that it is successful in allaying people's fears, whilst conciliation is sought to placate those who are bitter at the apparent injustice of globalised law and economics.

Introduction

NOT-FOR-PROFIT ORGANISATIONS AND WHAT THEY REPRESENT

In the area of corporate responsibility, not-for-profit companies[277] mostly have a stewardship role for members and this does not have different governance implications from business corporations. A not-for-profit organisation[278] has a fundamental difference in its relationship with company members to the relationship of profit organisation and its company members. Non-for-profit organisations, formed to collect money to give aid to developing countries, aid for earthquake crisis situations, aid to the poor and homeless, to build schools, hospitals, etc., have members whose commitment to the company is to donate money to the company . These members must exercise rights for the beneficiaries who are helped by the company. This is their stewardship role.

---

277 There are more than 153, 000 charities registered with the UK Charities Commission. and the UK government donated £2 billion to them. http://www.public technology.net, article 'Governmentfunding.org.uk operative & has £120 million to give away'., 27 April 2004.

278 These are 30, 000 companies limited by guarantee without share capital, and some do not have to state the word 'Ltd' in their name, under section 30, Companies Act 1985. There are also 58, 000 unincorporated companies, 28, 000 trusts and 88, 000 others., estimated at £12 billion income a year.

On the other hand, for-profit organisations have the interest of the shareholders as priority. Consumer interests are only pursued to the extent that these consumer interests are also the same interests of the members of the company.

Directors of not-for profit organisations must have some ultra vires doctrine with which to constrain them; they do not have the remit to increase shareholders value, as with for-profit organisations; their remit must be, in the case of money for aid companies, to efficiently distribute aid to the most deserving and to pursue fund raising activities to sustain such aid to the needy.. Another duty of directors of such not-for-profit organisations is prevention of the majority from stopping the company from achieving optimum efficiency. These aims cannot be achieved by for-profit directors because, although efficiency may be considered as an important objective in company contracts, it never suffices and there is a balance between company law interference and the freedom of contract principle.

That directors of not-for-profit companies need constraints is illustrated by incidents of church pastors stealing funds. UK theft and fraud, usually discovered during the audit and submission of annual accounts to the Charity Commission, is perpetrated by cunning people who can hide debts and window-dress the accounts without raising suspicion, especially in the church sector where trust is implied.

Example of False Accounting in UK Not-For-Profit Organisations

The Victory Centre in London, a charity,[279] submitted cessation accounts in 2002. It was discovered that it had debts of £200, 000 even though it had an income of £3, 500, 000.00 in 2001. The preacher of this church received a salary from a trust[280] of which he was also a trustee, as do many preachers in many churches in England and Wales. The preacher lived a lavish lifestyle which was very much beyond his known means and this led members to ask for an investigation by the Charity Commission. Incidents like this have forced the Charity Commission[281] to implement further regulations to charity accounts to make charities transparent and more accountable.

The investigation by the Charity Commission was to establish if there was fraud and to establish the level of responsibility of the trustees in the management and administration of the charity. They found evidence of management misconduct and mismanagement, examples of which were unauthorised salary payments and other benefits to the preacher and some others, the preacher being the sole signatory to the cheques, a breach of the Charity's constitution. There were no financial controls of cash collections and there were expenses not accounted for. The Charity Commission appointed a Receiver and Manager under section 18(1)[282] of the Charities Act 1993. The church was closed down in December 2002 with no identifiable assets and the Commission did not order the restitution of benefits, as it did not think it appropriate in this case.

---

279 A charity has the advantage of being exempt from income, corporation and capital gains tax and land and buildings occupied by the charity are rated at 50% for general and water purposes.

280 A charitable trust such as a church as this is, is a trust whose object is to provide benefit to the public, in this case, by way of the advancement of religion, one of the four categories as per Lord Macnaughten in Income Tax Commissioners v Pemsel [1891]AC531, 581. The rule in the context of religion is that the benefits should be available to any suitable personwho wishes to take advantage of them.

281 The Charity Commission can be said to be a pro-active regulator. Proactive enforcement strategies will discover deviance from the rules if they are obvious and can help the regulated as well as teach the regulator how the charity really works. Theorists, Black(1973), Alderson (1979), Cranson (1979), Hawkins(1984) and Hutter(1986), state that it is difficult to quantify the value of such pro-active strategies . The writer later illustrates the estimated quantification of the money laundering pro-active strategy in the only area where such money laundering can succeed—in the unregulated not-for-profit sector and proves this same point; that the costs of such pro-active regulator strategies far outweigh any benefit whatsoever and so disagrees strongly with the concept of proactive enforcement strategies in Hutter's 1986 paper, 'An inspector calls', British Journal of Criminology, Volume 26 No.2, April 1986.

282 The powers on its own initiative to change charities' trustees and freeze their assets.

But the Commission stated that a charity is entitled to the objective judgement of its trustees, and that such judgement must be exercised solely in the interests of the charity, with no conflict of interest. Normally, a trustee who benefits from a position of trust without the necessary authority is liable to repay the benefit which he has received.

They opined that churches need to practice good corporate governance. A trusted and respected spiritual leader must not use "undue influence" in his capacity or, induce members to give him money directly nor should he help himself to money contributed to the church.[283] The UK has new regulations that compel charities that give financial advice or sell insurance, to register with the regulator the Financial Services Authority from January 2005.

In line with America's fight against money laundering[284] and terrorism, the UK has implemented its Terrorism Act 2000, the Anti-Terrorism, Crime and Security Act 2001, and UN Financial Action Task Force measures against money laundering, freezing $100 million of 'terrorist' assets, now released mostly to the government of Afghanistan.

CHARITY LAW IN THE UNITED STATES

In the United States, unlike the UK, charitable giving is big business, estimated at over $120 billion a year by individuals, including the billionaire businessman Bill Gates and billionaire investor Warren Buffet, spawning whole sectors devoted to taxation and trust law for charities. This is apart from corporate bequests, limited to 10% of its taxable income. A corporation can give stock, equipment, property and money. In total, this not-for-profit sector contributes $785 billion a year to the US economy.[285]

The US federal income tax laws allow up to 50% of a person's annual income to go tax free to charity. and 100% tax free to go to charity on one's death. Motivation for giving ranges from tax planning by way of trusts for future generations of family to minimising estate tax through charitable split-interest trusts, for example. Bequests may be from a person in another country, to persons in another country, to governments of other countries, and the tax rules are complex. There are tax rules as to what can type of asset can be bequeathed.[286] There is extensive case-law on disallowed tax deductions, disallowed types of trusts and disallowed purpose of the bequest.[287] It is the international activities[288] of US charitable organisations that were of concern to state security dealing with terrorism. Before September 2001, the US trust

---

283 The making of a donation to a church is a fundamental right of any individual and these donations are sometimes the lifeblood for such institutions that mostly do fine and noble work. Distinctions need to be drawn between donating money to a church and direct gifts to one of its members, even the spiritual leader. Principles of guidance need to be established by churches with regard to donations by members to individual members such as the spiritual leader

284 Money laundering laws enacted a decade ago to stop drug trafficking and now terrorism, are to my mind, more relevant to the stem of illegal money flows which grow trans-national illegal organisations, hidden behind the veil of personal privacy and bank secrecy of increasingly wealthy, criminal corporate offenders. Charities too, are heavily used by wealthy persons as tax-exempt vehicles to transport their legal and illegal gains to their future generations. The whole complex and extremely expensive system organised to facilitate giving, throws out some benefits to the poor and needy but mostly have ulterior motives., . Such motives are not usually altruistic but selfish. Therefore the writer examines the transaction to discover whether there is gain which far outweighs the hefty and labour intensive financial and psychological cost of checking our money.

285 Weiner. S, (2003), 'Proposed legislation: its impact on Not-For-Profit board governance', CPA Journal, November 2003.

286 For example, certain intangible property cannot be included with other assets and bequeathed copyright, trademark, franchise, programmes or data or memoranda., for tax deduction in a bequest, although they can be bequeathed with tax deducted.(73 CJS Property 5, section 963(h)(3)(b).

287 For example, in Edwards v Phillips, 373F.2d 616 (10ᵗʰ circuit). Mr Hansen bequeathed his entire estate to a District Parish in Denmark. It was held that bequests to subdivided countries, ie foreign governments or political subdivisions of a foreign country, were not intended by Congress to be tax deductible. But a bequest to a US organisation abroad is deductible, as in the case Montessori School of Paris, Inc v Commissioner, 75 T.C.480(1980).

288 The US has over 600 national organisations, foundations, corporate philanthropy programmes, representing hundreds of thousands of charities in every state in America with over 160 NGOs operating in each developing country.

accountants and tax authorities did not perform due diligence tests on the nature or destination of bequests abroad.[289] There were bequests to the Red Cross as well as to organisations such as the Holy Land Foundation for Relief. Since July 2004, the new rules provide that a contribution that is deductible as per the Internal Revenue Code is allocated and apportioned only to the US source for foreign tax credit purposes. But this is only a small step in the fight against money laundering for terrorism purposes.[290]

There are new rules for the corporate governance of all companies including Not-For-Profit companies. All companies must now have Audit committees and strict financial controls and reporting, independent directors, independent auditors, compensation committee. There are other rules peculiar to each state. For instance, companies listed on NASDAQ are required to have at least one member with past employment experience in finance and accounting and all foreign issuers must disclose any exemption to NASDAQ's corporate governance requirements at start and yearly.

In September 2004, 3 years after the terrorist assault on the US, the Non—Profit Integrity Act was passed, imposing Sarbanes—Oxley type provisions, applicable to charitable corporations, charitable trusts, unincorporated charity fundraisers and fundraiser counsels on pain of fines for non-compliance. But hospitals, institutions and religious organisations are exempt.

Before this, and shortly after 9/11, the federal government issued an Executive Order[291] to freeze the assets of all involved with terrorism. In October 2001 the US Patriot Act 2001 criminalized the financing of terrorism[292] with fines and imprisonment. Further steps to stop money laundering and thus terrorism were the extended trade embargoes, which, if violated by charitable and humanitarian organisations, even inadvertently, are subject to civil and criminal penalties. The 2003 Tax Code amendments provide for automatic suspension of tax-exempt status of any charity suspected of helping to finance terrorism. The USAID, United States Agency for International Development now has a certification procedure so that countries which receive aid must sign and declare that they are not aiding terrorism.

---

289 Charitable trusts are formed to donate money for terrorist activities, drug trafficking and money laundering. There are many not-for-profit companies which trade with each other, invest the excess in property, shipping, computers, etc., and increasing in number as profits grow. These profits are in fact illegal untaxed money and this corporate activity is organised crime., using trade to move money between accounts and across borders by way of charities, companies, financial trusts and offshore accounts. One such organisation was the "Tvind used clothes chain "of for-profit and not-for-profit companies which operated in the US, Canada, France, UK, Sweden, Holland.

290 Since the 2003 case Madigan v Telemarketing Associates, it is now illegal for fundraisers to intentionally mislead donors. But this did not stop US donations to charity to rise by 2% from 2002 to 2003. However, in 2003-4, many non-profits have had reduced state funding.
See The Howe and Hutton Report, (2004), 'Analysing the news of importance to the non-profit community', Volume 2004, Issue 7, July 2004.

291 Global Terrorism Sanctions Regulations, 31 C.F.R. Part 594, issued under the International Emergency Economic Powers Act, 50 U.S.C. s 1701-1707.

292 The Patriot Act is an amalgam of measures to identify and root out money laundering and to strengthen existing laws which prohibit the provision of material or financial support to terrorists and terrorist organisations. Material support is defined as 'currency or monetary instruments or financial securities, financial services, lodging, training, expert advice or assistance, safe-houses, false documentation or identification, communications equipment, facilities, weapons, lethal substances, explosives, personnel transportation, and other physical assets, except medicine or religious materials. In 2003, the Supreme Court, in Humanitarian Law Project v United States Department of Justice, 352 Fed 382 (9th Cir.2003), held that the terms 'personnel' and 'training' in this definition were vague and unconstitutional. In the two and a half years to March 2004, the Executive Order has resulted in lists on which are 1500 names of suspected terrorists, 200 names of terrorist US organisations and 280 names of foreign terrorist organisations. Four of these names were US public charities who now have no tax-exempttion.

Comparative Analysis of Cost of New Legislation in Each Country

The estimated analysis, using the various estimates, calculations, interpolations and extrapolations have given an idea of the costs of the money laundering legislation implemented in the various countries. and only the USA and the UK have actually given more in total donations than was spent on anti-terrorism and money laundering which, can be argued was only relevant to the non-banking, unregulated sector such as charities.. It shows that unless there are some other purpose in giving, such as a tax shelter, tax exemption or for the sake of posterity, charitable donations seem futile.

But if charitable giving is such a large part of the economy[293] as in the UK and the US, there must be substance to such hearsay as that 'there are as many unregistered charities in the US as there are registered charities'.[294] In that case, the legislation implementation in the US and the UK would have been worthwhile, even if only to bring all unregistered charities into the legal system. But it is dishonest to make emergency and mandatory changes to a country's financial systems using people's real fear, rather than through democratic debate as to the soundness of this action.

As the accountancy requirements and controls feed back into the sector, transparency allows donors to notice any discrepancies in accounts. As the state laws impact and there is disclosure as to fund destination, those undesirable recipients, if any, will disappear.

With regard to France and Germany, it is clear that they did not choose the harsh US route of new legislation because they do not have charity sectors that are such a significant proportion of the countries' Gross Domestic Product. France and Germany have had a recent overall reform of their financial regulatory systems but this is not to combat terrorism or money laundering but to consolidate for regularisation of systems and for economies of scale reasons. Certainly France has opened up its equity market to non-EU countries and Germany has new regulation of hedge funds, mainly because a large portion of Germany's hedge fund business relates to the unregulated US transactions.

Since Germany has always had a highly regulated banking system, there was no need for money laundering legislation to combat terrorism. There have been no money laundering episodes uncovered in these countries' charity sector in the past 3 years, except in Canada where there was a $ US 1 million event, a mere 0.015% of the amount given (1/6500). and another million in the UK, a tiny 0.06% of donor gifts. So at an estimated cost to the 5 countries of $US642.17 Billion or $642, 000, 000, 000 dollars, two million dollars of money laundering attempt was discovered and that cannot be justified, just 0.0003%.

Canada—Using Another Method to Combat Money Laundering in the Charity Sector

The Canadian government implemented the Anti-Terrorism Act punishable under provisions in the Canadian Criminal Code, Foreign Missions Amendment Act, Public Safety Act and Proceeds of Crime Act.

The way that Canada prohibits charities from terrorist funding and other money laundering activities, is not through stricter governance rules[295] or financial supervision and regulation, but by making a charity a personality that can be subject to prosecution under the stricter Criminal Code. The types of situations that charities can find themselves culpable are—

-   A charity, through a fundraiser, may solicit funds by using a food aid programme to benefit terrorists.

-   Medical aid might be obtained by a charity to help wounded terrorists.

---

293 The CPA Journal, (2003), 'Proposed legislation:its impact on Not-For-Profit Board Governance', November 2003.. The article states that this sector is the third largest of the US economy.

294 ibid.

295 Charities may be subject to recordkeeping and reporting duties as per the regulations in the Proceeds of Crime Act which state which entities must do such recording, these being authorised foreign banks, cooperative credit societies, life insurance companies, Savings and Loans companies, trusts, loan companies, stock brokers, investment services, foreign exchange traders, accountants, lawyers, casinos, government post offices, and employees of these entities.

- Funds raised for a hospital to operate go towards caring for the sick who are radical student protesters.

- A religious charity gives funds to another church which uses it to give student protesters somewhere to sleep.

- Church members go to an abortion clinic and threaten and intimidate the patients.

- A charity helps an asylum seeker with money, not knowing that the refugee's brother is a terrorist.

The punishment would be a listing under the Security Information Act, loss of charitable status, freezing of its assets, restraint and seizing of its property. Anyone found guilty of terrorism in Canada will have a 10 year maximum prison sentence, or directors, a fine up to h$100, 000 plus a one year prison sentence for non-directors.

There has been no act of terrorism in Canada, nor is there any name on the Securities Act List. No charities have been found guilty of breach of the Criminal Code. A total of $100 million was reported in Canada as suspicious cases of terrorist financing, but only one million found was attributed to money laundering by charities.[296]

The only matter that makes for anxiety in Canada is that lawsuit following the New York terrorist attack on 11 September 2001. It names some Canadian charities in third party liability claims.[297] If found guilty, these charities will be listed terrorists' cells; they will lose their charitable status, their property will be seized and their cash will be frozen.

France and Germany's Not-For-Profit Organisations

France has implemented new rules for not-for-profit companies which increase the incentive for charity giving and does not address the money laundering issue. There are tax credits of 90% to businesses who buy artworks for the nation and so keep their art in France. France has given generous tax incentives of 50% relief on donations to public organisations to a maximum of 10% of taxable income. N G O's are now allowed to pay up to 3 directors a maximum of 1 million Euro a year in salary and all their income below 60, 00 Euro is tax free.

Like France, Germany has incentivised its charities by making changes to its Federal Civil Code in 2002. There is now an entity called a 'foundation' which can be a legal personality subject to government authorisation and supervision. and tax reform is planned.

Conclusion

From the evidence above, it is clear that the United States, after the 2001 terrorist action, has been vigorous in implementing every possible measure to counter terrorism and money laundering which it perceives to aid terrorism. Largely, the United Kingdom and Canada have done almost as much in legislation and regulations. But France and Germany have instead fortified their charity sector and acted to enable these organisations to fulfil their aims and objectives of social good . France's attitude is consistent with the opening up of the French market and Germany's new company 'foundation' is part of the total efficiency drive and overall that Germany needs to encourage investment. In the past 3 years there have been no terrorist attacks in any of these countries and no money laundering to speak of, (the UK seized 1 million from an Afghan during the war on suspicion that it would be used by terrorists and has since returned that money to the Afghan government) although all have contingency plans in place, legally trained personnel and security in place.

The US had an excellent security system in place even as the attack happened.[298] The analysis is silent on the more realistic threat of cyber terrorism, which, if it takes place, needs no money laundering to facilitate it, but only a few highly

---

296 Dawson. A, (2002), 'Agency flagges $100 million in illicit cash', The National Post, 6 November 2002.. Apart from this the past 3 years in Canada have been uneventful.

297 Bell. S, (2002), 'Canadian organisations named in US $1 trillion law suit over september 11', The National Post, 29 August 2002.

298 The Advisory Panel to Assess Domestic Response Capabilities for terrorisminvolving weapons of mass destruction. Federal Response Plan, 2000.

intelligent, well qualified computer scientists, facilitated by the world wide web, a place of no jurisdiction, difficult to monitor[299] and changeable at a faster rate than a person can think, digitally attacking target entities. The symptoms are already to be seen in the United Kingdom which reported over £40 Billion fraud loss in 2003, a two hundred percentage change from fraud loss in the UK in 2002, and the Telecom sector at the 2004 Conference on Anti-fraud Strategies in London on 21st September 2004, reported that over £20 Billion pounds fraud loss was through their sector. The writer 's experience in the study of anti-fraud techniques and theories reveal the folly of over-supervision and hysteria in the banking system .It is operationally simple(but expensive) and visible to implement the new money laundering laws, lending confidence to the population that needs to visibly see anti-terrorism action. It is this false air of confidence that is being paid for by the same populations that fear terrorisms, because, banks are profit-making organisations, operating money laundering law on government's behalf and putting the cost on their Profit and Loss Accounts, where it erodes shareholders dividends. The problem lies in electronic technology which must immediately plug the gaps in the electronic systems that allow Billions of dollars of fraud loss. It would take a different study to enquire whether the telecom industry has a vested interest in leaving the gaps and loopholes in their electronic systems, especially when the telecom industry has revealed that it expects global telecom to be at an intelligent estimate of nearly £2 Trillion,[300] by the year 2007 in 85 countries. The telecom industry knows that over 50% of fraud loss comes from the United States.

There are many, highly intelligent, superbly qualified persons in poor, disadvantaged countries who are well aware of their own plight and with the motivation to undermine the West's business networks. The US's assessment report on terrorism risk discusses the nuclear black market which, like the neural computer networks, does not need money, only motivation.

A third point that all legislation is silent on, is that it is possible to hold some insurance against risk. I did not see a statute that included mandatory insurance cover. Fourthly, psychological operations and deceptions by way of business intelligence, through disinformation, misinformation and commonplace frauds resembles the old cold war, now played out between conglomerates, not governments.

The excellent, scholarly work of Hird (1991), Hopkins (1991) and Hahn (1996) on the cost of implementing new legislation was followed by their study of the cost of implementation of the US Federal government's asset-freezing Executive Order. . If we look at the regulatory cost of combating money laundering in order to avoid another terrorism attack, in the context of the unregulated charity industry, the following picture emerges (taking data in the public domain)—

---

299 There are 4 points that make a cybercrime different—these are the cheapness of waging information war; there are no boundaries in cyberspace; perception is esaily changed in cyberspace; information warfare can easily happen as it only needs access into the system.

300 Wraith. J, (2004), 'An overview of telecoms fraud and working within the wider fraud community', unpublished Paper given at The 7th Annual 'Strategies to combat fraud' (2004) Conference, Millenium Knightsbridge, London, 21st–22nd September 2004.

Giving per Capita, Cost of New Legislation per Capita

Year 2003	France	Germany	UK	US	Canada
GDP per capita—$US	28, 146	27, 913	26, 984	27, 964	29, 498
Giving per capita .$ US	151	185	508	819	200
Cost of implementing anti-terrorism and anti-money laundering laws	1008	1009	968	1373	1079
Ratio of Giving to cost of law implementation	1/10	2/10	5/10	6/10	2/10

So, overall, more was spent on anti-terrorism mandatory measures including anti-money-laundering, than people gave to charity.

Bibliography

Advisory Panel to Assess Domestic Response Capabilities for Terrorism Involving WMD, (2000), Federal Govt .US.

AGCAS, (2004), 'Voluntary Sector Report'.

Alderson. J, '(1979), 'Policing Freedom', Plymouth: Macdonald and Evans.

Association of Fundraising Professionals, (1955-1997), 'Research & statistics'

Australia Bureau of Statistics, (1997), 'Australian Social Trends'.

Black, D.J. (1973), 'The Mobilization of Law', Journal of Legal Studies, 2, 125-149.

Bussenius, A. (2004), 'Money Laundering by Defence Counsel—The Decision of the Federal Constitutional Court', Vol 5 No.9, German Law Journal, September 2004.

Carter, T.S. (2004), 'Charities and Compliance with Anti-Terrorism Legislation in Canada: The Shadow of the Law', Quarterly Journal of the International Centre for Not-For-Profit Law, Volume 6, Issue 3, June 2004.

Charities Commission, (2004), 'The Charities Bill', HMSO.

Cranston, R.(1979), 'Regulating Business: Law and Consumer Agencies', London: Macmillan.

Day Berry and Howard foundation Inc, (2004), 'Handbook of Counter-Terrorism Measures: What Non-Profits and Grantmakers Need to Know'.

Energy R & D Trends and Policies, (2004), Statistics.

Ezrati. M. (2004), 'The costs of terrorism', Lord Abbett 's Economic Insight, 8 October 2004. www. Lrdabbett. com.

Federal Deposit Insurance Corporation, (2004), 'Basel II Capital Requirements'.

Fein, R.A. and Vossekuil, B. (2000), 'Protective Intelligence and Threat Assessment Investigations: A Guide for State and Local Law Enforcement Officials', National Institute of Justice.

Gardner. S, (2003), 'Introduction to the Law of Trusts', Oxford University Press.

Global Policy Forum, (2004), 'EU names counter-terrorism Tsar', Reuters, 29 March 2004.

Hawkins, K. (1984), 'Environment and Enforcement: Regulation and the Social Definition', Oxford: Clarendon Press.

Hutter, B.M. (1986), 'An Inspector Calls', British Journal of Criminology, Vol 26 No 2April 1986.

Nakajima. C and Sheffield. E, (2002), 'Conflicts of Interest and Chinese Walls', London: Butterworths.

NASDAQ, (2003, 'Corporate Governance Summary Rules Changes', November 2003.

Nelken. D, (1994), 'White Collar Crime', Aldershot: Dartmouth.

PGDC, (2003), '2003 Federal Income Tax Rate Schedules for Trusts, Estates and Individuals'.

PGDC Newsletters, 2003-4.

Pollard, .N. (2000), 'The next President's Terrorism Policy', The Terrorism Research Centre Inc., US.

Quillen. C, (2000), 'State-Sponsored WMD Terrorism: A Growing Threat?', The Terrorism Research Centre Inc., US.

The Howe and Hutton Report, (2004), 'Not-For-Profit Law Development', Volume 2004, Issue 6.

Silk, T, (2004), 'Corporate Philanthropy and Law in the United States: A practical Guide to Tax Choices and an Introduction to Compliance with Anti-Terrorism Laws', International Journal of Not-For-Profit Law, Volume Six, Issue Three, June 2004.

Weiner, S. (2003), 'Proposed Legislation: Its impact on Not-For-Profit Board Governance', The CPA Journal, November 2003.

Whitehouse, Office of the President of the United States, (2004), 'Report to Congress on the Costs and Benefits of Federal Regulations', Whitehouse Home.

World Fact-book, (2004), 'Country Reports'.

Appendix 1—Estimated Cost of Implementing Terrorism and Money Laundering Legislation against the Previously Unregulated Charity Giving

Year 2003	France	Germany	USA	Canada	UK
Total giving (US$ Billions)	9.14	7.04	240	6.5	32 (converted)
environmental costs	31.39	42.92	207.71	18.11	31.48
other social costs	11.79	16.12	78.03	6.8	11.83
economic costs	15.45	21.12	102.21	8.91	15.49
paperwork &disclosure	2.16	2.95	14.29	1.24	2.17
Total cost	60.79	83.11	402.24	35.06	60.97
Deficit(US $ Billions)	(51.65)	(76.07)	(162.24)	(28.56)	(28.97)
Costs in US $ billions as proportion of Giving for each country	six times more than giving	eleven times more than giving	just less than amount of giving	five times more than giving	just less than amount of giving

Sources: OECD data; Sector Briefings for the UK; Association of Fundraising Professionals, Centre of Philanthropy Research Data, Indiana University, US.; Hurd and Hahn study of compliance costs of Banking Legislation (1991), Herd and Hahn study of Federal Executive Orders' compliance costs(1997) using their 1991 methodology—'Report to Congress on the Costs and Benefits of Federal Regulations', Whitehouse, Washington DC. ; USA Statistics; Federal Deposit Insurance Corporation-Report on Risk-Based Capital Requirement 2003; Bank of England Press Release, September 2004; World Fact-book—Country Statistics.

Appendix 2—Statutes and Conventions and Caselaw

Anti-Terrorism Act 2001 (Canada)

Anti-Terrorism, Crime and Security Act 2001 (UK)

Canadian Criminal Code (amendments) 2001

Charities Act 1993 (UK)

Companies Act 1985 (UK)

Foreign Missions Amendment Act 2001 (Canada)

German Federal Civil Code (amendments) 2002

International Emergency Economic Powers Act 2001 (US)

Non-Profit Integrity Act 2004 (US)

Patriot Act 2001 (US)

Proceeds of Crime Act 2001 (Canada)

Proceeds of Crime Act 2002 (UK)

Public Safety Act 2001 (Canada)

Terrorism Act 2000 (UK)

CASELAW

Edwards v Phillips, 373F.2d 616 (10th Circuit)	US case
Humanitarian Law Project v United States Department of Justice, (2003), 352 F.ed 382(9th Circuit)	US case
Income Tax Commissioners v Pemsel [1891] AC531	UK case
Madigan v Telemarketing Associates (2003)	US case
Montessori School of Paris, Inc. v Commissioner, 75 T.C.480(1980)	US case

CHAPTER 3

SHORT ARTICLES ON CONTEMPORARY TOPICS

3.1—What is Fraud?

WHAT IS FRAUD

English law does not provide a definition of fraud, nor is there a substantive offence of fraud at criminal law. There are a number of offences that cover fraudulent activity. Fraudulent conduct involves deception and dishonesty. When the term fraud is used it can cover a wide spectrum of criminal activity ranging from minor offences such a benefit fraud to sophisticated frauds involving complicated financial transactions and large sums of money. The offences of theft and deception are contained in the Theft Acts of 1968 and 1978. There is also the common law offence of conspiracy to defraud. There are also offences of fraudulent trading. There is the Theft Amendment Act 1996 which aims to close the cases of mortgage frauds due to the impact of technology and electronic banking where the courts held that money transfers between banks by cheque or by electronic means were not offences under the Theft Acts because they did not involve the specific transfer of "property belonging to another".

There used to be offences of fraud in wagering under the Gaming Act 1845, an example of such a case being <u>R v Clucas and O'Rourke [1959]</u> . In this case C and O were convicted of a number of offences of fraud in wagering, operating a scheme whereby one of them would contact a book-maker, giving a false name and pretending to be engaged on a works contract; the bookmaker would be asked to accept bets on behalf of the men on the site from C and O. When there were winnings, C and O collected them, and when there were losses of any substantial amount, they moved on to another place. Section 17 of the Gaming Act 1845 provided that "every person who shall, by any fraud…in wagering on the event of any game, sport, pastime or exercise, win from any other person to himself, or any other or others, any sum of money or valuable thing, shall be deemed guilty of obtaining such money or valuable thing by a false pretence." The question put to the jury was "Were the accused at the time they made these bets with bookmakers intending to cheat and defraud those bookmakers by not paying losses?" And so the appeal failed. This is an example of deceit; concealment of their intention to move on without paying if they lost on the bets. It was known as the offence of fraud in wagering.

Fraud is concealed stealing and serious fraud is no more than fraud of a very large amount. Fraud may be defined as any behaviour by which one person intends to gain a dishonest advantage over another. It includes such diverse acts as petty theft, pilfering, extortion, embezzlement, forgery, unfair competition, commercial espionage and other white—collar crimes. Serious frauds consist of the most serious of these types of crime, namely complex embezzlement, long firm frauds and commercial and organised crimes. Serious frauds can also occur through terrorist offences and drug offences by way of money laundering. Other serious frauds are examples of blatantly dishonest financial conduct such as the unauthorised sale of financial products, market manipulation, the abuse of discretionary client account management, the churning of insurance or pension products and the continued promotion of unsuitable products in order to generate greater commission such as fraudulent pension transfers.

All frauds fall naturally into identifiable categories because, over time, all frauds have been shown to be of certain types, even though modern methods give them new leases of life by particular embellishments.

Reduced to its basic level, fraud is simple; its objective is to gain a dishonest advantage by reducing the victim's assets, that is, a debit to the net worth of the victim. Fraud follows an incremental pattern limited only by the perpetrator's greed, opportunities and success or otherwise in concealing previous losses. Greed is the motivation. Concealment is an essential part of most large-scale, prolonged frauds, this being concealment of losses, concealment of blame, misrepresentation or manipulation.

3.2—The Test for Deception

THE TEST FOR DECEPTION

The Theft Act 1968 creates three offences of obtaining by deception and the Theft Act 1978 adds another four offences. So what is deception?

The Theft Act 1968 section 15(4) states: "…'deception' means any description (whether deliberate or reckless) by words or conduct as to fact or as to law, including a deception as to the present intentions of the person using the deception or any other person." If we take at look at cases in which the judge explains what such fraud is we find that as far back as 1889 in a case Derry versus Peek, Lord Herschell said: "…fraud is proved when it is shown that a false representation has been made

(1) knowingly;

(2) without belief in its truth;

(3) or recklessly, careless whether it be true or false…". This was a case where damages were sought for fraudulent misrepresentations of the defendants because of which the plaintiff was induced to take shares in the company.

In 1891 in the case Angus versus Clifford, Lord Justice Bowen said about a fraudster: "…did he know that the statement was false, was he conscious when he made it that it was false, or if not, did he make it without knowing whether it was false and without caring?"

Examples of deception are identity theft, corporate espionage, bank fraud and even cash-flow forecasts. A cash flow forecast is a statement of a sort and may be true or false, depending on whether it relates to existing facts, past or present. The making of a forecast, like that of a promise, will normally lead the recipient to draw certain inferences as to existing facts. It is clearly deceptive to make a forecast knowing that it will not come true. The making of a false statement is an offence in itself under the Financial Services Act, section 200(1) and whether it is deceptive depends on how its recipient understands it and is intended or expected to understand it as the judge said in the 1994 case Regina versus Morris "where…the charge is one of fraudulent trading, not requiring proof that any particular person was deceived, the question in issue must be as to the interpretation which a reasonable reader would, or might, put upon a document".

For someone to claim that they were deceived and to claim damages for the deceit, we can look for example at the case of someone, a plaintiff, who made a loan to another, the defendant, on the strength of such a statement.

The plaintiff will have to establish that the defendant made a representation to the plaintiff. The plaintiff would have to have evidence of this document, eg the cash-flow forecast or at least a witness statement as to the representation and its having been made to the plaintiff. The plaintiff would have to establish that he acted on that document. He would need the documentation or a witness statement evidencing how he made the loan as a result of the document supplied. He would have to prove that he suffered damage by acting on that document, so he would need to have evidence such as his bank statements showing his financial position before and after he acted on the misrepresentation. He would also have to establish that the representation by way of, for example, the cash-flow statement was untrue, so he would have to have that document, the cash-flow statement, for example, or a witness statement as to the circumstances in which the representation was made.

The only possible defence the defendant would have is that

the defendant did not intend to make a representation or that it was mere puff;

the defendant was not aware that it was untrue

or that the defendant believed it was true at the time.

As accounting technicians, it would be very advisable to create a sub-file in the client's file when making a cash-flow forecast. The sub-file should include all supporting documentation used to furnish figures in the forecast. Apart from the past year's financial statements, supporting figures such as the current interest rates, the current margins for that particular trade or sector, real figures as to the client's out-goings based on his mortgage statements, his car purchase details, all documentation relating to other debts he may have at the time, all current bank statements as to all bank accounts, tax liability statements, statements to show provision for VAT liabilities, should be kept in this sub-file . To protect oneself, a signed statement from the client that he has given you all relevant details and is aware of what the cash-flow statement says would be a cautious step to take.

3.3 Common Frauds

COMMON FRAUDS

There is no single offence of fraud but there are broad categories of offences in which numerous types of fraud are found. Here are some of these fraud offences.

1.   False Accounting.

False accounting is used to obtain more finance from banks. It is also used to raise share price, to appear more successful, to obtain performance-related bonuses, to cover up theft, to mislead auditors and to hide losses. False accounting is charged under the Theft Act 1968, section 17(1) which states "a person dishonestly with a view to gain for himself or another or with intent to cause loss to another—

(a) destroys, defaces, conceals or falsifies any account or record or document made or required for any accounting purpose; or

(b) in furnishing information for any purpose, produces or makes use of any account, or any such record or document as aforesaid, which to his knowledge is or may be misleading, false or deceptive in a material particular...."

2. Theft can also be theft by fraud. The common patterns for theft by fraud are direct theft of cash or any asset of the business, theft of stock, theft of computer equipment, theft of intellectual property, theft of price lists and customer lists, theft by making false expense claims, and by diverting payroll payments to ex-employees or fictitious employees and theft by increasing one's own salary.

Other fraud offences are:

2.   False statements by company directors. This offence is charged under the Theft Act 1968, section 19, which states:

"...an officer of a body corporate or incorporated association (or person purporting to act as such), with intent to deceive members or creditors of the body corporate or association about its affairs, publishes or concurs in publishing a written statement of account which to his knowledge is or may be misleading, false or deceptive in a material particular..."

3.   There is the offence of obtaining property by deception, under section 15 of the Theft Act 1968.

4.   The offence of "carrying on business with intent to defraud" comes under section 458 of the Companies Act 1985.

5.   "Insider dealing" comes under the Criminal Justice Act 1993.

6.   "Fraudulent trading" is charged under Companies Act 1985, section 458 ; this section states "...any business of a company is carried on with intent to defraud creditors of the company or creditors of any other person, or for any fraudulent purpose...".

7. "Fraudulent misappropriation of funds" is charged under the Proceeds of Crime Act 2002.

8. "Engaging in a course of conduct which creates a false or misleading impression as to market or price or value of investments" is charged as being contrary to section 47(2) of the Financial Services Act.

9. Cheque and credit card frauds are offences under the Theft Act 1968, section 15.(obtaining property by cheque or credit card fraud); Theft Act 1968, section 16 (obtaining pecuniary advantage by cheque or credit card fraud); under the Criminal Justice Act 1987, section 12 (Conspiracy to commit cheque or credit card fraud); under the Theft Act 1987, section 12 (obtaining services by cheque or credit card fraud); and under the Theft Act 1968, section 15A (obtaining a money transfer by cheque or credit card fraud).

10. "Obtaining property by deception (apart from cheque and credit card fraud) is caught under the Theft Act 1968, section 16.

11. Conspiracy to defraud (apart from cheque and credit card fraud) is caught under the Common Law and the Criminal Justice Act, section 12.

12. "Suppression of documents" is caught under the Theft Act 1968, section 20.

13. "Obtaining services by deception" is caught under the Theft Act 1978, section 1.

14. "Evasion of liability by deception" is an offence brought to the courts under the Theft Act 1978, section 2.

15. "Making off without payment" is an offence under the Theft Act 1978, section 3.

16. "Assisting another to retain the benefit of criminal conduct" is an offence under the Criminal Justice Act 1988, section 93A.

17. "Obtaining a money transfer by deception" is an offence under the Theft Act 1968, section 15A.

There are many other fraud offences.

How can fraud be frustrated? By putting controls in place, controls such as procedures to frustrate attempts to over-ride controls, segregation of responsibilities, controls of reconciliations and journal entries—a key control, use of pre-numbered, sequential documents, review of audit logs, pre-employment screening, internal audits, authorisation limits for cheques, dual signatories for all cheques, regular back-up of data, surveillance, job rotations and a fraud procedure in place.

A good employee will be prepared to sign a confidentiality agreement which states that he has a duty of confidentiality to the company and its clients and that information received in the course of employment will not be disclosed to persons outside the group and will not be used for an employee's own benefit or the benefit of others. If a company has a fraud ethics policy and reporting procedures in place, attempted frauds will be nipped in the bud, thus avoiding a scrupulous person from being forced to go to the police or to other authorities with the matter, as it will not arise if nipped in the bud.

3.4—Fraudulent Evasion

FRAUDULENT EVASION

Auditors of banks, insurance companies and charities have a duty to make reports to regulators. The Pensions Act 1995 established important responsibilities for pension scheme auditors. The Auditing Practices Board has established principles and set standards for the profession through the Statement of Auditing Standards 620, "The Auditors right and duty to report to regulators in the financial sector."

The principle determinant of the duty to report is whether a breach is likely to be of material significance to the regulator (level of materiality).

The Statement of Auditing Standards 620 states 'the term "material significance" requires interpretation in the context of the specific legislation applicable to the regulated entity. A matter or group of matters is normally of material significance to a regulator's functions when, due either to its nature or its potential financial impact, it is likely of itself to require investigation by the regulator.'

So, essentially, this is a matter of judgement for the auditor.

The first ever prosecution for the criminal offence of fraudulent evasion to be brought by the Occupational Pensions Regulatory Authority was 2002 case against Peter Lavender, a director of SSL(Patient Transport Systems Ltd, who used the company's occupational pensions to prop up the failing company.

The Director's defence was that he was not aware that the pension contributions were not being paid over to the pension scheme. He claimed that it was the bank that had stopped the direct debits of contributions to the scheme because of a shortage of funds in the account but in fact, he had instructed the bank to stop these direct debits.

He was found guilty of fraudulent evasion and was fined £1000, disqualified from being a director for four years. He had to pay some of the prosecution's costs and some compensation to three pension scheme members.

But another pension scheme fraud case, Woodland-Ferrari v UCL Group Retirement Benefits [2002], was decided against the pension scheme. In this case, a discharged bankrupt who was the former trustee of UCL Group Retirement Benefits, applied to set aside the statutory demand for sums which were claimed to be owed to UCL Group Retirement Benefits, following the Pensions Ombudsman decision that certain investments made by Woodland—Ferrari were made in breach of trust. Woodland-Ferrari stated that he had been made bankrupt after the date of the breaches of trust and given the fact that his bankruptcy had been discharged, he was no longer liable to make good the breaches of trust because he was released from all his bankruptcy debts on his discharge. The Pensions Ombudsman had decided that this was a "wilful default", but since "wilful default" was not the same as "fraudulent breach of trust" as per the Insolvency act, the judge decided that the demand had to be set aside.

Another important case was the case of Balfron Trustees v Peterson, in which a firm of solicitors applied to the court to strike out claims that it was liable for the alleged wrongful acts of its employee, a solicitor. The claim arose in relation to the misappropriation of funds from a pension scheme. As a result of the misappropriation, the scheme had become underfunded. A certain trustee of the scheme sought compensation because the solicitor had been instructed to act for Balfron Trustees Ltd, a company whose sole valuable asset was its interest in the scheme and the solicitor had drafted an agreement, part of a plan to use the assets of the pension scheme.

The Court did not strike out the claim that this solicitor had knowingly assisted in breaches of trust.

Since then, there has been a Pensions Bill 2004, which is expected to be enacted in November 2004 and which hopes to establish a Pension Protection Fund to protect members of private sector defined benefit schemes whose firms become insolvent with insufficient funds in their pension scheme so that they can be reassured that they will still receive most of the benefits which they are expecting. It will focus on protecting the benefits of pension scheme members and it will concentrate on those schemes where it is considered that there is a high risk of fraud, bad governance or poor administration. The Fund will come with a Pensions Regulator which will focus on under-funding, fraud and maladministration that can threaten members' benefits. The Regulator will start its job in April 2005. It will consist of a Chairman and six other board members and will have a committee of non-executive board members for specified functions such as reviewing the strategic direction of the Regulator. The difference between OPRA and the proposed Pensions Regulator is that whilst OPRA can only wind up a scheme or appoint an independent trustee, the new Regulator will be able to freeze the pension scheme for a time in order to investigate.

Employer-based or "occupational" pension schemes are a significant part of UK pensions with an estimated £776 billion in assets and between ten and eleven million employees as active participants, according to the Select Committee on Work and Pensions.

3.5—Fraudulent Trading

FRAUDULENT TRADING

The DTI brought a case against an accountant, a solicitor and a farmer in 2003 for fraudulent trading contrary to section 458 of the Companies Act 1985.

They were all involved in running three haulage companies in the Midlands and in Kent. The companies went into administration owing factoring companies two million pounds. The companies had been financed almost entirely from factored funds and false invoices had been raised and passed to the factoring companies to generate cashflow.

The Prosecution were able to ascertain these facts from old computer disks of the companies. From the financial data on the disks the prosecution team were able to recreate the management information that was available to the directors and produce for the court management accounts that formed an audit trail by analysing the movement of debtors, creditors, cash and the movement of balances with factoring companies. Far from being invisible, each disk left electronic fingerprints that led to conviction.

It is to be noted that a director's liability for fraudulent trading can only arise if the company is in administration or liquidation.

Directors have duties to act in the company's best interests, to be diligent, to take early legal advice if the company gets into financial difficulty, to avoid conflicts of interest, to hold regular board meetings and to keep proper minutes, to satisfy themselves about administration and financial information.

The penalties for breaches of duties and responsibilities are criminal penalties, civil penalties and disqualification, as in this case. It is a criminal offence to be involved in fraudulent trading and to recklessly make misleading statements in or omissions from public documents such as in filed accounts.

The breach of directors' duties to creditors that cause these creditors to suffer loss as a consequence, enables the creditors to sue for damages. The courts will disqualify a person for acting as a company director if he commits the offence of fraudulent trading because such a director is considered unfit for office., although disqualification is discretionary and the maximum period of disqualification is fifteen years.

The Court has a duty to disqualify a director for fraudulent trading under section 6 of the Company Directors Disqualification Act 1986, which reads as follows:

> "The court shall make a disqualification order for a period of not less than two years nor more than fifteen years against a person if, on application by the Secretary of State or at his discretion by the Official Receiver where a company is being wound up by the court in England and Wales, the court is satisfied that—
>
> (a) such person is or has been a director of a company which has at any time become insolvent (whether while he was a director or subsequently); and
>
> (b) his conduct as a director of the company (taken alone or together with his conduct as a director of any other company or companies) makes him unfit to be concerned in the management of a company."

Unfitness of a director is determined by the above section of the Company Directors Disqualification Act 1986 and other facts such as outstanding debts for VAT, PAYE and NIC, are considered important in determining unfitness.

The courts have seen cases where unfitness was determined by a breach of commercial immorality, by really gross incompetence, by recklessness and when a director was seen as a danger to the public if he were allowed to continue to be involved in the management of companies

Important factors in determining unfitness are:

• The amount of debts outstanding and not paying debts so as to continue trading;

- The number of companies that the director has been involved in and the number of liquidations he has been involved in;

- To what extent the accounts have been kept up to date and returns made to Companies House;

- The personal circumstances of the director.

Finally, it must be stated that there is an objective standard of unfitness, as per the dicta of Justice Gibson in the case Re Bath Glass [1988], when he said

> "To reach a finding of unfitness the court must be satisfied that the director has been guilty of a serious failure or serious failures, whether deliberately or through incompetence, to perform those duties of a director which are attendant on the privilege of trading through companies with limited liability. Any misconduct of the respondent qua director may be relevant."

This is an objective test because serious failure of a company can occur due to a director's incompetence. If a person is incapable of performing the duties of a director through incompetence, the standard will be breached and he will be disqualified similar to a competent but fraudulent director.

Companies House keeps a register of disqualified directors and this can be consulted by anyone.

3.6—Document Destruction

DOCUMENT DESTRUCTION IN BUSINESS

Being deeply involved with the figures as accountants and accounting technicians can often lead us to miss the importance of the very documents we use to get to the accounts we deal with.

When things go wrong, contemporary documents are of the utmost value. It is to documents that the legal people look with special care when there is any issue with accounts. Oral testimony alone is less reliable. Documents are the means of tracing a contemporary record going to the thing in issue. That is why no documents should be destroyed.

In certain cases, the destruction of documents is illegal. For example, a company officer who destroys or falsifies a document affecting the company's property or affairs is liable to prosecution under the Companies Act 1985, section 450, unless he can prove that he did not intend to deceive by doing so. Section 450 of the Companies Act states:

"Punishment for destroying, mutilating, etc, company documents.

(1) An officer of a company who

(a) destroys, mutilates or falsifies or is privy to the destruction, mutilation or falsification of a document affecting or relating to the company's property or affairs, or

(b) makes, or is privy to the making of a false entry in such a document,

is guilty of an offence, unless he proves that he had no intention to conceal the state of affairs of the company or to defeat the law.

(2) Such a person as above mentioned who fraudulently either parts with, alters or makes an omission in any such document or is privy to fraudulent parting with, fraudulent making of an omission in any such document, is guilty of an offence.

(3) A person guilty of an offence under this section is liable to imprisonment or a fine, or both.

(4) Section 732 (restriction on prosecutions), section 733 (liability of individuals for corporate default) and section 734 (criminal proceedings against unincorporated bodies) apply to an offence under this section.

(5) In this section "document" includes information recorded in any form.

And if a dispute has already arisen, it is very dangerous to destroy any documents. In some cases a deliberate decision to destroy documents if it is extremely likely that a dispute is soon to arise or after a dispute has arisen could make one liable under the criminal offence of obstructing or perverting the course of justice.

Anyway, missing documents usually leave tell-tale indications of their existence because they are often referred to in surviving documents. If the case goes to court, one has to list not only documents in one's possession, custody or power, but also those which were but are no longer.

Destruction of documents can lead to the case being found against you by inference. Such a case was the 1985 case of Infabrics versus Jaytex, a case of copyright infringement of prints for shirts It was discovered that after the case commenced, most of the invoices, stock records and similar documents had been destroyed.

The judge said:

> "I am not prepared to give the defendants the benefit of any doubt or to draw an inference in their favour where a document, if not destroyed, would have established the matter beyond doubt."

It speaks for itself.

Companies should have document retention policies and should not be haphazard as to what they keep and what they decide not to keep. It used to be the case that we could look to the Limitation Act 1980 for how long we should keep files, most professions keeping papers for at least six years. But the recent case of Brocklesby versus Armitage makes it possible now for someone to bring a case in respect of say, a bad piece of accounting advice, long after the six year limit.

What are the documents that the Companies Act mentions in section 450? Well, documents can include text messages and emails. In the Guinness case in 1986, Mr Saunders was charged with destroying a jottings book, some correspondence, some pages from an address book and a 1986 diary, among other things. They were seen to be documents. In this case the judge said

> "Section 450 is the part of the heavy artillery of the Companies Act. It carries a maximum of a seven year sentence. No other Companies Act offence carries a higher maximum sentence….This section (450) is also unusual in that it places the burden of making out the statutory defence on the defence. Under this section, the prosecution need merely prove that the documents destroyed affected or related to the company's property or affairs…The onus is then on the defendant to show that he had no intention to conceal the state of affairs of the company or to defeat the law."

The judge went on to decide that Mr Saunders' diary, etc. were documents as per section 450. He went on to say "Those words 'affecting or relating to the company's property or affairs' show that the embargo against destruction goes beyond the formal documents that are the company's documents, to the officer's private documents, provided they affect or relate to the company's property or affairs. In my judgement, the ordinary literal construction of the word 'document' is the correct one, it being the intention of the legislature to forbid all unjustifiable destruction of documents or other less formal documents, whether the company's documents or not, and whether in the company's possession or not". It couldn't have been stated more clearly.

Nowadays with advanced technology at our hands, it would be wise to preserve files using scanners and other electronic storage means rather than destroy them. A written policy on document destruction and retention, to be applied consistently, is a wise move.

3.7—Cartels

CARTELS

Cartel activity has become a criminal offence since the Enterprise Act 2002 which brought widespread changes to competition regulation in the UK. The punishment for operating cartels is now a maximum of five years imprisonment and/or a fine

A cartel is a group of companies which have entered into an agreement to fix their prices or to share the market so that they can raise prices by removing and/or reducing the competition around. There are price fixing cartels, bid-rigging cartels and market sharing cartels.

The prosecution of the cartel offence of market sharing against the bus companies Arriva plc and First-group plc is the most recent and indeed the first of the OFT fines under the new Act, and in this case the parties were found guilty and fined for engaging in a route-swapping cartel. Arriva was fined £318, 000 and First group was also fined but First-group's fine was dropped on appeal. The cartel offence was that the two bus companies had agreed between them to withdraw from certain bus routes in Leeds and Wakefield. They had had a meeting in a hotel and agreed that Arriva would withdraw five buses from two complete routes in return for First-group withdrawing from another two routes.

The Office of Fair Trading investigation into this cartel activity was triggered by an anonymous letter. Because First-group plc had co-operated with the Office of Fair Trading by becoming a whistle-blower as per the Enterprise Act, they were granted leniency. Arriva's fine was also reduced because Arriva also decided to co-operate

Market sharing cartels such as this are often an agreement to decide the market share each company is to enjoy and to decide which company will win which contract in order to maintain that market share. and is known as bid-rigging when it is to do with tendering for contracts

But cartel activity is nothing new; it is just the criminality of it that is new. in that under the Enterprise Act, not only will the guilty parties be fines but they can be imprisoned for up to five years. Persons found guilty will most likely be directors, being agents of the company.

There was the 1995 case of the Director of Fair Trading v Pioneer Concrete (UK) Ltd in which Pioneer Concrete (UK) Ltd had, at a senior level, put compliance procedures in place in order to comply with the Restrictive Trade Practices Act 1976, but some employees ignored these instructions and did otherwise. The company was prosecuted. The case went to the House of Lords and it was decided that the actions of a company's employees acting in the course of their employment, amounts to the the carrying on of business by the company. So, despite the compliance procedures being in place, the company was still liable for the acts of its employees in the same way as a company is liable when one of its employees makes a defective product .So what better compliance procedures would have prevented the employees from committing this offence? A good compliance programme will have four features—support of senior management, appropriate policy and procedures, staff training and regular evaluation of the programme's effectiveness; and the compliance manual should explain the legislation and give examples of prohibited conduct. The compliance programme should be much more than just a policy document and should regularly positively encourage whistle-blowing, so that the company can see the areas of risk and address those as a priority.

The Enterprise Act now allows criminal sanctions and so calls for individual responsibility for compliance with competition law. This is a compelling reason for the upgrade and instatement of compliance programmes.

To remind us, the Enterprise Act 2002, section 188 gives the definition of a cartel offence:

(1) An individual is guilty of an offence if he dishonestly agrees with one or more other persons to make or implement, or to cause to be made or implemented, arrangements of the following kind relating to at least two undertakings (A and B).

(2) The arrangements must be ones which, if operating as the parties to the agreement intend, would—

(a) directly or indirectly fix a price for the supply by A in the United Kingdom (otherwise than to B) of a product or service,

(b) limit or prevent supply by A in the United Kingdom of a product or service,

(c) limit or prevent production by A in the United Kingdom of a product,

(d) divide between A and B the supply in the United Kingdom of a product or service to a customer or customers,

(e) divide between A and B customers for the supply in the United Kingdom of a product or service, or

(f) be bid-rigging arrangements.

(3) Unless subsection (2)(d), (e) or (f) applies, the arrangements must also be ones which, if operating as the parties to the agreement intend, would-

(a) directly or indirectly fix a price for the supply by B in the United Kingdom (otherwise than to A) of a product or service,

(b) limit or prevent supply by B in the United Kingdom of a product.

(4) In subsections (2)(a) to (d) and (3), references to supply or production in the appropriate circumstances(for which see section 189).

(5) "Bid-rigging arrangements" are arrangements under which, in response to a request for bids for the supply of a product or service in the United Kingdom, or for the production of a product in the United Kingdom-

(a) A but not B may make a bid, or

(b) A and B may each make a bid but, in one case or both, only a bid arrived at in accordance with the arrangements.

(6) But arrangements are not bid-rigging arrangements if, under them, the person requesting bids would be informed of them at or before the time when a bid is made.

(7) "Undertaking" has the same meaning as in Part 1 of the 1998 Act.

3.8—Charity Bill

CHARITY LAW

The law affecting charities in England and Wales is about to change. When the Charity Bill of the 21st December becomes law, there will be new regulations for the preparation of accounts for charities.

The wheels of justice turn very slowly in this area of law and some professionals may remember the tax avoidance schemes of the 1970's, many of which abused charity law. The "Rossminster" case was one in which some professionals became millionaires by making tax avoidance schemes available to small business persons as well as to the wealthy. Using the charitable trust as an artificial vehicle for tax avoidance accounted for losses to the exchequer of £500 million each year during the 1970's. Apart from the status as 'charitable trust' being used as a tax avoidance vehicle there are also cases of charitable donations used as trustees' personal slush funds even though the 1993 Charities Act and the Charities SORP sought to bring accountability and transparency . Examples of cases that were investigated in 2003 and 2004 were the 'Victory Centre in London', Registered Charity No.800130 and the 'Light of the Word Ministries' Charity No. 803515.

Discovery of Charity fraud, like Corporate fraud, depends mainly on whistle blowers and recent research reveals that 26.3% of financial fraud discovery is through employees whistle-blowing, 18.6 % through internal audit, 15.4% by internal accounting control systems, and 11.5% by external audit, a staggering 71.8% of fraud discovery due to accounting systems and personnel., the remaining 28.2% of fraud discovery by law enforcement, by accident and through customers. This is why the Charity Bill is important

The 2004 Charity Bill to fully regulate charities was a long time coming.

The word 'charity' now has a legal definition for England and Wales.

A charity will not be registered by the Charity Commission unless it falls into one of these categories—prevention or relief of poverty; advancement of education, health, citizenship or community development, arts, heritage or science, amateur sport, human rights, conflict resolution or reconciliation, environmental protection or improvement, animal welfare, the relief of the young, old, sick, poor or homeless and other currently charitable purposes.

The Charities Bill has 72 clauses, and only clauses 27 and 28 of Chapter 6 concern the accounts and audit. Clause 27 says that an independent examination is required and Clause 28 is effectively a compulsory whistle-blowing duty by way of a written report to the Charities Commission, even if the independent examiner is no longer connected to that charity. As far as sports clubs and such recreational charities are concerned, they will not have charitable status and are deemed to be 'clubs'.

For the first time in English legislation, whistle-blowing will be fully protected in that auditors and independent examiners (and their staff) will have protection against suits of 'breach of confidence' and 'defamation'. This is a tremendous step taken to protect whistle-blowers; to date one can be sued for defamation even if the report only goes to the police. On the subject of whistle-blowing which the government is encouraging all of us to do, there are already many new laws that include compulsory whistle-blowing, the Pensions Act 2004, the Public Disclosure Act 1998, the Pensions Act 1995, the Children's Act 1989, the Financial Services and Markets Act 2000, Investment Regulations 2004 and the Money Laundering regulations.

However, the Charity Bill does not define exactly what a whistle-blower can report.

We need to know what exactly are the levels of materiality (in a large audit of £500 million turnover the level of materiality could be that anything under £10, 000 is not material enough to be queried) who exactly at the Charity Commission one must report to, what exactly are the steps that the Charity Commission have taken to safeguard the whistle blower's confidentiality. It needs to be precise. Employees of accountancy firms will be ruined if they fear dismissal for raising suspicions (statistics show that most whistle—blowers lose their jobs, are shunned, vilified and cannot find other jobs) and the firms will be in breach of the law if they fail to report suspicions or findings to the Charity Commission. If serious fraud is found, will it be for the Charity Commission to notify the police or should the accountant do so as well as notifying the Charity Commission?

The Bill is silent as to the penalty for non-reporting of financial irregularities but exempts such reporting from any "breach of confidentiality". Other aspects of law which would apply to this whistle-blowing would be the requirement to report under the money laundering regulation, the Public Disclosure Act for employees, your institute or association's guide to professional conduct and in matters of pensions. For instance, the Pensions Act 2004 imposes a duty to report breaches of the law. This duty applies to a trustee or manager of a pension scheme, a person involved with the administration of the pension scheme and a professional advisor, on pain of a civil penalty for non-disclosure.

But for lack of these details, this is indeed a very bright day for the conscientious whistle-blower and it remains to be seen whether legislation can force ethics into business.

3.9—European Company

THE EUROPEAN COMPANY

Abstract

The new European Company Statute has allowed the formation of a European company, the SE, *societas europaea*. The writer has researched the present position of company law of three member states, UK, France and Germany to find that, as far as shareholder rights, there is very little difference despite the embedded notion that companies in these three member states must be different because they have different legal systems. The analysis also reveals that worries about new employee rights are unfounded as employee rights are already being converged by the International Labour Organisation and by trans-national companies in these member states.

Since its formation, the European Union has been one outside force which has issued directives to harmonise member states and resulted in changes in corporate law. The incorporation of the OECD's internationally ratified code of corporate conduct, the Principles of Corporate Governance, has been another outside factor that has changed corporate law in different countries. The billions of US dollars lost through fraud, using the internet and tele-marketing, for example in trading in commodity futures contracts in stock markets the world over, has forced all countries to begin to standardise and share information There is a universal drive towards financial regulation in terms of monetary regulation, banking, securities and insurance regulation. This is global financial regulation to ensure markets that accurately reflect the forces of supply and demand free of disruptive and fraudulent activity and that violations are detected and prevented.

This new type, formed by the European Company Statute, is now available to commercial organisations with operations in more than one business state. The Statute came into force on 8th October 2004 and it is thought that companies with registered offices in one or more member states will form one European company, 'societas europaea' or SE, registered in one member state only, with one currency and under the law of that one state including matters of directors' duties, capital and capital maintenance, preparation of accounts, audit of accounts, publication of accounts and compliance penalties, instead of the costly liquidation process they must go through at present. There will be options on rules on board structure, rules on enhanced creditor and minority shareholder protection, currency of capital and currency in which accounts are to be drawn up. One currency will be used but it can be the Euro or another, not both.

Other costs to be saved will be administrative costs and taxation. Only the tax rules of the member state in which the SE is registered will apply, which will mitigate certain national taxes such as capital gains tax on cross-border re-structuring. Also, the Interest and Royalties Directive (2003/49/EC) which provides relief from with-holding tax on interest and royalty payments made between associated companies of different member states will be extended to the SE.

There is an Employee Involvement Directive attached to the SE which will require that each SE must have a negotiating body made up of managers and employees and which will enable all employees of the SE to adopt the highest standards of that SE's employees. So, for example, if the SE has an office in the UK and one in Latvia, the Latvian employees must have the same employment rights as the UK workers of the SE. The one factor that managers will be worried about is the potential for demands for European-wide collective bargaining.

UK, France and Germany—corporate law

The UK has a common law legal system and its company law vests control of the company primarily with company shareholders. Since 1844 the UK has had codified company law. since 1862 It has also had the London Stock Exchange which has played a role in regulating the financial market and ensuring shareholder primacy. Entry requirements are by the registration system. The law set broad limits for the allocation of control rights and left it to shareholders to change them within these limits. Minimum corporate capital and mandatory pre-emptive rights only became law later in the 1980's in response to the EU directive. There has always been litigation on company law issues and the UK has a fine body of case law, developed over many years. Recently, there has been consolidation of financial regulation and the Financial Services Authority is the financial regulating body of the UK. In an attempt to identify best legal practice the FSA is overseen by the International Monetary Fund, IMF, which is due to investigate its processes at regular intervals to advise on shortfalls in compliance areas.

Germany is a civil law country and has a formal legal system, and a General Commercial Code since 1861. It has developed its financial market largely internally with very little borrowing. Entry requirement is by the registration system. As to legal rights in company law, Germany leaves that to the law and not to the shareholders and company law dictates the rights and obligations of shareholders. There have been corporate governance rules in place well before other developed countries. There is modest company law litigation in Germany but the shareholder must first make a formal complaint to the supervisory board and not unless the matter is unresolved can it go to expensive litigation. Shareholders cannot litigate on behalf of the company, for example they cannot file a lawsuit against the BaFin regulatory body. Nevertheless Germany has a good amount of company case law for closed corporations.

German companies must have legal capital. Legal capital is the amount of capital that shareholders contribute to the company's assets when they acquire shares. The provision of legal capital is a big issue worldwide and regulation for, especially, stipulate minimum legal capital.

France, like Germany, has a civil law system and had its code de commerce, including a code on corporations, since 1807.Entry requirement is by the registration system and in France its highly mandatory company law determines the allocation of control rights. as well as stipulating the requirements for disclosing annual reports to company shareholders and the rights and responsibilities of shareholders.

There is little company law litigation in France, although shareholders can file lawsuits on behalf of the company.

In summary form, the similarities in company law between the UK, France and Germany are tables as follows:

SHAREHOLDER PROTECTION IN UK, FRANCE and GERMANY

	UK	France	Germany
Proxy by mail	yes	no	no
Cumulative voting	no	no	no
Blocking of shares	no	no	no-
Shareholder litigation	yes	yes	yes
Pre-emptive rights	yes	yes	no
Minority shareholder extraordinary meeting	yes	no	no
Change in company law	1998	1999	1998
Legal capital	yes	yes	yes
Capital decrease	no	no	no
Capital increase	no	no	no
Issuing authorised shares	no	Board	75%
Share repurchase	no	Regulator clearance required	no

3.10—Revealing Facts—Computer Crime Conference

REVEALING FACTS, PRESENTING EVIDENCE

The Computer and Internet Crime Conference 2004 which took place in London on the 30th and 31st March was a very necessary and timely conference. Ed Gibson, Agent of the FBI and now at the US Embassy, gave a presentation, the opening address made by the Assistant Commissioner of the Metropolitan Police Tarique Ghaffer.

Cybercrime such as internal and external hacking,[301] spam and computer viruses are widely acknowledged. Hacking is a growing problem for businesses which store confidential client and customer details electronically. External hackers can access confidential information, deface websites and steal financial company information.

Often, white collar crime is carried out by internal hackers but a larger proportion is through an outside source of security breaches. Employees can steal intellectual property from their employers. Intellectual property theft includes theft of e-mail address books, proposal documents used as marketing tools of solicitors, client databases and contact information. An indication on how serious the problem of white collar crime has become is the recent issue of "The Lawyer" which concentrated on the war on fraud and featured so many expert witnesses on white collar crime.

In what way are hackers' activities illegal? In the UK, it is a Data Protection Act offence to send unsolicited e-mails. There is a new European Commission Directive introduced in 2003 which makes it a criminal offence to send unsolicited e-mails. In the UK, this EC Directive has been implemented by the Privacy and Electronic Communications Regulations 2003. Will these regulations deter the sending of spam? Only if the source of the spam can be pin-pointed. Spam is particularly sinister. At present spammers have created virtual countries' websites[302] and virtual banks even. Spammers can blackmail companies. Current anti-spam devices can filter spam. Spam also damages businesses by taking up valuable business time in dealing with them and also because they can carry malicious viruses which cause even more major disruption to businesses. Viruses in a business's computer system are very costly in terms of data recovery, slow-down in productivity, necessary software upgrades as well as loss of business, not to mention the lowering of staff morale and the damage to the business reputation.[303] Internet filtering and e-mail monitoring software, anti-virus software, backing-up of data, and systems security policies are steps to controlling any potential damage. Staff policies must be put in place. The consequences of e-mail misuse must be set down in company policies.

If staff, for example, use e-mail to circulate ridicule about other staff members, this would amount to gross misconduct and dismissal. Such e-mails would amount to intrusions into employee privacy as per Article 8 of the European Convention on Human Rights.

When things go wrong, electronic documents, spread-sheets and e-mails hold the relevant material for litigation. More and more in court cases, evidence is found to be exclusively in electronic format. Forensic technology therefore needs to be a large part of the investigation. Forensic technology can recover, for example, deleted material. Forensic techniques can recover multiple versions of the same document from traces left on electronic media. Small differences between the altered versions can be used to build up a picture of what changes were made and when. The time-line of document creation and differing versions can be used to corroborate or disprove the chronology of events. Electronic evidence must prove the provenance of the material and the entire history of electronic material can be collated to produce robust evidence in court. The evidence must be collected under the UK evidence laws. Metadata is hidden within electronic files,

---

301 Deloitte-Touche Tohmatsu 2003 Global Security Survey. 41% breaches carried out by outside sources, 24% of unknown sources and 35% by internal means.

302 The Assistant Commisioner of the Metropolitan Police said that recently a virtual country called "The Principality of Ceylon" was set up as a website.

303 The world's most valuable brands are as follows:
Coco Cola $70.45 billion, Microsoft $65.17 billion, IBM $51.77 billion, GE $42.34 billion, Intel $31.11 billion, Nokia $29.44 billion, Disney $28.04 billion, McDonald's $ 24.70 billion, Marlboro $22.18 billion, Mercedes $21.37 billion.
Source: Interbrand 100 Best Global Brands 2003.

examples of which are entries in e-mails, dates embedded in documents and links to other files. In the case of e-mails, a full audit trail does exist and can be retrieved.

It is now possible for forensic technology specialists to use forensic tools to sift large volumes of material for electronic files and filter such material to reveal potential disclosable material. The volume of material in large businesses can be in tetabytes in size. This material can be sifted on live computer servers without disrupting business or alerting any suspects.

And when a fraud case comes before the courts, evidence is displayed in court on large computer screens to the jury and the defence, rather than on paper. However, most successful prosecutions rely on more than one stream of computer-derived evidence. What is needed is more than one independent stream of evidence, oral, paper and computer-derived, which collaborate each other. There are cases where e-mails have been forged and it is no longer the case that because it is in electronic form, it must be true. A recent case in the UK is <u>R v Bhatt (unreported) Canterbury Crown Court [2003]</u>. During the trial, the defence illustrated to the court how such an e-mail is forged by simulating a link to the Internet to create and explain how electronic communications can be manipulated in real time. The simulated e-mail was "read" with a standard e-mail client, Microsoft Outlook Express and it appeared no different from the paper e-mails that the prosecution offered as "proof" that the e-mail had in fact been sent by Bhatt. Only a full technical examination of the "headers" within Outlook Express system would have revealed the forgery, and only after a significant amount of network investigation.

So what can accounting departments do? A fraud policy can be formulated. A fraud policy is a formal, written statement recording the company's attitude to fraud. It should make clear that fraud is unacceptable and that all instances of suspected fraud will be treated seriously and dealt with swiftly. Staff should be required to indicate their awareness of and compliance with the fraud policy on an annual basis. The policy will serve a useful purpose as a deterrent. The company should also have a contingency plan setting out the steps that should be taken in the event that fraud is suspected. This plan should be known to all staff.

3.11—International Accounting Standards

A FLAVOUR OF THE FORTHCOMING REPORT AND ACCOUNTS OF LISTED COMPANIES COMPULSORILY TO BE PREPARED USING INTERNATIONAL ACCOUNTING STANDARDS AS FROM JANUARY 2005 AND THE AUDIT STATEMENT ACCOMPANYING IT.

From January 2005 all UK listed companies must produce their financial statements using the International Accounting Standards.

There is only one format for the Balance Sheet, a choice from two formats for the Income Statement, a choice from two formats for Statement of Recognised Gains and Losses and one format for the Cash-Flow statement.

Example of an IAS Balance Sheet:

ABC Group—Balance Sheet as at 31 December 2006

(in thousands of currency units)

	2006	2006	2005	2005
ASSETS			x	
Non-current assets	x		x	
Property, Plant and Equipment	x		x	
Goodwill	x		x	
Manufacturing licences	x		x	
Investments in associates	x		x	
Other financial assets	x		x	
	x	x	x	x
Current assets	x		x	
Inventories	x		x	
Trade and other receivables	x		x	
Prepayments	x		x	
Cash and cash equivalents	x		x	
		x		x
Total assets		x		x
EQUITY AND LIABILITIES				
Capital and Reserves				
Issued Capital	x		x	
Reserves	x		x	
Accumulated profits/(losses)	x		x	
		x		x
Minority interest	x		x	
Non-current liabilities				
Interest bearing loans	x		x	
Deferred tax	x		x	
Retirement benefit obligation	x		x	
		x		x
Current liabilities				
Trade and other payables	x		x	
Short-term borrowings	x		x	
Current portion of interest bearing borrowings	x		x	
Warranty provision	x		x	
		x		x
Total equity and liabilities	x		x	

ABC GROUP—INCOME STATEMENT FOR THE YEAR ENDED 31 DECEMBER 2006

(illustrating the classification of expenses by function)

(in thousands of currency units)

	2006	2006	2005	2005
Revenue	x		x	
Cost of sales		(x)		(x)
Gross profit		x		x
Other operating income	x		x	
Distribution costs	(x)		(x)	
Administrative expenses	(x)		(x)	
Other operating expenses	(x)		(x)	
Profit from operations		x		x
Finance cost		(x)		(x)
Income from associates	x		x	
Profit before tax	x		x	
Income tax expense		(x)		(x)
Profit after tax		x		x
Minority interest	(x)		(x)	
Net profit from ordinary activities	x		x	
Extraordinary items		x		x
Net profit for the period	x		x	

NB: Dividends do not show under IAS but are in the memoranda. Note that this is an illegal way to show dividends under Companies Act.

ABC GROUP—INCOME STATEMENT FOR THE YEAR ENDED 31 DECEMBER 2006

(illustrating the classification of expenses by nature)

(in thousands of currency units)

	2006	2006	2005	2005
Revenue	x		x	
Other operating income	x		x	
Changes in inventories of finished goods and work in progress		(x)		(x)
Work performed by the enterprise and capitalised	x		x	
Raw material and consumables used		(x)		(x)
Staff costs		(x)		(x)
Depreciation and amortisation expense	(x)		(x)	
Other operating expenses	(x)		(x)	
Profit from operations		x		x
Finance cost		(x)		(x)
Income from associates	x		x	
Profit before tax	x		x	
Income tax expense		(x)		(x)
Profit after tax		x		x
Minority interest	(x)		(x)	
Net profit or loss from ordinary activities	x		x	
Extraordinary items		x		x
Net profit for the period	x		x	

ABC GROUP–STATEMENT OF CHANGES IN EQUITY FOR THE YEAR ENDED 31 DECEMBER 2006

(in thousands of currency units)

	Share capital	Share premium reserve	Reval-uatiosn reserve	Transl-ation reserve	Accum-ulated	Total
Balance at 31 December 2004	x	x	x	(x)	x	
Changes in accounting policy					(x)	(x)
Restated balance	x	x	x	(x)	x	x
Surplus on revaluation of properties		x				x
Deficit on revaluation of investments		(x)				(x)
Currency translation differences				(x)		(x)
Net gains and losses not recognised in the income statement			x	(x)		x
Net profit for the period					x	x
Dividends					(x)	(x)
Issue of share capital	x	x				x
Balance at 31 December 2005	x	x	x	x	x	x
Deficit on revaluation of properties			(x)			(x)
Surplus on revaluation of investments			x			x
Currency translation differences				(x)		(x)
Net gains and losses not recognised in the income statement			(x)	(x)		(x)
Net profit for the period					x	x
Dividend					(x)	(x)
Issue of share capital	x	x				x
Balance at 31 December 2006	x	x	x	x	x	x

ABC GROUP—STATEMENT OF RECOGNISED GAINS AND LOSSES FOR THE YEAR ENDED 31 DECEMBER 2006

(in thousands of currency units)

	2006	2006	2005	2005
Surplus/(deficit) on revaluation of properties		(x)		x
Surplus/(deficit) on revaluation of investments	x		(x)	
Exchange differences on translation of the financial statements of foreign entities	(x)		(x)	
Net gains not recognised in the income statement		x		x
Net profit for the period	x		x	
Total recognised gains and losses	x		x	
Effect of changes in accounting policy			x	

THE UK situation at present (2003)

At present there are nine Statements of Standard Accounting Practice (SSAP's) in force in the UK. They are as follows:

SSAP 4	Government grants
SSAP 5	VAT
SSAP 9	Stocks and long-term investments
SSAP 13	Research and development
SSAP 17	Post Balance Sheet events
SSAP 19	Investment properties
SSAP 20	Foreign currency translation
SSAP 21	Leases and hire purchase
SSAP 25	Segmental reporting.

There are also 19 Financial Reporting Standards (FRS's)in force in the UK. They are:

FRS 1	Cash flow statements
FRS 2	Subsidiary undertakings
FRS 3	Reporting financial performance
FRS 4	Capital instruments
FRS 5	Reporting substance
FRS 6	Mergers and acquisitions
FRS 7	Fair values in acquisition accounting
FRS 8	Related party disclosures
FRS 9	Associates and joint ventures
FRS 10	Goodwill and intangible assets
FRS 11	Impairment of fixed assets

FRS 12	Provisions
FRS 13	Derivatives
FRS 14	Earnings per share
FRS 15	Tangible fixed assets
FRS 16	Current tax
FRS 17	Retirement benefits
FRS 18	Accounting policies
FRS 19	Deferred tax.

To assist in preparing accounts under International Accounting Standards, it would be useful to note the following similarities with the UK SSAP's and FRS's:

IAS		similar to FRS/SSAP
1	Presentation of Financial Statements	FRS 18
2	Inventories	SSAP 9
7	Cash flow statements	FRS 1
10	Events after the Balance Sheet date	SSAP 17
12	Income taxes	FRS 19
20	Accounting for government grants	SSAP 4
22	Business combinations	FRS 6
26	Accounting for retirement benefit plans	FRS 17
27	Consolidated Financial Statements	FRS 7
32	Financial instruments—disclosure and presentation	FRS 4
36	Impairment of assets	FRS 11
37	Provisions, contingent liabilities and contingent assets	FRS 12
38	Intangible assets	FRS 10
39	Financial instruments—recognition and measurement	FRS 4
40	Investment properties	SSAP 19

It is to be noted that even though all UK accounts for listed companies must be prepared using International Accounting Standards as from January 2005, these accounts will not meet the requirements of the UK Companies Act 1985 and so, for taxation purposes, the usual tax accounts will also have to be prepared until such time as the Companies Act is changed as to its requirements.

In January 2003 the Institute of Chartered Accountants in England and Wales (ICAEW) issued a technical release (Audit 01/03) in which they recommended that auditors should from now on include the following text (or similar text in effect) in their audit reports:

"This report is made solely to the issuer's members, as a body, in accordance with section 235 of the Companies Act 1895. Our audit work has been undertaken so that we might state to the issuer's members those matters we are required to state to them in an auditor's report and for no other purpose. To the fullest extent permitted by law, we do not accept or assume responsibility to anyone other than the issuer and the issuer's members as a body, for our audit work, for this report, or for the opinions we have formed"

It remains to be seen whether cases of negligent misstatement come to court after 2005 when the IAS kicks in and where securities are being admitted to the Official List of the UK Listing Authority and the offering document contains accounts so qualified and whether this ICAEW technical release would be subject to the test of reasonableness imposed by section 2 of the Unfair Contract Terms Act 1977.

3.12—Serious Fraud Office

THE SERIOUS FRAUD OFFICE

The Serious Fraud Office (SFO) came into being in April 1988. At the same time every fraud squad in the United Kingdom became part of what is now known as the Fraud Investigation Group (FIG) and the FIG works under the Crown Prosecution Service. These fraud squads are policed by policemen who have volunteered for the positions.

One of the findings of the Fraud Trials Committee Report (the Roskill Report) was that the system for bringing frauds to trial was poor. The opening section of the Roskill Report set out the scale of the problem: "The public no longer believes that the legal system in England and Wales is capable of bringing perpetrators of serious frauds expeditiously and effectively to book. The overwhelming weight of evidence laid before us suggests that the public is right .In relation to such crimes and to the skilful and determined criminals who commit them, the present legal system is archaic, cumbersome and unreliable. At every stage during investigation, preparation, committal, pre-trial review and trial, the present arrangements offer an open invitation to blatant delay and abuse. While petty frauds, clumsily committed, are likely to be detected and punished, it is all too likely that the largest and cleverly executed crimes escape unpunished. The Government has encouraged and continues to encourage ordinary families to invest their savings in the equity markets, particularly in the equities of formerly state-owned enterprises. If the Government cherishes the vision of an "equity owning democracy", then it faces an inescapable duty to ensure that financial markets are honestly managed, and that transgressors in these markets are swiftly and effectively discovered, convicted and punished. Self-regulatory mechanisms designed to encourage honest practices are now coming into force. Where these mechanisms are abused, the law must deliver retribution, swift and sure."

The Report then continued with over one hundred recommendations, only one of which has not so far been implemented—the proposal for a frauds trial tribunal to replace trial by jury in cases of complex fraud.

The most important recommendation of the Roskill Report was for a "formation of a single, unified organisation responsible for all the functions of detection, investigation and prosecution of serious fraud. It stated that the advantages of such an organisation would be that fewer serious frauds would be allowed to escape prosecution by slipping through the net of a series of independent organisations working in this field (for example, the Fraud Investigation Group, the Department of Trade and Industry, the Inland Revenue, HM Customs and Excise) and that this would help investigations to lead to more effective prosecutions.

After the Roskill Report there was the Criminal Justice Act 1987 which created the Serious Fraud Office. The purpose of the Criminal Justice Act was to make further provisions for the investigation of and trials for fraud and for connected purposes. It set down the procedure for transferring a fraud case from the Magistrate's Court to the Crown Court. Under the Act, notice of transfer to the Crown Court has to be issued before the Magistrate's hearing starts. Pre-trial reviews were now treated as part of the trial.

The judge now had very wide powers. He could decide whether a case should be discharged. He could now make orders for the production of a case statement from the prosecution and order defendants to produce statements setting out in broad terms the nature of their defence and where they take issue with the prosecution. He could now decide the admissibility of evidence and questions of law relating to the case. He could adjourn a preparatory hearing from time to time, order the production of charts and visual aids to help the jury in their comprehension of the case later on and he now has the power at trial to refer back to the cases disclosed at the preparatory hearing if those cases are suddenly altered so that the jury would be alerted that one or both sides had decided to take a different course.

These are the laid out rules relating to the trials of serious fraud cases which the SFO brings. The SFO does not refer or defer to the Director of Public Prosecutions and is only responsible to the Attorney General.

After operating for five years, there was a report, published in 1994, called the GRAHAM Report, which was carried out by the Royal Commission on the Criminal Justice System and included the SFO . The report was a feasibility study into the merger of the SFO and the FIG. The FIG had been established in 1985 under the aegis of the Director of Public Prosecutions. It was the FIG which began the use of a multi-disciplinary approach to fraud investigation used today by the SFO. The only difference between the two agencies is that the SFO has the use of section 2, Criminal Justice Act, for compulsory interviews of defendants. The Report was in favour of the continuation of the SFO as a separate agency. It established that 40% of the FIG's work was not serious or complex fraud and recommended that in FIG cases of serious and complex fraud should be merged with the SFO's caseload.

Later, a Committee was set up to examine whether the SFO should be preserved as an agency. This Committee reported (the DAVIE Report of 1995) ; it said……"The SFO has developed a speciality which needs to be preserved and not diluted. The mere fact that two organisations are involved in the prosecution of fraud in this area is not, of itself, a conclusive reason for change. There have been a number of developments since the establishment of the SFO and indeed a number of improvements in both the Fraud Division and the SFO since the GRAHAM Report. The Committee believes there is scope for building on these and for introducing further changes in order to meet the requirements identified."

The Report identified an urgent change needed which was the relatively unstructured way in which cases were assigned between the SFO and the Crown Prosecution Service. If the SFO had a full workload it would generally accept the biggest cases. The DAVIE Report stated that this ad hoc approach was unsatisfactory and needed to be addressed quickly. It proposed a new set of criteria including the lowering from £5 million to £1 million of the SFO's financial threshold to be used when assessing if a case was suitable for the SFO.

It recommended that the SFO should continue. The Report was accepted on 31st March 1995 by Sir Nicholas Lyell on behalf of the government when he said…

"…in its seven years in existence to date, the SFO has brought to trial one hundred and forty one major cases including three hundred and nine defendants of whom one hundred and ninety one have been convicted. In over 75% of cases brought to trial by the SFO, at least one person has been convicted, usually the principal defendant."

How does the SFO decide which cases to take?

The statutory criteria for accepting cases came to be formalised in the light of criteria agreed by the law officers following the DAVIE Report on the merits and feasibility of merging all or part of the Fraud Divisions of the Crown Prosecution Service (CPS) and the SFO. The key criterion for deciding whether the SFO should accept a case is that the suspected fraud is such that the direction of the investigation should be in the hands of those responsible for the prosecution. Factors taken into account are–

-   cases where the monies at risk are at least one million pounds;

-   cases likely to give rise to national publicity and widespread public concern;

-   cases requiring highly specialised knowledge of stock exchange practices or regulated markets;

-   cases with an international dimension;

-   cases where legal, accountancy and investigative skills need to be brought together; and

-   cases which are complex and in which the use of Section 2 powers may be appropriate.

The Serious Fraud Office is unique in the criminal justice system. It investigates allegations of crime and it takes the decision to prosecute and pursue cases through the courts.

3.13—The Fraud Offence

THE FRAUD OFFENCE in the United Kingdom

Introduction

The UK is to have a fraud offence on its statute books, this having been recommended by the Law Commission. This new offence may appease the public who are dismayed by the rising rate of "fraud". The new offence will be based on misrepresentation, non-disclosure and abuse of trust. There is to be a new offence also of obtaining services dishonestly and this offence will not require the proof of misrepresentation and of non-disclosure as the fraud offence will require.

The Law Commission had rejected the offence of conspiracy to defraud, stating that conspiracy is too close to dishonesty.

But let us unpack this new fraud offence and compare it with the old offence of conspiracy to defraud to see exactly what the differences are that warrant a new offence of fraud.

THE FRAUD OFFENCE

1. Any person who, with intent to make a gain or to cause loss or to expose another to the risk of loss, dishonestly

    (1)   makes a false representation, or

    (2)   fails to disclose information to another person which

        (a)   he or she is under a legal duty to disclose, or

        (b)   is of a kind which the other person trusts him or her to disclose, and is information which in the circumstances it is reasonable to expect him or her to disclose, or

    (3)   abuses a position in which he or she is expected to safeguard, or not to act against, the financial interests of another person, and does so without the knowledge of that person or of anyone acting on that person's behalf,

    should be guilty of an offence of fraud.

2. Fraud should be triable either way, and on conviction on indictment should be punishable with up to ten years imprisonment.

OBTAINING SERVICES BY DECEPTION

3. Any person who by any dishonest act obtains services in respect of which payment is required, with intent to avoid payment, should be guilty of an offence of obtaining services dishonestly.

4. The offence of obtaining services dishonestly should be triable either way, and on conviction on i8ndictment should be punishable with up to five years' imprisonment.

5. All the deception offences under the Theft Acts 1968-1996, and conspiracy to defraud, should be abolished."

The new fraud offence has the *mens rea* of intention on the part of the defendant. Conspiracy to defraud is the attempting to defraud and the incitement to defraud—the same elements as the fraud offence. The fraud offence intends that all the deception offences under the Theft Acts and conspiracy to defraud will be abolished. But what of the cases where the offence occurred abroad?

At present the charge of conspiracy to defraud is the most used charge by the Serious Fraud Office because in a conspiracy to defraud charge it is only necessary to prove the essentials of a charge. (Tax and VAT evasion schemes, for example, are particularly likely to be caught by conspiracy to defraud charge). To bring complexity to the charge, conspiracy to defraud can occur over more than one territory. An agreement formed in one territorial area may be aimed at people in another area or other areas, or may reach into such areas in the course of its performance or plot. This is an aspect of criminal conspiracy that has made it difficult to relate to the theory of territoriality which has so much influence on common law rules concerning the administration of criminal justice. The Criminal Justice Act 1993 makes provision for such problems by making provision about the jurisdiction of courts in England and Wales in relation to certain offences of dishonesty and blackmail.

It states that Group A offences are offences under the Theft Act 1968, under the Theft Act 1978, under the Forgery and Counterfeiting Act 1981 and under the common law offence of cheating in relation to the public revenue. It states that Group B offences are conspiracy to commit Group A offences, conspiracy to defraud, attempting to commit a Group A offence and incitement to commit a Group A offence. It does not matter whether a guilty person is British or not, as long as the offence had effect in England and Wales and gives extended jurisdictions over certain conspiracies. If persons conspire to defraud and that fraud is to be committed abroad, as long as they conspire in the UK, they can be charged with an offence, although they planned to commit the offence in other countries. Before the Criminal Justice Act 1993, they would be charged in the UK only if they conspired to defraud in the UK, even if the conspiracy to defraud occurred abroad.

THE NEW FRAUD OFFENCE ADJUSTS THIS 1993 ACT. For instance, it deletes from section 2 Criminal Justice Act 1993, the parts relating to sections 15 and 16 of the Theft Act 1968 but it still leaves the following in section 2, namely that Group A offences are—

Section 1 Theft Act–theft;

Section 17 Theft Act–false accounting,

Section 19 Theft Act–false statements by company directors,

Section 20 (2) Theft Act–procuring execution of valuable security by deception,

Section 21 Theft Act–blackmail, and

Section 22 Theft Act—handling stolen goods.

This is ambiguous; it means that theft is not fraud, that false accounting is not fraud, that false statements by company directors are not frauds, that procuring execution of valuable security by deception is not a fraud, etc. We know that this cannot be so.

The case of Barings Futures (Singapore) pte Ltd v Deloitte and Touche is a case that illustrates the false statement by a company director. If an accountant signs off incorrect audits, those statements are false statements and a fraud.

In the UK, the common law offence of conspiracy to defraud can technically be committed by a limited company, even though this has not occurred since 1944 in the case of R v ICR Haulage Ltd[304] in which the limited company and nine individuals were charged with conspiracy to defraud by overcharging and in the case of Director of Public Prosecutions v Kent and Sussex Contractors Ltd[305] in which Lord Caldecote CJ said "The real point we have to decide ..is whether a company is capable of an act of will or of a state of mind, so as to be able to form an intention to deceive or to have

---

304 [1944]KB 551
305 [1944] KB 146

knowledge of the truth or falsity of the statement…The offences created by regulation are those of doing something with intent to deceive or of making a statement known to be false in a material particular. There was ample evidence on the facts as stated in the special case, that the company, by the only people who could act or speak or think for it, had done both these things, and I can see nothing in any of the authorities to which we have been referred which requires us to say that a company is incapable of being found guilty of the offences with which the respondents have been charged." And Justice McNaughten said in the same case, "It is true that a corporation can only have knowledge and form an intention through its agents, but circumstances may be such that the knowledge and intention of the agent must be imputed to the body corporate…If the responsible agent of a company, acting within the scope of his authority, puts forward on its behalf a document which he knows to be false and by which he intends to deceive, I apprehend that according to the authorities that my Lord has cited, his knowledge and intention must be imputed to the company".

On this matter of fraud by a company, the Bill is silent

Now let us look at the mechanics of recording crime to see what will result from a new fraud offence. Even in 1999, The New Law Journal editorial (21 May) said that "…there is not even an authoritative measure of the extent of fraud in the UK. Police and private sector estimates vary from £400 million a year to £5 billion and the Association of British Insurers puts the total at nearer £16 billion….Even within the police there is no agreed definition or consistent recording practice. The City of London Police statistics are analysed by value according to type of fraud. The West Yorkshire Police figures cover 6 monthly periods and are broken down…and analysed by victim type…,"

The DTI submitted that 1000 persons were charged in 1993 with the offence "conspiracy to defraud" and that 321 were convicted in the UK.[306] In the UK Commons Hansard Written answers for 25 January 2001, the figures given for the common law offence of conspiracy to defraud were 1003, 1069,1119,1175,1174 persons charged during the years 1995,1996,1997,1998 and 1999 respectively and that the actual convictions were 383, 477,500,466,420 respectively for those same years. In a population of over 63 million persons, this is hardly cause for alarm and the charge of conspiracy to defraud cannot be the culprit for the extent of fraud nor for the lack of conviction for fraud crimes.

The Home Office Counting Rules for Recording crime give the standard ways in which the Home Office counts fraud and forgery for the UK. For Home Office statistics, the following are counted as "fraud and forgery":[307]

- frauds by company directors, (recorded as crime type 51—maximum sentence 7 years);
- false accounting,(recorded as crime type 52-maximum sentence seven years);
- cheque and credit card fraud,(recorded as crime type 53A);
- other frauds,(recorded as crime type 53B);
- bankruptcy and insolvency offences,(recorded as crime type 55-maximum sentence seven years);
- forgery of drug prescription,(recorded as crime type 60-maximum sentence ten years);
- other forgery,(recorded as crime type 61-maximum sentence ten years); and
- fraud, forgery associated with vehicle or driver records(recorded as crime type 814-maximum sentence two years).

These offences counted under the eight above headings, comprise offences under the Theft Act 1968, Companies Act 1985, Protection of Depositors Act 1963, Theft Act 1978, Criminal Justice Act 1987,Fraudulent Mediums Act

306 Memorandum submitted by Dr Elaine M Drage, Director, Trade Policy 2,DTI, to Select Committee on International Development, 2000.
307 Home Office Research Development & Statistics Directorate, April 2003.

1951,Public Stores Act 1875,Post Office Act 1953,Stamp Duties Management Act 1891, Agricultural Credits Act 1928, Gaming Act 1845Law of Property Act 1925, Land Registrations Act 1925, Criminal Justice Act 1988,Social Security Administration Act 1992, Computer Misuse Act 1990, Enterprise Act 2002,Deeds of Arrangement Act 1914, Insolvency Act 1986,Forgery and Counterfeiting Act 1981,Mental Health Act 1983, Coinage Act 1971,Hallmarking Act 1973, Protecting the Euro Against Counterfeiting Regulations 2001(SI 3948/2001),Road Traffic Act 1988, Vehicle Excise and Registration Act 1994, Transport Act 1968, Goods Vehicles Act 1995 and Road Traffic Regulation Act 1984.

The new fraud offence is silent as to whether it makes the relevant sections of all these acts repealed, except that it states that:

The Fraud Act will

(1) abolish the common law offence of conspiracy to defraud, Criminal Justice Act 1988;

(2) the Visiting Forces Act 1952 section 3, will have inserted "the Fraud Act 2002" in paragraph 3;(this is not included in the Home Office list under fraud);

(3) the Theft Act 1968 will have omitted s 15 and 16, and sections 24 and 25 will be altered;

(4) the Criminal Law Act 1977 will omit section 5(2) ; (this is not counted by the Home Office as fraud);

(5) the Theft Act 1978 will omit section 4(2)(a) and 5(1);

(6) the Limitation Act 1980 will have section 5(b) altered ; (this is not counted as fraud by the Home Office);

(7) the Finance Act 1982 section 11(1) will change ; (this is not counted by the Home Office as fraud);

(8) the Nuclear Materials Act 1983 section 1(1)(d) is altered;(this does not feature in Home Office Counting rules;

(9) the Police and Criminal Evidence Act 1984 section 1(8)is altered; and

(10)   the Criminal Justice Act 1987 section 12 is omitted ;(this is on the Home Office Counting rules);

In total, the new Fraud Act will repeal Theft Act 1968 sections 15, 15A, 15B, 16, 18(1), 20(3), 24A(3), Criminal Law Act section 5(2), Nuclear Material Offences Act 1983 section 1(1)(d), Criminal Justice Act 1987 section 12, Criminal Justice Act 1993section 1(2)(b) and 2(b),5(b),6(1) and 6(5)., Theft Amendment Act 1996 sections 1,3(2) and 4 and Criminal Justice and Court Services Act 2000, schedule 6 paragraph 1.

This will not clear up the confusion of recording fraud by the Home Office, not to mention the confusion that occurs when various police forces count crimes in various ways and so the public will be none the wiser about the true extent of fraud.

According to the Home Office Counting Rules, the maximum ten year sentence now applies to the offences of

53/1—False statements by company directors,

53/4—Giving false information knowingly or recklessly when applying for a Confidentiality Order, etc.

60/21—Forgery of a drug prescription or copying a false drug prescription

60/22—Using a false drug prescription or a copy of ac false drug prescription

61/21—Forgery or copying false instrument (other than drug prescription)

61/27—Possessing materials or dies to make counterfeit coins or note

61/31—Counterfeiting etc of dies or marks (other forgery etc)

Conspiracy to defraud at common law also carries the maximum of ten years sentence.

It can be argued that since conspiracy to defraud charge was only used in just over one thousand instances, consistently, in recent years' figures, that, the offence is not the problem. It may be that the problem is one of evidence gathering, entrapment and breaches through inadequacies of following the PACE guidelines and prosecution presentation. The new fraud offence would still leave many other "fraud" offences under various statutes or the status quo. Are conspiracy to defraud trials lengthy because of the charge used[308] or because of prosecution defects in bringing a case to trial without breaching PACE or breaching the Human Rights Act 1998?

3.14—Money-laundering and trafficking
MONEY LAUNDERING RULES USED TO TACKLE THE TRAFFICKING OF WOMAN AND CHILDREN

The definition of trafficking in human beings in the United Nations Protocol to Prevent, Suppress and Punish Trafficking in Persons, especially Women and Children(2000) states:

"1. (a) 'Trafficking in persons' shall mean the recruitment, transportation, transfer, harbouring or receipt of persons, by means of threats or use of force or other forms of coercion, of abduction, of fraud, of deception, of the abuse of power or of a position of vulnerability or of the giving or receiving of payments of benefits to achieve the consent of a person having control over another person, for the purposes of exploitation. Exploitation shall include, at a minimum, the exploitation of the prostitution of others or other forms of sexual exploitation, forced labour or services, slavery or practices similar to slavery, servitude or the removal of organs. The consent of the victim of trafficking in persons to the intended exploitation set forth in sub-paragraph (a) of this article shall be irrelevant where any of the means set forth in sub-paragraph (a) have been used.

(b) The recruitment, transportation, transfer, harbouring or receipt of a child for the purpose of exploitation shall be considered 'trafficking in persons' even if this does not involve any of the means set forth in sub-paragraph(a) of this article.

(c) 'Child' shall mean any person under eighteen years of age."

The United Nations estimate that 1.2 million children are trafficked each year. The reasons for trafficking people are mainly for prostitution, domestic servitude, to beg on the streets, for cheap labour, for restaurant work, as drugs contraband mules and to carry out benefit fraud."

The Police have decided to tackle the slavery of trafficking women and children by establishing dedicated financial investigation units to gather evidence that will convict gang-masters and organised criminals because it is very difficult to convict such criminals using the Sexual Offences Act or immigration laws .The Sexual Offences Act 2003 includes a specific offence of trafficking within the UK. They are going down the financial route because they have very little intelligence that can help them to catch the traffickers and because the UK Government has decided to opt out of the EU Directive on Illegal Immigration and Trafficking.

It has been estimated that people trafficking is the second most profitable crime after the trafficking of guns and drugs. The police feel that disruption is the most effective way of stopping this crime and that seizing the proceeds of crime and the suspected proceeds of crime is the most effective means of disruption. There have already been convictions for document forgery. There is a Serious Organised Crime Agency proposed and part of their agenda will be people trafficking offences. There is already a Trafficking Guide published for Chief Police Officers.

We in the accountancy profession can help to detect trafficking by being vigilant on the PAYE side, spotting large tranches of very low-paid workers in the accounts records, spotting payments to lorry companies in a non-transport company's records, spotting one-off payments to someone abroad, spotting mass purchase of cheap clothing and footwear, spotting money being deposited in many different branches of the company's bank, far away from the place of

308 Barbara Ann Hocking, "The fame, fortunes and future of the 'rump of the common law': Conspiracy to defraud and English Law", Justice Studies, Queensland, Australia 4058.

business, spotting sudden rises in income, spotting different modes of personal drawings, etc. It may seem far removed from the accountancy profession, but technicians have trained eyes and as the first port of call for the preparation of accounts, are better placed to discover such crimes than accountants.

What sort of accounts can reveal such organised crime? Any. From newsagents, tobacconists, doctors' accounts (sudden increase in patients), family firms with many low paid workers or much regular cash withdrawals, companies suddenly renting large cheap accommodation on the pretext of storage, sudden large purchases of cheap foodstuffs, clothing and footwear, sudden rises of income in any business from pornography retail outlets, massage parlours to market traders to new small subsidiaries abroad.

The UK's Proceeds of Crime Act 2002 cuts through all persons and companies and all crimes. It contains definitions of money laundering. A person commits an offence of concealing, disguising, converting or transferring criminal property. Criminal property is that which is had from criminal conduct or that which represents the benefit from criminal conduct and the offender knows or suspects that it constitutes or represents such a benefit. No offence is made if the person concerned makes a timely disclosure of the facts to the police, a customs officer or a person nominated for the purpose by the person's employer. It is also an offence to acquire, use or have possession of criminal property.

3.15—Fraud conference 2004

THE 2004 INTERNATIONAL FRAUD CONFERENCE IN LONDON

The 2004 Annual Fraud Conference entitled "STRATEGIES TO COMBAT FRAUD" took place this week in London, England. It was attended by fraud specialist investigators, police, regulatory agencies and corporations' senior compliance personnel.

I discovered that it was estimated by some that fraud in the UK was over £45 BILLION in 2003, of which a total of £7 billion was telecoms fraud. It was disconcerting to hear that the UK has the highest percentage of "card-not-present" (ie, spending by credit card on the internet) fraud in the world and also that the UK has the highest percent of internet gambling in the world, 60% of all internet gambling!

The most important bit of information is that most fraud is "an inside job". This means that corporations must put in place fraud policies, whistle-blowing policies and ethics policies, not forgetting to physically secure the corporate computer network and to control internet access.

One of the subjects at the Conference is the UK's newly formed Assets Recovery Agency. This new agency was formed after the UK's Proceeds of Crime Act 2002 came into force. The Proceeds of Crime Act 2002 significantly extended the scope of money laundering offences and introduced various reporting requirements and established the Assets Recovery Agency.

The Assets Recovery Agency is a non-ministerial department that is accountable to the Home Secretary. Its main role is to conduct investigations resulting in the retrieval of the proceeds of crime, the recovery of such proceeds by civil proceedings; and the taxing of criminal gains. The Civil Recovery Scheme empowers the Director of the Assets Recovery Agency to sue in the High Court to recover proceeds of unlawful conduct. The Director is able to apply to the High Court for an interim receiving order and freeze suspected assets that will ten be managed by an independent receiver. The Director will have to have a strong, arguable case that the property is derived from crime. A court may make a compensation order in favour of victims of crime, but in practice these are only made in straightforward cases and involve loss of control.

This new agency is seen as a useful weapon against fraud because it uses the civil court where the proof of the crime is on a balance of probability instead of the criminal conviction needing a proof beyond reasonable doubt. Financial institutions have faced particular difficulties in relation to efforts to combat money laundering. Section 333 of the Proceeds of Crime Act makes "tipping off" an offence.

Another subject discussed at the Conference at which Ros Wright, SFA Director, Robert Wardle, SFO Director and George Staples, former SFO Director spoke, was the very practical subject of how fraud can be detected in a computerised system of accounts. **Some of the classic tests for fraud are as follows:**

(a) **Sales Allowance and Credit Notes.**

Analyse customer accounts and identify all allowances and credit notes for both product and non-product items. Calculate the ratio of product A and non-product B as a percentage of sales. Print out customers by reference to the ratio of A/B, B/C, and (A+B)/C.

(b) **Pricing.**

Identify the lowest prices charged (for a selection of products) to customers (including intra-company transactions). Print details of customers with the lowest prices or lowest gross margins.

(c) **Free Issues and Consignment Stocks.**

Identify free issues (consignment stocks, free samples, warranty replacements) to customers. Summarise these as a ratio of free issues : total sales.

(d) **Sales of Scrap Goods (and Fixed Assets)**

Identify sales of scrap (raw materials, components, finished goods), summarise by customer : showing product description, date and price.

(e) **Bad Debt Write-offs.**

Identify bad debt write-offs. Summarise by customer and authorised signatory.

(f) **Inflated Sales.**

For each customer, calculate the ratio of sales in the fourth quarter (A) as a percentage of annual sales (B). Aggregate the credit notes in the first quarter of the subsequent year (c) and calculate C/A. Print out customers and branches with the highest ratios (possibly indicating fictitious sales in the fourth quarter).

(g) **As regards purchasing, the risks are that purchasing agents may misuse their authority to favour vendors with whom they are in collusion, including fictitious entities. So you can make a check file for purchasing thus:**

Database Field	Comment
VENDOR NO. VENDOR NAME VENDOR ADDRESS VENDOR TEL NO. DATE ENTERED ON FILE VAT REF	Standing data. One file each year to monitor Changes.
COST CODE	To identify department or individual authoriser
INDIVIDUAL PURCHASE ORDERS FOR PAST 3 YEARS	Vendor no., Purchase Order No., Invoice No., date, gross amount, Net amount, product code, product Description, quantity, gross price, Net price.
GOODS RECEIVED FILE FOR PAST YEAR	Vendor No., Purchase Order No., Invoice no., date, gross amount, Product code, product description, Quantity, gross price, net price. Goods received date.
INDIVIDUAL PURCHASE INVOICES FOR PAST 3 YEARS	Vendor no., purchase order no., invoice No., date, gross amount, net amount, tax, Product code, product description, Quantity, gross price, net price. Any Special transaction codes. Goods Received date.
CREDIT NOTES FOR PAST 3 YEARS	Vendor no., credit note no., date, gross amount, net amount, tax, product code, product description, quantity, gross price, net price.
PURCHASE LEDGER FOR PAST 3 YEARS	Vendor no., vendor name, gross and Net purchases, adjustments, credit notes an payment details. Bad debt write Offs.
PAYMENTS FILE (RECURRING & NON-RECURRING)	Beneficiary Account No., (Customer no., supplier no., employee no., etc.), beneficiary name, date of payment, transaction reference (cheque no.), amount, bank name, bank sort code, bank reference.

Then compare key fields (post codes, addresses, bank accounts) in the vendor master file (and if appropriate, miscellaneous vendors) with the employees' master file. Print out matching fields and details of suppliers where key data is missing.

You can also identify budgets which have over-run in the previous year. List all transactions

UNDER THESE HEADINGS, IDENTIFY THE SUPPLIERCONCERNED

SUMMARISE TURNOVER.

    (h) Test for round amounts of money transactions.

        Examine the purchase transaction file and identify all round amount items where the two least significant digits and decimal points are all zeros (15,000.00).Summarise by supplier and authorised signatory. This test identifies a classic fraud profile of fraudulent invoices and advance payments.

        This is just a small part of forensic accounting. There is more to be learnt at these conferences.

3.16—United Kingdom transfer pricing legislation among transfer pricing developments in other countries.

UNITED KINGDOM TRANSFER PRICING

Introduction

Transfer Prices are remuneration for the transfer of goods, intangibles and the provision of services and loan capital among related enterprises.. The concept and definition of transfer pricing is relevant for business economics and for taxation purposes. Almost 70% of cross-border trade in the world takes place between related enterprises and most multinationals consider that transfer pricing is the most important international tax issue. Fears that companies would move their profits to subsidiaries in countries with low tax rates in order to pay less tax, have caused many countries, including the UK, to update their laws on transfer pricing.

Hungary recently introduced new transfer pricing regulations; so did the Netherlands; Argentina, Brazil, Columbia, Peru, Venezuela, Russia, Kazakhstan, and U.S made Transfer Pricing Amendments in 2003; Mexico made transfer pricing amendments and also made new requirements for Transfer Pricing Documentation.

On year ago, the UK made changes to the law relating to transfer pricing.

Transfer Pricing Method

There are, and have been since 1979,at least five transfer pricing methods.

(1) the comparable, uncontrolled price method, (CUP);

(2) the cost-plus method;

(3) the resale price method;

(4) the profit-split method and

(5) the comparable profit method.

The CUP is thought to be the ideal method, but was not always practical because evidence of comparable prices on the open market is rare. The cost-plus method is often used, based on the cost price of the product or service to which a profit mark-up was added. The mark-up represents guarantees, market risk and foreign exchange risk. The resale price method starts from the price for which the goods are resold to an independent third party. The gross margin of the reselling related party is deducted from that price. The result is the transfer price for which the related producing enterprise supplies to the reselling company.

The profit-split method compared net profits. It was a method used to estimate approximately what the transfer pricing would be, until the exact transfer pricing could be determined by investigation.

Transfer pricing was much used by United States multinational companies to save on taxation by using countries with much lower tax rates than the US. The US was forced to pass a law, The Tax Reform Act 1986 in order to stop the treasury loss, requesting extensive documentation on pain of automatic penalties. They started to use a fifth transfer pricing method, the comparable profit method (CPM). The CPM is based on the operating profit level of uncontrolled taxpayers engaged in similar business transactions under similar circumstances. To allow tax reduction, the arm's length principle must be proved and to prove this more than one result becomes available. The arm's length rule is proved when comparable figures are available in the open market. Documentation showing the audit trail which led to the findings must be secured and if this is not full documentation, a penalty charge is made by the United States Revenue Office. The US treats the tax assessment for transfer pricing as a criminal offence, forcing the customer to prove that the Revenue's figure is incorrect. The US transfer pricing rules caused great anxiety in Europe that the US government would get the largest slice of multinational taxation. They lobbied the OECD on the unfairness of this and finally, in 1995, the OECD produced new Transfer Pricing guidelines.

As there were many transfer pricing methods, there was still the possibility of double taxation as one country used one method and another country used another. As can be expected those rich countries with good administrative infrastructure to carry out strict investigation, were able to collect the most taxes, making them even richer. Also, the US choice of transfer pricing method, the CPM became the most used method in the world because it was deemed the best method. When there is a cross-border transaction within a multinational, the market is searched for comparable gross and net margins of products of the same type, risk and function.

Even today, there is no uniform agreement about transfer pricing. For instance, the US uses a transfer pricing method, the CPM, which Europe does not consider to be fair. Germany and Sweden still use the transfer pricing method it used in 1983, before the OECD recommendation of 1995 and allows the manager of the MNE to choose a *reasonable* method which a Sound Business Manager would use (SBM). The Netherlands also apply this method BUT Belgium applies the CPM, although the tax authorities there will not require a detailed analysis using a functional analysis and search of comparable figures before a margin can be accepted.

The Arm's Length Principle

This is the establishment of the facts that the two entities which contracted are independent of each other. The concept was created to make all enterprises equal as regards taxation. The OECD Guidelines state that

> "...the application of the Arm's Length Principle is generally based on a comparison. In order for such to be comparable means that none of the differences between the situations being compared could materially affect the condition being examined in the methodology or that reasonably accurate adjustments can be made to eliminate the effect of any such differences."

And some argue that it is close to the operation of the open market. Others argue that the arm's length principle is against all economic reality and that it is unfair that a business forms itself as a multinational enterprise to gain economies of scale which are promptly taken away and usurped by taxation, and sometimes double taxation.

Transfer Pricing in the United Kingdom

The trial of the case <u>Lankhorst—Hohorst GmbH v Finanzampt Steinfort (Case C-324/00) [2003] STC 607 </u>revealed that the UK Transfer Pricing Rules, in force since 1951, were illegal and in breach of the European Treaty.[309] The government quickly changed the law to read that from 1st April, 2004, UK to UK business transactions were no longer exempt from tax on the difference in prices except for transactions between small[310] and medium sized[311] companies.[312] This means that if a branch of a company incurs a loss on its Profit and Loss Account for £1000, it cannot carry forward this loss to another UK branch. It must restrict only carry forward losses made in the UK to other branches of the same company only. And if a branch in the UK paid interest to the parent company which is based outside the UK, the interest on the loan it borrowed is treated as the parent company's dividend if the borrowing exceeded a given debt to equity ratio. The legislation applies to all parent companies abroad with branches in the UK and also to all branches in the UK of a company based outside the UK.

Small and Medium Sized Companies

With medium sized businesses, the Revenue will have the power to require transfer-pricing adjustments in "*exceptional*" cases. "*Exceptional*" is not defined. The exemption applies at the time of filling a tax return, but the Revenue reserves the right to conduct an investigation if it turns out that there is "*significant*" tax at stake. "*Significant*" is not defined

Documentation for Cross-Border transactions

The documentation necessary would be primary accounting records;

Records of any adjustments made for tax purposes;

A record of the transaction covered by the legislation;

And evidence to demonstrate arms 's length result.

---

309 LH was a German company whose ultimate shareholder was a Netherlands company LTBV .In Dec.1996, loaned 3 million DM to LH, repayable over 10 years in annual instalments. In its Corporation Tax assessment notices, of June 1999,with regard to 19978, the German tax authorities decided that the interest paid to LTBV for the loan was equal to a covert distribution of profits within the, meaning of para 8a(1).LH brought proceedings in Germany. His case was that para 8(a) breached his human right of freedom of establishment. The German court sent the case to Court of Justice of the European Union. Where it was decided against the German government and said that a reduction in tax revenue did not constitute an overriding reason in the public interest which could justify a measure which was contrary to a fundamental freedom. The legislation in issue does not have the specific purpose of preventing wholly artificial arrangements, designed to circumvent German tax legislation, from attracting a tax benefit, but applies generally to any situation in which the parent company has its seat outside Germany. This not not necessarily constitute tax evasion., because that company still has tax liability to the state in which it is based. Since the lower court had found no such abuse, they would agree that there is no such abuse. Furthermore LH had made a loss in 1996, 1997 and 1998., which loss more than the interest paid on the loan. It is also clear that this was an arm's length one. Article 9 OECD provides that profits must include income from a linked company.

310 The definition of a 'small' business:—
"Small businesses are those having fewer than 50 employees and either turnover or assets of less than 10 million Euro."

311 "Medium sized businesses are those having fewer than250 employees and either turnover of less than50 million Euro, or assets of less than 43 million Euro". Commission Recommendation 2003/361/EC of 6 May 2003.

312 Under the new rules, companies who have borrowed from an UK Company or overseas parent will need to show that the loan could have been made on a stand-alone basis or face possible transfer pricing penalties.

Only the first three types of documentation are required and only when you are you file your tax return. The Arm's length transaction[313] documentation only needs to be produced if the Revenue requests it in the course of an investigation. If the first three types of documents cannot be produced, there is a penalty of 3000 Euro for failure to keep and preserve adequate records. The penalty of a fine for fraud or neglect can be whatever the Revenue deems fit, even 100% of the under—paid tax. An example of neglect is if the company filed a tax return based on incorrect transfer pricing without good reason for believing it to be correct. Even Germany has just made new rules and harsher penalties for transfer pricing documentation. German tax law now includes harsh penalty provisions for taxpayers who fail to meet the legal requirements since December 31st, 2003. The documentation requirement is now

Transfer Pricing documentation relating to the manner and content of their international business relationships with related parties; a narration of the economic and legal facts that relate to the arm's length principle, to be submitted within 60 days of the tax authorities' request, along with extraordinary transactions, contemporaneously documented within 6 months of occurrence. There are penalties for failure to comply, these being 5% to 10% of the income adjustment and up to 1 million euro for late submission and 100 euro a day for overdue documentation.

If a company incurs a penalty, there is a two-year period of grace, which means that <u>no penalty is to be paid until 1 April 2006. But this does not apply if the penalty is for fraud or neglect.</u> Alternatively, an UK company can agree its pricing policies in advance with its local Inspector of Taxes. This option would be easier and cheaper to negotiate than an advance pricing agreement.

The old Transfer Pricing law allowed a UK group to be treated as a single entity to determine what level of debt it could carry, but the new law, a company's debt capacity is considered in isolation. This new UK law represents a tax planning opportunity also. It is not just a compliance or audit-avoidance strategy. A transfer pricing study can help management focus on the overall value of the company's transfer—pricing activities and locations and improve decision—making, aimed at maximising total returns.

3.17—Compulsory whistle-blowing in EU financial markets
COMPULSORY WHISTLE-BLOWING IN EU FINANCIAL MARKETS

The Public Disclosure Act 1998 protects individuals who make certain disclosures of information in the public interest. It protects them from victimisation.

It protects workers who are employees and also protects persons who

"(a) work or worked for a person in circumstances in which–

  (i) he is or was introduced or supplied to do that work by a third person, and

  (ii) the term on which he is or was engaged to do the work are or were in practice substantially determined not by him but by the person for whom he works or worked by the third person or by both of them…"

This would seem to only apply in the employment sphere however .

There is compensation to be claimed if an employee were dismissed because of whistle-blowing. If he or she finds that a criminal offence has been committed or that a person has failed to comply with any legal obligation, and he or she reports it, it will be deemed to be a protected disclosure against which that person has protection from dismissal. The disclosure qualifies for protection so long as "the worker makes the disclosure in good faith, he reasonably believes that the information disclosed and any allegations contained in it, are substantially true, and he does not make the disclosure for purposes of personal gain", according to the Public Disclosure Act.

---

313 Any companies that became dormant after 31 January 2004 were caught by the transfer pricing rules. solution, is to document, as evidence of proper compliance, why a UK company believes its transfer pricing policy is as close as possible to the arm's length standard.

Under the Act, allegations may be raised through a variety of procedures some being, to the employer, to a prescribed person, to a legal advisor or to a Minister of the Crown.

One example of an obligation to whistle-blow is found in the Pensions Act 1995, which states in section 48 that "(1) If the auditor or actuary of any occupational pension scheme has reasonable cause to believe that–1

(a) any duty relevant to the administration of the scheme imposed by any enactment or rule of law on the trustees or managers, the employer, any professional advisor or any prescribed person acting in connection with the scheme has not been or is not being complied with, and

(b) the failure to comply is likely to be of material significance in the exercise by the Authority of any of their functions,

he must immediately give a written report of the matter to the Authority."

So, in auditing, in a case where a sample check is done for deductions from members pay for pension contributions, if you were to discover that those contributions were not paid over in the statutory time limit, you would have a duty to whistle-blow so that the matter must be reported to OPRA. Audit firms must have procedures for technicians who discover such matters to have it actioned immediately and reported to OPRA.

There has been a recent case in the courts in 2002, RBG Resources PLC v Rastogi and others, in which it was decided that a senior employee owes a duty to "blow the whistle" on a major fraud that was being perpetrated upon his employer by its directors. This duty to "blow the whistle" overrides his obligation of confidence.. The senior employee, the financial controller, was sued by the company RBG Resources PLC for breach of duty. The case came about as a result of 400 million US dollars having been siphoned off by the directors.

Auditors also owe a duty to report evidence of fraud and/or misconduct. The case of SASEA Finance Ltd v KPMG in 1999 made the decision that the nature and scope of the duty of auditors was such that they should blow the whistle on fraud discovered during the course of conducting an audit and that they should not wait until they have signed off the accounts but should blow the whistle immediately. SASEA Finance Ltd was a part of a group of companies which collapsed in 1992 in circumstances of a huge fraud carried out by one of its directors. KPMG was retained to prepare SASEA'a 1989 accounts and carried out this work in 1990, signing off the accounts in November 1990. The obvious reason why KPMG should have disclosed the fraud immediately was that the client might be spared further losses.

The net is closing, it seems, in areas of securities, insurance and banking. The EU Financial Instruments Markets Directive, adopted and in force since April 2004, must be implemented by EU member states by 30th April 2006. Essentially, investment firms must take all reasonable steps to obtain, when executing orders, the best possible results for their clients, taking into account price, costs, speed, likelihood of execution and settlement, size and nature or any other consideration relevant to the execution of the order. This is the way they must conduct business from April 2006. By another name, it is a means of fighting security fraud. It means that companies offering securities for sale must tell the public the truth about their businesses, the securities they are selling and the risks involved in investing.

This Directive interacts with the EU Market Abuse Directive 2003/6/EC. The UK's Criminal Justice Act 1993 and Financial Services and Markets Act 2000 are not adequate to meet the new obligations of whistle-blowing in respect of authorised persons who arrange or execute a transaction in financial instruments. The UK Treasury and the Financial Services Authority, FSA, propose legislative and rule book changes, including compulsory whistle-blowing, by April 2005 with civil implementation instead of criminal.

Market abuse can be argued to be a risk of detriment to the general public and any directors found guilty of such market abuse should be disqualified under section 8 of the Directors Disqualification Act 1986, blunt instrument this may be. The company could be restrained from engaging in the specified business activity or restrained from carrying out all or part of its business activity which breaches the FSA proposed market abuse rules from 2005. This is arguably more expedient in the public interest, ie. cut the cancer out before it spreads or let it be an example to others. This could be imposed as well as the proposed FSA fine. It can be argued that a fine would just be factored into the company's administrative costs and relayed back to the public.

Since this is a public interest matter, and with pensions mis-selling fresh in the public's mind, are the meetings to agree the FSA rule changes going to be open to the public and the news media? Will the civil actions of the FSA include the return of illegal profits? What sanctions will there be for persons who repeatedly violate such new rules? What provisions will be made to ensure the professional security of the whistle-blowers in these situations? Will the whistle-blowers be compelled to give evidence, or will their suspicions be anonymous? What is the written criteria for whistle-blowing? Will the FSA advertise a list of all companies found deficient and discovered through periodic inspections, complaints and whistle-blowing? Will the FSA report to the public which companies were found to have breached these new market abuse rules, the nature of the breach, the value of the breach and the sanctions imposed?

The FSA must make clear the way in which this compulsory whistle-blowing on market abuse will operate with stated criteria for whistle-blowing, safeguards for whistle-blowers as well as clear criteria on what are valid suspicions, what will be treated as malicious, and what sort of whistle-blowing might constitute anti-competitive practices. This would save time, money and unnecessary business disruption by weeding out non-credible allegations as soon as the whistle-blowing occurs.

Finally, defamation issues must be mentioned. Will the Public Interest Disclosure Act 1998 protect market abuse whistle-blowers or can they be sued for defamation? Is the FSA a "prescribed person" under the Public Interest Disclosure Act 1998? Defamation cases are extremely expensive to defend and are not covered by professional indemnity insurance.

3.18—The Electronic Invoice

THE ELECTRONIC INVOICE

Before journeying into the mechanics of the electronic invoice, it is as well to recap the present electronic situation for business in the United Kingdom. The electronic age is well and truly established and for litigation purposes, desktop computers, laptops, mobile phones, personal digital machines are just a few of the many sources of electronic business data. Statistics reveal that for the year 2000, 97.3% of all documents were created electronically with 35% of these never converted into hard copy. In the United Kingdom overall, there were 263 million email mail-boxes and 31 billion emails were sent worldwide.

In law, a document is anything on which information is recorded. .

Derby v Weldon [1991] was the court case in which was established that a computer database is a document. This decision is still valid today.

Council Directive 2001/115/EC deals with business invoices related to the European Union. There are new mandatory provisions which are:

The customer's VAT number

The mandatory sequencing of invoices

The full name and address of the buyer.

Furthermore, all invoices must be translated into the local language and must be kept for a period of at least four years; maximum time being 15 years. The storage of the invoice must be such that it can be made available to the authorities. This change means that all UK business computers must be configured. It is a sobering thought that, had all invoices been sequenced and showing the buyer's full name and address, it might have prevented the huge multi million pound "mobile telephone fraud",[314] the total sum of which was 5 billion pounds

---

314 Telegraph Newspaper 10th July 2003. The article states that the Office for National Statistics said that imports into the United Kingdom from the European Union were £11 billion a year higher over the past four years than had been realised and that this meant that the United Kingdom's trade deficit for the year 2002 was £4.5 billion, or 4.5% of Gross Domestic Product. The trade figures had to be revised after an investigation into the fraudulent imports into the UK of mobile telephones through the exploitation of non-payment of Value Added Tax on these products. This particular fraud was said to create a loss to the United Kingdom's Treasury of £2 billionin unpaid taxes in the year 2002 alone.

This EU Directive, agreed to be fully implemented by January 2005, is fraught with the same fraud potential that it originally sought to eradicate due to these reasons:

1. There is no one date by which all twenty five EU Member States must comply.

2. There is no statistical collection of data, actual or planned.

3. The EU Accession States, with their negotiated three year grace to 2007, have also negotiated to establish VAT rates and they are using provisional rates until 2007. These provisional rates differ significantly with the fifteen original Member States rates of VAT. The effect of this is obvious. Fraudsters have two years to the year 2007 to exploit various Member States' differing rates of VAT. They can do this by forming a European Company with its seat in one of the Accession Member States with low tax rate, since only the law of the state where a company's seat lies would apply to the business. (The only Member State that has not implemented the Directive yet is Turkey).

EU rates of Value Added Tax

State	Super reduced	Reduced	Standard
Austria	-	10	20
Belgium	-	6	21
Cyprus	-	5	15
Czech Rep	-	5	22
Denmark	-	-	25
Estonia	-	5	18
Finland	-	8	22
France	2.1	5.5	19.6
Germany	-	7	16
Greece	4	8	18
Hungary	-	12	25
Ireland	4.3	13.5	21
Italy	4	10	20
Latvia	-	9	18
Lithuania	-	5	18
Luxemburg	3	6	15
Malta	-	5	15
Netherlands	-	6	19
Portugal	-	5	19
Slovak Rep	-	-	19
Slovenia	-	8.5	20
Spain	4	7	16
Sweden	-	6	25
United Kingdom	-	5	17.5

4. If the invoices are stored in a program which updates itself automatically, all the original document "metadata" will be lost. Electronic documents, even graphic formats such as TIFF and PDF, can be altered or forged with a fraction of the effort it would take to do the same with traditional hard-copy materials.

5. We must lobby for an "Authentication Protocol" for electronic documents from all Member States.

6.   We must all agree to one uniform Evidence Retention and Document Destruction Protocol.

In this way, when the Authorities ask for past documents, we would be assured that the documents will be produced, in good order, with original substance, and so will the Authority's.

3.19—Terrorism and the Accounting Community
TERRORISM AND THE ACCOUNTING COMMUNITY

The Terrorism Act 2000 was the UK law against political violence. It established a permanent regime and with emphasis on combating international terrorism. After September 11th 2001, the government passed the Anti-terrorism, Crime and Security Act 2001. We in the UK can say we know about terrorism, having endured many years of IRA antics. We had derogated Article 15 of the Human Rights Convention since 1988 and had been detaining terrorist suspects without the full protection of legal advice, etc. We are no strangers to legislating or addressing the problem. One new facet of the Anti-terrorism laws passed recently is section 1(2) (e) of the 2001 Act which is designed to take account of cyber-terrorism. It had been opined by experts in the field that this part of the legislation is draconian and treats modes of political expression as illegal and as terrorist activity.

But the threat of terrorism has changed and crimes such as identity frauds, "*phishing*" and electronic sabotage by alleged sophisticated, trained, organised, trans-national groups are now real fears. This Terrorism Act contains what we in the business community know as "risk management" and this is part of the pro-active steps taken by the United Kingdom to assuage public fear.

So how does the Act work? Well, it has powers of forfeiture of property and seizure of cash and freezing of foreign property held by UK institutions. It also stops any claims of asylum seeking. It enables the police to retain fingerprints in asylum and immigration application cases. It allows detention without trial of *foreign persons* who have been denied asylum on national security grounds. Note that it provides no protection against British terrorists or British cyber-terrorists.

The National High-Tech Crime Unit (NHTCU) gathers evidence from communications providers. So does MI15, the Security Service, and MI16, the Secret Intelligence Service. There is a Terrorist Finance Team (TFT) in the Economic Crime Unit (ECU) at the National Criminal Intelligence Service (NCIS) The Chief Police Officers (CPO's) have a National Counter-Terrorism Security Service (NaCTSO) for training police and Special Branch Police. There is a processing centre called the Joint Terrorism Analysis Centre (JTAC).

So do you feel safe? Well my opinion is that identity theft is rife, as is borne out in newspapers and this is not mainly by thieves rifling through your waste bins but mostly by electronic means. This 'mostly internet based' theft refers to using information about a company or person to engage in false applications for loans, credit cards, withdrawals from bank accounts and internet shopping. An identity thief can use personal data to open a bank account, deposit stolen cheques, withdraw the money electronically, lease vehicles, etc.

The only way to stop them is to keep personal information from others; avoid telephone salespersons, deal in writing as much as possible, avoid using your mobile in public, avoid cash machines, etc.

More intelligence preventative steps consist of

1.   Requesting a Credit Report from Credit Agencies (*Equifax* and *Experian* are two of these) periodically.

2.   Maintaining careful records of banking and financing accounts, keeping copies of cheques and other transactions.

3.   Keeping all your personal and business records for seven years to ensure the greatest protection. Original records are extremely valuable in any dispute to do with a financial transaction. Consider how difficult it would be to find this

particular transaction among the millions in a large organisation, even if they do have a search facility you can pay for. Even if ordered to produce a record they could have lost it and you will be able to do nothing about it.

4. And finally, even if you have been vigilant but become a target, swift action, informing the bank, stopping the account, requesting <u>in writing by recorded delivery</u>, that all your accounts 'numbers be changed and changing all your passwords;

5. informing the police and obtaining a police incident number for insurance purposes;

6. informing your insurers or the credit card insurers;

7. ` informing *Experian* that a fraud has been committed;

8. informing DHSS to secure your NHS number;

9. inform the Citizen Advice Bureau who might know of Victim Centres;

10. and obtaining advice from a solicitor after taking all of these steps;

11. are all actions you can take to safeguard yourself.

Your motto should be <u>***"Be vigilant and act quickly if your identity is stolen"***</u>.

It may be the first step in a terrorist move or it may be the first step in a move to steal from your employer, a larger and more lucrative target.

THE END

Appendix

Prevention of Terrorism Act 2005

An Act to provide for the making against individuals involved in terrorism-related activity of orders imposing obligations on them for purposes connected with preventing or restricting their further involvement in such activity; to make provision about appeals and other proceedings relating to such orders; and for connected purposes.

[11th March 2005]

Be it enacted by the Queen's most Excellent Majesty, by and with the advice and consent of the Lords Spiritual and Temporal, and Commons, in this present Parliament assembled, and by the authority of the same, as follows:—

Control orders

1 Power to make control orders

(1) In this Act "control order" means an order against an individual that imposes obligations on him for purposes connected with protecting members of the public from a risk of terrorism.

(2) The power to make a control order against an individual shall be exercisable—

    (a) except in the case of an order imposing obligations that are incompatible with the individual's right to liberty under Article 5 of the Human Rights Convention, by the Secretary of State; and

    (b) in the case of an order imposing obligations that are or include derogating obligations, by the court on an application by the Secretary of State.

(3) The obligations that may be imposed by a control order made against an individual are any obligations that the Secretary of State or (as the case may be) the court considers necessary for purposes connected with preventing or restricting involvement by that individual in terrorism-related activity.

(4) Those obligations may include, in particular—

    (a) a prohibition or restriction on his possession or use of specified articles or substances;

    (b) a prohibition or restriction on his use of specified services or specified facilities, or on his carrying on specified activities;

    (c) a restriction in respect of his work or other occupation, or in respect of his business;

    (d) a restriction on his association or communications with specified persons or with other persons generally;

    (e) a restriction in respect of his place of residence or on the persons to whom he gives access to his place of residence;

    (f) a prohibition on his being at specified places or within a specified area at specified times or on specified days;

    (g) a prohibition or restriction on his movements to, from or within the United Kingdom, a specified part of the United Kingdom or a specified place or area within the United Kingdom;

    (h) a requirement on him to comply with such other prohibitions or restrictions on his movements as may be imposed, for a period not exceeding 24 hours, by directions given to him in the specified manner, by a specified person and for the purpose of securing compliance with other obligations imposed by or under the order;

(i) a requirement on him to surrender his passport, or anything in his possession to which a prohibition or restriction imposed by the order relates, to a specified person for a period not exceeding the period for which the order remains in force;

(j) a requirement on him to give access to specified persons to his place of residence or to other premises to which he has power to grant access;

(k) a requirement on him to allow specified persons to search that place or any such premises for the purpose of ascertaining whether obligations imposed by or under the order have been, are being or are about to be contravened;

(l) a requirement on him to allow specified persons, either for that purpose or for the purpose of securing that the order is complied with, to remove anything found in that place or on any such premises and to subject it to tests or to retain it for a period not exceeding the period for which the order remains in force;

(m) a requirement on him to allow himself to be photographed;

(n) a requirement on him to co-operate with specified arrangements for enabling his movements, communications or other activities to be monitored by electronic or other means;

(o) a requirement on him to comply with a demand made in the specified manner to provide information to a specified person in accordance with the demand;

(p) a requirement on him to report to a specified person at specified times and places.

(5) Power by or under a control order to prohibit or restrict the controlled person's movements includes, in particular, power to impose a requirement on him to remain at or within a particular place or area (whether for a particular period or at particular times or generally).

(6) The reference in subsection (4)(n) to co-operating with specified arrangements for monitoring includes a reference to each of the following—

(a) submitting to procedures required by the arrangements;

(b) wearing or otherwise using apparatus approved by or in accordance with the arrangements;

(c) maintaining such apparatus in the specified manner;

(d) complying with directions given by persons carrying out functions for the purposes of those arrangements.

(7) The information that the controlled person may be required to provide under a control order includes, in particular, advance information about his proposed movements or other activities.

(8) A control order may provide for a prohibition, restriction or requirement imposed by or under the order to apply only where a specified person has not given his consent or approval to what would otherwise contravene the prohibition, restriction or requirement.

(9) For the purposes of this Act involvement in terrorism-related activity is any one or more of the following—

(a) the commission, preparation or instigation of acts of terrorism;

(b) conduct which facilitates the commission, preparation or instigation of such acts, or which is intended to do so;

(c) conduct which gives encouragement to the commission, preparation or instigation of such acts, or which is intended to do so;

(d) conduct which gives support or assistance to individuals who are known or believed to be involved in terrorism-related activity;

and for the purposes of this subsection it is immaterial whether the acts of terrorism in question are specific acts of terrorism or acts of terrorism generally.

(10) In this Act—

"derogating obligation" means an obligation on an individual which—

(a) is incompatible with his right to liberty under Article 5 of the Human Rights Convention; but

(b) is of a description of obligations which, for the purposes of the designation of a designated derogation, is set out in the designation order;

"designated derogation" has the same meaning as in the Human Rights Act 1998 (c 42) (see section 14(1) of that Act);

"designation order", in relation to a designated derogation, means the order under section 14(1) of the Human Rights Act 1998 by which the derogation is designated.

2 Making of non-derogating control orders

(1) The Secretary of State may make a control order against an individual if he—

(a) has reasonable grounds for suspecting that the individual is or has been involved in terrorism-related activity; and

(b) considers that it is necessary, for purposes connected with protecting members of the public from a risk of terrorism, to make a control order imposing obligations on that individual.

(2) The Secretary of State may make a control order against an individual who is for the time being bound by a control order made by the court only if he does so—

(a) after the court has determined that its order should be revoked; but

(b) while the effect of the revocation has been postponed for the purpose of giving the Secretary of State an opportunity to decide whether to exercise his own powers to make a control order against the individual.

(3) A control order made by the Secretary of State is called a non-derogating control order.

(4) A non-derogating control order—

(a) has effect for a period of 12 months beginning with the day on which it is made; but

(b) may be renewed on one or more occasions in accordance with this section.

(5) A non-derogating control order must specify when the period for which it is to have effect will end.

(6) The Secretary of State may renew a non-derogating control order (with or without modifications) for a period of 12 months if he—

(a) considers that it is necessary, for purposes connected with protecting members of the public from a risk of terrorism, for an order imposing obligations on the controlled person to continue in force; and

(b) considers that the obligations to be imposed by the renewed order are necessary for purposes connected with preventing or restricting involvement by that person in terrorism-related activity.

(7) Where the Secretary of State renews a non-derogating control order, the 12 month period of the renewal begins to run from whichever is the earlier of—

(a) the time when the order would otherwise have ceased to have effect; or

(b) the beginning of the seventh day after the date of renewal.

(8) The instrument renewing a non-derogating control order must specify when the period for which it is renewed will end.

(9) It shall be immaterial, for the purposes of determining what obligations may be imposed by a control order made by the Secretary of State, whether the involvement in terrorism-related activity to be prevented or restricted by the obligations is connected with matters to which the Secretary of State's grounds for suspicion relate.

3 Supervision by court of making of non-derogating control orders

(1) The Secretary of State must not make a non-derogating control order against an individual except where—

(a) having decided that there are grounds to make such an order against that individual, he has applied to the court for permission to make the order and has been granted that permission;

(b) the order contains a statement by the Secretary of State that, in his opinion, the urgency of the case requires the order to be made without such permission; or

(c) the order is made before 14th March 2005 against an individual who, at the time it is made, is an individual in respect of whom a certificate under section 21(1) of the Anti-terrorism, Crime and Security Act 2001 (c 24) is in force.

(2) Where the Secretary of State makes an application for permission to make a non-derogating control order against an individual, the application must set out the order for which he seeks permission and—

(a) the function of the court is to consider whether the Secretary of State's decision that there are grounds to make that order is obviously flawed;

(b) the court may give that permission unless it determines that the decision is obviously flawed; and

(c) if it gives permission, the court must give directions for a hearing in relation to the order as soon as reasonably practicable after it is made.

(3) Where the Secretary of State makes a non-derogating control order against an individual without the permission of the court—

(a) he must immediately refer the order to the court; and

(b) the function of the court on the reference is to consider whether the decision of the Secretary of State to make the order he did was obviously flawed.

(4) The court's consideration on a reference under subsection (3)(a) must begin no more than 7 days after the day on which the control order in question was made.

(5) The court may consider an application for permission under subsection (1)(a) or a reference under subsection (3)(a)—

(a) in the absence of the individual in question;

(b) without his having been notified of the application or reference; and

(c) without his having been given an opportunity (if he was aware of the application or reference) of making any representations to the court;

but this subsection is not to be construed as limiting the matters about which rules of court may be made in relation to the consideration of such an application or reference.

(6) On a reference under subsection (3)(a), the court—

(a) if it determines that the decision of the Secretary of State to make a non-derogating control order against the controlled person was obviously flawed, must quash the order;

(b) if it determines that that decision was not obviously flawed but that a decision of the Secretary of State to impose a particular obligation by that order was obviously flawed, must quash that obligation and (subject to that) confirm the order and give directions for a hearing in relation to the confirmed order; and

(c) in any other case, must confirm the order and give directions for a hearing in relation to the confirmed order.

(7) The directions given under subsection (2)(c) or (6)(b) or (c) must include arrangements for the individual in question to be given an opportunity within 7 days of the court's giving permission or (as the case may be) making its determination on the reference to make representations about—

(a) the directions already given; and

(b) the making of further directions.

(8) On a reference under subsection (3)(a), the court may quash a certificate contained in the order for the purposes of subsection (1)(b) if it determines that the Secretary of State's decision that the certificate should be contained in the order was flawed.

(9) The court must ensure that the controlled person is notified of its decision on a reference under subsection (3)(a).

(10) On a hearing in pursuance of directions under subsection (2)(c) or (6)(b) or (c), the function of the court is to determine whether any of the following decisions of the Secretary of State was flawed—

   (a) his decision that the requirements of section 2(1)(a) and (b) were satisfied for the making of the order; and

   (b) his decisions on the imposition of each of the obligations imposed by the order.

(11) In determining—

   (a) what constitutes a flawed decision for the purposes of subsection (2), (6) or (8), or

   (b) the matters mentioned in subsection (10),

   the court must apply the principles applicable on an application for judicial review.

(12) If the court determines, on a hearing in pursuance of directions under subsection (2)(c) or (6)(b) or (c), that a decision of the Secretary of State was flawed, its only powers are—

   (a) power to quash the order;

   (b) power to quash one or more obligations imposed by the order; and

   (c) power to give directions to the Secretary of State for the revocation of the order or for the modification of the obligations it imposes.

(13) In every other case the court must decide that the control order is to continue in force.

(14) If requested to do so by the controlled person, the court must discontinue any hearing in pursuance of directions under subsection (2)(c) or (6)(b) or (c).

4 Power of court to make derogating control orders

(1) On an application to the court by the Secretary of State for the making of a control order against an individual, it shall be the duty of the court—

   (a) to hold an immediate preliminary hearing to determine whether to make a control order imposing obligations that are or include derogating obligations (called a "derogating control order") against that individual; and

   (b) if it does make such an order against that individual, to give directions for the holding of a full hearing to determine whether to confirm the order (with or without modifications).

(2) The preliminary hearing under subsection (1)(a) may be held—

   (a) in the absence of the individual in question;

   (b) without his having had notice of the application for the order; and

   (c) without his having been given an opportunity (if he was aware of the application) of making any representations to the court;

   but this subsection is not to be construed as limiting the matters about which rules of court may be made in relation to that hearing.

(3) At the preliminary hearing, the court may make a control order against the individual in question if it appears to the court—

   (a) that there is material which (if not disproved) is capable of being relied on by the court as establishing that the individual is or has been involved in terrorism-related activity;

(b) that there are reasonable grounds for believing that the imposition of obligations on that individual is necessary for purposes connected with protecting members of the public from a risk of terrorism;

(c) that the risk arises out of, or is associated with, a public emergency in respect of which there is a designated derogation from the whole or a part of Article 5 of the Human Rights Convention; and

(d) that the obligations that there are reasonable grounds for believing should be imposed on the individual are or include derogating obligations of a description set out for the purposes of the designated derogation in the designation order.

(4) The obligations that may be imposed by a derogating control order in the period between—

(a) the time when the order is made, and

(b) the time when a final determination is made by the court whether to confirm it,

include any obligations which the court has reasonable grounds for considering are necessary as mentioned in section 1(3).

(5) At the full hearing under subsection (1)(b), the court may—

(a) confirm the control order made by the court; or

(b) revoke the order;

and where the court revokes the order, it may (if it thinks fit) direct that this Act is to have effect as if the order had been quashed.

(6) In confirming a control order, the court—

(a) may modify the obligations imposed by the order; and

(b) where a modification made by the court removes an obligation, may (if it thinks fit) direct that this Act is to have effect as if the removed obligation had been quashed.

(7) At the full hearing, the court may confirm the control order (with or without modifications) only if—

(a) it is satisfied, on the balance of probabilities, that the controlled person is an individual who is or has been involved in terrorism-related activity;

(b) it considers that the imposition of obligations on the controlled person is necessary for purposes connected with protecting members of the public from a risk of terrorism;

(c) it appears to the court that the risk is one arising out of, or is associated with, a public emergency in respect of which there is a designated derogation from the whole or a part of Article 5 of the Human Rights Convention; and

(d) the obligations to be imposed by the order or (as the case may be) by the order as modified are or include derogating obligations of a description set out for the purposes of the designated derogation in the designation order.

(8) A derogating control order ceases to have effect at the end of the period of 6 months beginning with the day on which it is made unless—

(a) it is previously revoked (whether at the hearing under subsection (1)(b) or otherwise under this Act);

(b) it ceases to have effect under section 6; or

(c) it is renewed.

(9) The court, on an application by the Secretary of State, may renew a derogating control order (with or without modifications) for a period of 6 months from whichever is the earlier of—

(a) the time when the order would otherwise have ceased to have effect; and

(b) the beginning of the seventh day after the date of renewal.

(10) The power of the court to renew a derogating control order is exercisable on as many occasions as the court thinks fit; but, on each occasion, it is exercisable only if—

 (a) the court considers that it is necessary, for purposes connected with protecting members of the public from a risk of terrorism, for a derogating control order to continue in force against the controlled person;

 (b) it appears to the court that the risk is one arising out of, or is associated with, a public emergency in respect of which there is a designated derogation from the whole or a part of Article 5 of the Human Rights Convention;

 (c) the derogating obligations that the court considers should continue in force are of a description that continues to be set out for the purposes of the designated derogation in the designation order; and

 (d) the court considers that the obligations to be imposed by the renewed order are necessary for purposes connected with preventing or restricting involvement by that person in terrorism-related activity.

(11) Where, on an application for the renewal of a derogating control order, it appears to the court—

 (a) that the proceedings on the application are unlikely to be completed before the time when the order is due to cease to have effect if not renewed, and

 (b) that that is not attributable to an unreasonable delay on the part of the Secretary of State in the making or conduct of the application,

the court may (on one or more occasions) extend the period for which the order is to remain in force for the purpose of keeping it in force until the conclusion of the proceedings.

(12) Where the court exercises its power under subsection (11) and subsequently renews the control order in question, the period of any renewal still runs from the time when the order would have ceased to have effect apart from that subsection.

(13) It shall be immaterial, for the purposes of determining what obligations may be imposed by a control order made by the court, whether the involvement in terrorism-related activity to be prevented or restricted by the obligations is connected with matters in relation to which the requirements of subsection (3)(a) or (7)(a) were satisfied.

5 Arrest and detention pending derogating control order

(1) A constable may arrest and detain an individual if—

 (a) the Secretary of State has made an application to the court for a derogating control order to be made against that individual; and

 (b) the constable considers that the individual's arrest and detention is necessary to ensure that he is available to be given notice of the order if it is made.

(2) A constable who has arrested an individual under this section must take him to the designated place that the constable considers most appropriate as soon as practicable after the arrest.

(3) An individual taken to a designated place under this section may be detained there until the end of 48 hours from the time of his arrest.

(4) If the court considers that it is necessary to do so to ensure that the individual in question is available to be given notice of any derogating control order that is made against him, it may, during the 48 hours following his arrest, extend the period for which the individual may be detained under this section by a period of no more than 48 hours.

(5) An individual may not be detained under this section at any time after—

 (a) he has become bound by a derogating control order made against him on the Secretary of State's application; or

 (b) the court has dismissed the application.

(6) A person who has the powers of a constable in one part of the United Kingdom may exercise the power of arrest under this section in that part of the United Kingdom or in any other part of the United Kingdom.

(7) An individual detained under this section—

(a) shall be deemed to be in legal custody throughout the period of his detention; and

(b) after having been taken to a designated place shall be deemed—

(i) in England and Wales, to be in police detention for the purposes of the Police and Criminal Evidence Act 1984 (c 60); and

(ii) in Northern Ireland, to be in police detention for the purposes of the Police and Criminal Evidence (Northern Ireland) Order 1989 (SI 1989/1341 (NI 12));

but paragraph (b) has effect subject to subsection (8).

(8) Paragraphs 1(6), 2, 6 to 9 and 16 to 19 of Schedule 8 to the Terrorism Act 2000 (c 11) (powers and safeguards in the case of persons detained under section 41 of that Act) apply to an individual detained under this section as they apply to a person detained under section 41 of that Act, but with the following modifications—

(a) the omission of paragraph 2(2)(b) to (d) (which confers powers on persons specified by the Secretary of State, prison officers and examining officers);

(b) the omission of paragraph 8(2), (5) and (5A) (which relates to the postponement of a person's rights in England and Wales or Northern Ireland); and

(c) the omission of paragraphs 16(9) and 17(4) and (4A) (which make similar provision for Scotland).

(9) The power to detain an individual under this section includes power to detain him in a manner that is incompatible with his right to liberty under Article 5 of the Human Rights Convention if, and only if—

(a) there is a designated derogation in respect of the detention of individuals under this section in connection with the making of applications for derogating control orders; and

(b) that derogation and the designated derogation relating to the power to make the orders applied for are designated in respect of the same public emergency.

(10) In this section "designated place" means any place which the Secretary of State has designated under paragraph 1(1) of Schedule 8 to the Terrorism Act 2000 (c 11) as a place at which persons may be detained under section 41 of that Act.

6 Duration of derogating control orders

(1) A derogating control order has effect at a time only if—

(a) the relevant derogation remains in force at that time; and

(b) that time is not more than 12 months after—

(i) the making of the order under section 14(1) of the Human Rights Act 1998 (c 42) designating that derogation; or

(ii) the making by the Secretary of State of an order declaring that it continues to be necessary for him to have power to impose derogating obligations by reference to that derogation.

(2) The power of the Secretary of State to make an order containing a declaration for the purposes of subsection (1)(b)(ii) is exercisable by statutory instrument.

(3) No order may be made by the Secretary of State containing such a declaration unless a draft of it has been laid before Parliament and approved by a resolution of each House.

(4) Subsection (3) does not apply to an order that contains a statement by the Secretary of State that the order needs, by reason of urgency, to be made without the approval required by that subsection.

(5) An order under this section that contains such a statement—

(a) must be laid before Parliament after being made; and

(b) if not approved by a resolution of each House before the end of 40 days beginning with the day on which the order was made, ceases to have effect at the end of that period.

(6) Where an order ceases to have effect in accordance with subsection (5), that does not—

(a) affect anything previously done in reliance on the order; or

(b) prevent the Secretary of State from exercising any power of his to make a new order for the purposes of subsection (1)(b)(ii) to the same or similar effect.

(7) In this section—

"40 days" means 40 days computed as provided for in section 7(1) of the Statutory Instruments Act 1946;

"the relevant derogation", in relation to a derogating control order, means the designated derogation by reference to which the derogating obligations imposed by that order were imposed.

7 Modification, notification and proof of orders etc

(1) If while a non-derogating control order is in force the controlled person considers that there has been a change of circumstances affecting the order, he may make an application to the Secretary of State for—

(a) the revocation of the order; or

(b) the modification of an obligation imposed by the order; and it shall be the duty of the Secretary of State to consider the application.

(2) The Secretary of State may, at any time (whether or not in response to an application by the controlled person)—

(a) revoke a non-derogating control order;

(b) relax or remove an obligation imposed by such an order;

(c) with the consent of the controlled person, modify the obligations imposed by such an order; or

(d) make to the obligations imposed by such an order any modifications which he considers necessary for purposes connected with preventing or restricting involvement by the controlled person in terrorism-related activity.

(3) The Secretary of State may not make to the obligations imposed by a control order any modification the effect of which is that a non-derogating control order becomes an order imposing a derogating obligation.

(4) An application may be made at any time to the court—

(a) by the Secretary of State, or

(b) by the controlled person,

for the revocation of a derogating control order or for the modification of obligations imposed by such an order.

(5) On such an application, the court may modify the obligations imposed by the derogating control order only where—

(a) the modification consists in the removal or relaxation of an obligation imposed by the order;

(b) the modification has been agreed to by both the controlled person and the Secretary of State; or

(c) the modification is one which the court considers necessary for purposes connected with preventing or restricting involvement by the controlled person in terrorism-related activity.

(6) The court may not, by any modification of the obligations imposed by a derogating control order, impose any derogating obligation unless—

(a) it considers that the modification is necessary for purposes connected with protecting members of the public from a risk of terrorism; and

(b) it appears to the court that the risk is one arising out of, or is associated with, the public emergency in respect of which the designated derogation in question has effect.

(7) If the court at any time determines that a derogating control order needs to be modified so that it no longer imposes derogating obligations, it must revoke the order.

(8) The controlled person is bound by—

(a) a control order,

(b) the renewal of a control order, or

(c) a modification by virtue of subsection (2)(d) or (5)(c),

only if a notice setting out the terms of the order, renewal or modification has been delivered to him in person.

(9) For the purpose of delivering a notice under subsection (8) to the controlled person a constable or a person authorised for the purpose by the Secretary of State may (if necessary by force)—

(a) enter any premises where he has reasonable grounds for believing that person to be; and

(b) search those premises for him.

(10) Where the Secretary of State revokes a control order or modifies it by virtue of subsection (2)(b) or (c)—

(a) he must give notice of the revocation or modification to the controlled person; and

(b) the notice must set out the time from which the revocation or modification takes effect.

(11) A control order, or the renewal, revocation or modification of such an order, may be proved by the production of a document purporting to be certified by the Secretary of State or the court as a true copy of—

(a) the order; or

(b) the instrument of renewal, revocation or modification;

but this does not prevent the proof of a control order, or of the renewal, revocation or modification of such an order, in other ways.

8 Criminal investigations after making of control order

(1) This section applies where it appears to the Secretary of State—

(a) that the involvement in terrorism-related activity of which an individual is suspected may have involved the commission of an offence relating to terrorism; and

(b) that the commission of that offence is being or would fall to be investigated by a police force.

(2) Before making, or applying for the making of, a control order against the individual, the Secretary of State must consult the chief officer of the police force about whether there is evidence available that could realistically be used for the purposes of a prosecution of the individual for an offence relating to terrorism.

(3) If a control order is made against the individual the Secretary of State must inform the chief officer of the police force that the control order has been made and that subsection (4) applies.

(4) It shall then be the duty of the chief officer to secure that the investigation of the individual's conduct with a view to his prosecution for an offence relating to terrorism is kept under review throughout the period during which the control order has effect.

(5) In carrying out his functions by virtue of this section the chief officer must consult the relevant prosecuting authority, but only, in the case of the performance of his duty under subsection (4), to the extent that he considers it appropriate to do so.

(6) The requirements of subsection (5) may be satisfied by consultation that took place wholly or partly before the passing of this Act.

(7) In this section—

"chief officer"—

(a) in relation to a police force maintained for a police area in England and Wales, means the chief officer of police of that force;

(b) in relation to a police force maintained under the Police (Scotland) Act 1967 (c 77), means the chief constable of that force;

(c) in relation to the Police Service of Northern Ireland, means the Chief Constable of that Service;

(d) in relation to the Serious Organised Crime Agency, means the Director General of that Agency; and

(e) in relation to the Scottish Drug Enforcement Agency, means the Director of that Agency;

"police force" means—

(a) a police force maintained for a police area in England and Wales;

(b) a police force maintained under the Police (Scotland) Act 1967;

(c) the Police Service of Northern Ireland;

(d) the Serious Organised Crime Agency; or

(e) the Scottish Drug Enforcement Agency;

"relevant prosecuting authority"—

(a) in relation to offences that would be likely to be prosecuted in England and Wales, means the Director of Public Prosecutions;

(b) in relation to offences that would be likely to be prosecuted in Scotland, means the appropriate procurator fiscal;

(c) in relation to offences that would be likely to be prosecuted in Northern Ireland, means the Director of Public Prosecutions for Northern Ireland.

(8) In relation to times before the Serious Organised Crime Agency begins to carry out its functions, this section is to have effect as if—

(a) the National Crime Squad were a police force; and

(b) references, in relation to that Squad, to its chief officer were references to its Director General.

(9) In subsection (7)—

the Scottish Drug Enforcement Agency" means the organisation known by that name and established under section 36(1)(a)(ii) of the Police (Scotland) Act 1967; and

"the Director" of that Agency means the person engaged on central service (as defined by section 38(5) of that Act) and for the time being appointed by the Scottish Ministers to exercise control in relation to the activities carried out in the exercise of the Agency's functions.

9 Offences

(1) A person who, without reasonable excuse, contravenes an obligation imposed on him by a control order is guilty of an offence.

(2) A person is guilty of an offence if—

(a) a control order by which he is bound at a time when he leaves the United Kingdom requires him, whenever he enters the United Kingdom, to report to a specified person that he is or has been the subject of such an order;

(b) he re-enters the United Kingdom after the order has ceased to have effect;

(c) the occasion on which he re-enters the United Kingdom is the first occasion on which he does so after leaving while the order was in force; and

(d) on that occasion he fails, without reasonable excuse, to report to the specified person in the manner that was required by the order.

(3) A person is guilty of an offence if he intentionally obstructs the exercise by any person of a power conferred by section 7(9).

(4) A person guilty of an offence under subsection (1) or (2) shall be liable—

(a) on conviction on indictment, to imprisonment for a term not exceeding 5 years or to a fine, or to both;

(b) on summary conviction in England and Wales, to imprisonment for a term not exceeding 12 months or to a fine not exceeding the statutory maximum, or to both;

(c) on summary conviction in Scotland or Northern Ireland, to imprisonment for a term not exceeding 6 months or to a fine not exceeding the statutory maximum, or to both.

(5) In relation to an offence committed before the commencement of section 154(1) of the Criminal Justice Act 2003 (c 44), the reference in subsection (4)(b) to 12 months is to be read as a reference to 6 months.

(6) Where a person is convicted by or before any court of an offence under subsection (1) or (2), it is not to be open to the court, in respect of that offence—

(a) to make an order under section 12(1)(b) of the Powers of Criminal Courts (Sentencing) Act 2000 (c 6) (conditional discharge);

(b) to make an order under section 228(1) of the Criminal Procedure (Scotland) Act 1995 (c 46) (probation orders); or

(c) to make an order under Article 4(1)(b) of the Criminal Justice (Northern Ireland) Order 1996 (SI 1996/3160 (NI 24)) (conditional discharge in Northern Ireland).

(7) A person guilty of an offence under subsection (3) shall be liable—

(a) on summary conviction in England and Wales, to imprisonment for a term not exceeding 51 weeks or to a fine not exceeding level 5 on the standard scale, or to both;

(b) on summary conviction in Scotland or Northern Ireland, to imprisonment for a term not exceeding 6 months or to a fine not exceeding level 5 on the standard scale, or to both.

(8) In relation to an offence committed before the commencement of section 281(5) of the Criminal Justice Act 2003, the reference in subsection (7)(a) to 51 weeks is to be read as a reference to 6 months.

(9) In Schedule 1A to the Police and Criminal Evidence Act 1984 (c 60) (arrestable offences), at the end insert—

"27A Prevention of Terrorism Act 2005

An offence under section 9(3) of the Prevention of Terrorism Act 2005."

(10) In Article 26(2) of the Police and Criminal Evidence (Northern Ireland) Order 1989 (SI 1989/1341 (NI 12)) (offences for which an arrest may be made without a warrant in Northern Ireland), at the end insert—

"(o) an offence under section 9(3) of the Prevention of Terrorism Act 2005."

Appeals and other proceedings

10 Appeals relating to non-derogating control orders

(1) Where—

(a) a non-derogating control order has been renewed, or

(b) an obligation imposed by such an order has been modified without the consent of the controlled person,

the controlled person may appeal to the court against the renewal or modification.

(2) In the case of an appeal against a renewal with modifications, the appeal may include an appeal against some or all of the modifications.

(3) Where an application is made by the controlled person to the Secretary of State for—

(a) the revocation of a non-derogating control order, or

(b) the modification of an obligation imposed by such an order,

person may appeal to the court against any decision by the Secretary of State on the application.

(4) The function of the court on an appeal against the renewal of a non-derogating control order, or on an appeal against a decision not to revoke such an order, is to determine whether either or both of the following decisions of the Secretary of State was flawed—

(a) his decision that it is necessary, for purposes connected with protecting members of the public from a risk of terrorism, for an order imposing obligations on the controlled person to continue in force;

(b) s decision that the obligations to be imposed by the renewed order, or (as the case may be) the obligations imposed by the order to which the application for revocation relates, are necessary for purposes connected with preventing or restricting involvement by that person in terrorism-related activity.

(5) The function of the court on an appeal against a modification of an obligation imposed by a non-derogating control order (whether on a renewal or otherwise), or on an appeal against a decision not to modify such an obligation, is to determine whether the following decision of the Secretary of State was flawed—

(a) in the case of an appeal against a modification, his decision that the modification is necessary for purposes connected with preventing or restricting involvement by the controlled person in terrorism-related activity; and

(b) in the case of an appeal against a decision on an application for the modification of an obligation, his decision that the obligation continues to be necessary for that purpose.

(6) In determining the matters mentioned in subsections (4) and (5) the court must apply the principles applicable on an application for judicial review.

(7) If the court determines on an appeal under this section that a decision of the Secretary of State was flawed, its only powers are—

(a) power to quash the renewal of the order;

(b) power to quash one or more obligations imposed by the order; and

(c) power to give directions to the Secretary of State for the revocation of the order or for the modification of the obligations it imposes.

(8) In every other case, the court must dismiss the appeal.

11 Jurisdiction and appeals in relation to control order decisions etc

(1) Control order decisions and derogation matters are not to be questioned in any legal proceedings other than—

(a) proceedings in the court; or

(b) proceedings on appeal from such proceedings.

(2) The court is the appropriate tribunal for the purposes of section 7 of the Human Rights Act 1998 (c 42) in relation to proceedings all or any part of which call a control order decision or derogation matter into question.

(3) No appeal shall lie from any determination of the court in control order proceedings, except on a question of law.

(4) No appeal by any person other than the Secretary of State shall lie from any determination—

    (a) on an application for permission under section 3(1)(a); or

    (b) on a reference under section 3(3)(a).

(5) The Schedule to this Act (which makes provision relating to and for the purposes of control order proceedings and proceedings on appeal from such proceedings) has effect.

(6) In this Act "control order proceedings" means—

    (a) proceedings on an application for permission under section 3(1)(a);

    (b) proceedings on a reference under section 3(3)(a);

    (c) proceedings on a hearing in pursuance of directions under section 3(2)(c) or (6)(b) or (c);

    (d) roceedings on an application to the court by any person for the making, renewal, modification or revocation of a derogating control order;

    (e) proceedings on an application to extend the detention of a person under section 5;

    (f) proceedings at or in connection with a hearing to determine whether to confirm a derogating control order (with or without modifications);

    (g) proceedings on an appeal under section 10;

    (h) proceedings in the court by virtue of subsection (2);

    (i) any other proceedings in the court for questioning a control order decision, a derogation matter or the arrest or detention of a person under section 5;

    (j) proceedings on an application made by virtue of rules of court under paragraph 5(1) of the Schedule to this Act (application for order requiring anonymity for the controlled person).

(7) In this section "control order decision" means—

    (a) a decision made by the Secretary of State in exercise or performance of any power or duty of his under any of sections 1 to 8 or for the purposes of or in connection with the exercise or performance of any such power or duty;

    (b) a decision by any other person to give a direction, consent or approval, or to issue a demand, for the purposes of any obligation imposed by a control order; or

    (c) a decision by any person that is made for the purposes of or in connection with the exercise of his power to give such a direction, consent or approval or to issue such a demand.

(8) In this section "derogation matter" means—

    (a) a derogation by the United Kingdom from the Human Rights Convention which relates to infringement of a person's right to liberty under Article 5 in consequence of obligations imposed on him by a control order or of his arrest or detention under section 5; or

    (b) the designation of such a derogation under section 14(1) of the Human Rights Act 1998 (c 42).

12 Effect of court's decisions on convictions

(1) This section applies where—

    (a) a control order, a renewal of a control order or an obligation imposed by a control order is quashed by the court in control order proceedings, or on an appeal from a determination in such proceedings; and

    (b) before it was quashed a person had been convicted by virtue of section 9(1) or (2) of an offence of which he could not have been convicted had the order, renewal or (as the case may be) obligation been quashed before the proceedings for the offence were brought.

(2) The person convicted may appeal against the conviction—

    (a) in the case of a conviction on indictment in England and Wales or Northern Ireland, to the Court of Appeal;

    (b) in the case of a conviction on indictment or summary conviction in Scotland, to the High Court of Justiciary;

    (c) in the case of a summary conviction in England and Wales, to the Crown Court; and

    (d) in the case of a summary conviction in Northern Ireland, to the county court.

(3) On an appeal under this section to any court, that court must allow the appeal and quash the conviction.

(4) An appeal under this section to the Court of Appeal against a conviction on indictment—

    (a) may be brought irrespective of whether the appellant has previously appealed against his conviction;

    (b) may not be brought more than 28 days after the date of the quashing of the order, renewal or obligation; and

    (c) is to be treated as an appeal under section 1 of the Criminal Appeal Act 1968 (c 19) or, in Northern Ireland, under section 1 of the Criminal Appeal (Northern Ireland) Act 1980 (c 47), but does not require leave in either case.

(5) An appeal under this section to the High Court of Justiciary against a conviction on indictment—

    (a) may be brought irrespective of whether the appellant has previously appealed against his conviction;

    (b) may not be brought more than two weeks after the date of the quashing of the order, renewal or obligation; and

    (c) is to be treated as an appeal under section 106 of the Criminal Procedure (Scotland) Act 1995 (c 46) for which leave has been granted.

(6) An appeal under this section to the High Court of Justiciary against a summary conviction—

    (a) may be brought irrespective of whether the appellant pleaded guilty;

    (b) may be brought irrespective of whether the appellant has previously appealed against his conviction;

    (c) may not be brought more than two weeks after the date of the quashing of the order, renewal or obligation;

    (d) is to be by note of appeal, which shall state the ground of appeal;

    (e) is to be treated as an appeal for which leave has been granted under Part 10 of the Criminal Procedure (Scotland) Act 1995; and

    (f) must be in accordance with such procedure as the High Court of Justiciary may, by Act of Adjournal, determine.

(7) An appeal under this section to the Crown Court or to the county court in Northern Ireland against a summary conviction—

    (a) may be brought irrespective of whether the appellant pleaded guilty;

    (b) may be brought irrespective of whether he has previously appealed against his conviction or made an application in respect of the conviction under section 111 of the Magistrates' Courts Act 1980 (c 43) or Article 146 of the Magistrates' Courts (Northern Ireland) Order 1981 (SI 1981/1675 (NI 26)) (case stated);

    (c) may not be brought more than 21 days after the date of the quashing of the order, renewal or obligation; and

(d) is to be treated as an appeal under section 108(1)(b) of that Act or, in Northern Ireland, under Article 140(1)(b) of that Order.

(8) In section 133(5) of the Criminal Justice Act 1988 (c 33) (compensation for miscarriages of justice), at the end of paragraph (c) insert

"or

(d) on an appeal under section 12 of the Prevention of Terrorism Act 2005."

Supplemental

13 Duration of sections 1 to 9

(1) Except so far as otherwise provided under this section, sections 1 to 9 expire at the end of the period of 12 months beginning with the day on which this Act is passed.

(2) The Secretary of State may, by order made by statutory instrument—

(a) repeal sections 1 to 9;

(b) at any time revive those sections for a period not exceeding one year; or

(c) provide that those sections—

(i) *are not to expire at the time when they would otherwise expire under subsection (1) or in accordance with an order under this subsection; but*

(ii) *are to continue in force after that time for a period not exceeding one year.*

(3) Before making an order under this section the Secretary of State must consult—

(a) the person appointed for the purposes of section 14(2);

(b) the Intelligence Services Commissioner; and

(c) the Director-General of the Security Service.

(4) No order may be made by the Secretary of State under this section unless a draft of it has been laid before Parliament and approved by a resolution of each House.

(5) Subsection (4) does not apply to an order that contains a declaration by the Secretary of State that the order needs, by reason of urgency, to be made without the approval required by that subsection.

(6) An order under this section that contains such a declaration—

(a) must be laid before Parliament after being made; and

(b) if not approved by a resolution of each House before the end of 40 days beginning with the day on which the order was made, ceases to have effect at the end of that period.

(7) Where an order ceases to have effect in accordance with subsection (6), that does not—

(a) affect anything previously done in reliance on the order; or

(b) prevent the making of a new order to the same or similar effect.

(8) Where sections 1 to 9 expire or are repealed at any time by virtue of this section, that does not prevent or otherwise affect—

(a) the court's consideration of a reference made before that time under subsection (3)(a) of section 3;

(b) the holding or continuation after that time of any hearing in pursuance of directions under subsection (2)(c) or (6)(b) or (c) of that section;

(c) the holding or continuation after that time of a hearing to determine whether to confirm a derogating control order (with or without modifications); or

(d) the bringing or continuation after that time of any appeal, or further appeal, relating to a decision in any proceedings mentioned in paragraphs (a) to (c) of this subsection;

but proceedings may be begun or continued by virtue of this subsection so far only as they are for the purpose of determining whether a certificate of the Secretary of State, a control order or an obligation imposed by such an order should be quashed or treated as quashed.

(9) Nothing in this Act about the period for which a control order is to have effect or is renewed enables such an order to continue in force after the provision under which it was made or last renewed has expired or been repealed by virtue of this section.

(10) In subsection (6) "40 days" means 40 days computed as provided for in section 7(1) of the Statutory Instruments Act 1946.

14 Reporting and review

(1) As soon as reasonably practicable after the end of every relevant 3 month period, the Secretary of State must—

(a) prepare a report about his exercise of the control order powers during that period; and

(b) lay a copy of that report before Parliament.

(2) The Secretary of State must also appoint a person to review the operation of this Act.

(3) As soon as reasonably practicable after the end of—

(a) the period of 9 months beginning with the day on which this Act is passed, and

(b) every 12 month period which ends with the first or a subsequent anniversary of the end of the period mentioned in the preceding paragraph and is a period during the whole or a part of which sections 1 to 9 of this Act were in force,

the person so appointed must carry out a review of the operation of this Act during that period.

(4) The person who conducts a review under this section must send the Secretary of State a report on its outcome as soon as reasonably practicable after completing the review.

(5) That report must also contain the opinion of the person making it on—

(a) the implications for the operation of this Act of any proposal made by the Secretary of State for the amendment of the law relating to terrorism; and

(b) the extent (if any) to which the Secretary of State has made use of his power by virtue of section 3(1)(b) to make non-derogating control orders in urgent cases without the permission of the court.

(6) On receiving a report under subsection (4), the Secretary of State must lay a copy of it before Parliament.

(7) The Secretary of State may pay the expenses of a person appointed to carry out a review and may also pay him such allowances as the Secretary of State determines.

(8) In this section—

"control order powers" means—

(a) the powers of the Secretary of State under this Act to make, renew, modify and revoke control orders; and

(b) his powers to apply to the court for the making, renewal, revocation or modification of derogating control orders;

"relevant 3 month period" means—

(a) the period of 3 months beginning with the passing of this Act;

(b) a period of 3 months beginning with a time which—

   (i) *is the beginning of a period for which sections 1 to 9 are revived by an order under section 13; and*

   (ii) *falls more than 3 months after the time when those sections were last in force before being revived;*

(c) a 3 month period which begins with the end of a previous relevant 3 month period and is a period during the whole or a part of which those sections are in force.

15 General interpretation

(1) In this Act—

"act" and "conduct" include omissions and statements;

"act of terrorism" includes anything constituting an action taken for the purposes of terrorism, within the meaning of the Terrorism Act 2000 (c 11) (see section 1(5) of that Act);

"apparatus" includes any equipment, machinery or device and any wire or cable, together with any software used with it;

"article" and "information" include documents and other records, and software;

"contravene" includes fail to comply, and cognate expressions are to be construed accordingly;

"control order" has the meaning given by section 1(1);

"control order proceedings" has the meaning given by section 11(6);

"the controlled person", in relation to a control order, means the individual on whom the order imposes obligations;

"the court"—

(a) in relation to proceedings relating to a control order in the case of which the controlled person is a person whose principal place of residence is in Scotland, means the Outer House of the Court of Session;

(b) in relation to proceedings relating to a control order in the case of which the controlled person is a person whose principal place of residence is in Northern Ireland, means the High Court in Northern Ireland; and

(c) in any other case, means the High Court in England and Wales;

"derogating control order" means a control order imposing obligations that are or include derogating obligations;

"derogating obligation", "designated derogation" and "designation order" have the meanings given by section 1(10);

"the Human Rights Convention" means the Convention within the meaning of the Human Rights Act 1998 (c 42) (see section 21(1) of that Act);

"modification" includes omission, addition or alteration, and cognate expressions are to be construed accordingly;

"non-derogating control order" means a control order made by the Secretary of State;

"passport" means—

(a) a United Kingdom passport (within the meaning of the Immigration Act 1971 (c 77));

(b) a passport issued by or on behalf of the authorities of a country or territory outside the United Kingdom, or by or on behalf of an international organisation;

(c) a document that can be used (in some or all circumstances) instead of a passport;

"premises" includes any vehicle, vessel, aircraft or hovercraft;

"the public" means the public in the whole or a part of the United Kingdom or the public in another country or territory, or any section of the public;

"specified", in relation to a control order, means specified in that order or falling within a description so specified;

"terrorism" has the same meaning as in the Terrorism Act 2000 (c 11) (see section 1(1) to (4) of that Act);

"terrorism-related activity" and, in relation to such activity, "involvement" are to be construed in accordance with section 1(9).

(2) A power under this Act to quash a control order, the renewal of such an order or an obligation imposed by such an order includes power—

    (a) in England and Wales or Northern Ireland, to stay the quashing of the order, renewal or obligation pending an appeal, or further appeal, against the decision to quash; and

    (b) in Scotland, to determine that the quashing is of no effect pending such an appeal or further appeal.

(3) Every power of the Secretary of State or of the court to revoke a control order or to modify the obligations imposed by such an order—

    (a) includes power to provide for the revocation or modification to take effect from such time as the Secretary of State or (as the case may be) the court may determine; and

    (b) in the case of a revocation by the court (including a revocation in pursuance of section 7(7)) includes power to postpone the effect of the revocation either pending an appeal or for the purpose of giving the Secretary of State an opportunity to decide whether to exercise his own powers to make a control order against the individual in question.

(4) For the purposes of this Act a failure by the Secretary of State to consider an application by the controlled person for—

    (a) the revocation of a control order, or

    (b) the modification of an obligation imposed by such an order,

is to be treated as a decision by the Secretary of State not to revoke or (as the case may be) not to modify the order.

16 Other supplemental provisions

(1) This Act may be cited as the Prevention of Terrorism Act 2005.

(2) The following provisions are repealed—

    (a) sections 21 to 32 of the Anti-terrorism, Crime and Security Act 2001 (c 24) (suspected international terrorists);

    (b) in section 1(4) of the Special Immigration Appeals Commission Act 1997 (c 68), paragraph (b) (which refers to section 30 of the 2001 Act) and the word "or" immediately preceding it;

    (c) section 62(15) and (16) of the Nationality, Immigration and Asylum Act 2002 (c 41) and paragraph 30 of Schedule 7 to that Act (which amended sections 23, 24 and 27 of the 2001 Act); and

    (d) section 32 of the Asylum and Immigration (Treatment of Claimants, etc) Act 2004 (c 19) (which amended sections 24 and 27 of the 2001 Act).

(3) Subsection (2) comes into force on 14th March 2005.

(4) The repeals made by this Act do not prevent or otherwise affect—

    (a) the continuation of any appeal to the Special Immigration Appeals Commission under section 25(1) of the Anti-terrorism, Crime and Security Act 2001 that has been brought but not concluded before the commencement of those repeals;

(b) the bringing or continuation of a further appeal relating to a decision of that Commission on such an appeal or on any other appeal brought under section 25(1) of that Act before the commencement of those repeals; or

(c) any proceedings resulting from a decision on a further appeal from such a decision;

but no other proceedings before that Commission under Part 4 of that Act, nor any appeal or further appeal relating to any such other proceedings, may be brought or continued at any time after the commencement of the repeals.

(5) The Secretary of State may enter into such contracts and other arrangements with other persons as he considers appropriate for securing their assistance in connection with any monitoring, by electronic or other means, that he considers needs to be carried out in connection with obligations that have been or may be imposed by or under control orders.

(6) There shall be paid out of money provided by Parliament—

(a) any expenditure incurred by the Secretary of State by virtue of this Act; and

(b) any increase attributable to this Act in the sums payable out of such money under any other Act.

(7) This Act extends to Northern Ireland.

(8) Her Majesty may by Order in Council direct that this Act shall extend, with such modifications as appear to Her Majesty to be appropriate, to any of the Channel Islands or the Isle of Man.

SCHEDULE

CONTROL ORDER PROCEEDINGS ETC

Section 11

Introductory

1

(1) In this Schedule "the relevant powers" means the powers to make rules of court for regulating the practice and procedure to be followed in proceedings in the court, the Court of Appeal or the Inner House of the Court of Session, so far as those powers are exercisable in relation to—

(a) control order proceedings; or

(b) relevant appeal proceedings.

(2) In this Schedule "relevant appeal proceedings" means proceedings in the Court of Appeal or Inner House of the Court of Session on an appeal relating to any control order proceedings.

General duty applying to exercise of the relevant powers

2

A person exercising the relevant powers must have regard, in particular, to—

(a) the need to secure that the making and renewal of control orders and the imposition and modification of the obligations contained in such orders are properly reviewed; and

(b) the need to secure that disclosures of information are not made where they would be contrary to the public interest.

Initial exercise of relevant powers

3

(1) This paragraph applies—

    (a) on the first occasion after the passing of this Act on which the relevant powers are exercised in relation to control order proceedings and relevant appeal proceedings in England and Wales; and

    (b) on the first occasion after the passing of this Act on which they are so exercised in relation to control order proceedings and relevant appeal proceedings in Northern Ireland.

(2) On each of those occasions—

    (a) the relevant powers may be exercised by the Lord Chancellor, instead of by the person by whom they are otherwise exercisable; and

    (b) the Lord Chancellor is not required, before exercising the powers, to undertake any consultation that would be required in the case of rules made by that person.

(3) The Lord Chancellor must—

    (a) consult the Lord Chief Justice of England and Wales before making any rules under this paragraph in relation to England and Wales; and

    (b) consult the Lord Chief Justice of Northern Ireland before making any rules under this paragraph in relation to Northern Ireland.

(4) The requirements of sub-paragraph (3) may be satisfied by consultation that took place wholly or partly before the passing of this Act.

(5) Rules of court made by the Lord Chancellor by virtue of this paragraph—

    (a) must be laid before Parliament; and

    (b) if not approved by a resolution of each House before the end of 40 days beginning with the day on which they were made, cease to have effect at the end of that period.

(6) Where rules cease to have effect in accordance with sub-paragraph (5)—

    (a) that does not affect anything previously done in reliance on the rules;

    (b) the Lord Chancellor is to have power again to exercise the relevant powers, in relation to the proceedings in question, instead of the person by whom they are otherwise exercisable;

    (c) he may exercise them on that occasion without undertaking any consultation that would be required in the case of rules made by that person; and

    (d) the rules made by the Lord Chancellor on that occasion may include rules to the same or similar effect.

(7) The following provisions do not apply to rules made by the Lord Chancellor by virtue of this paragraph—

    (a) section 3(2) of the Civil Procedure Act 1997 (c 12) (negative resolution procedure);

    (b) section 56 of the Judicature (Northern Ireland) Act 1978 (c 23) (statutory rules procedure).

(8) In sub-paragraph (5) "40 days" means 40 days computed as provided for in section 7(1) of the Statutory Instruments Act 1946.

Special powers to make rules of court

4

(1) Rules of court made in exercise of the relevant powers may, in particular—

    (a) make provision about the mode of proof in control order proceedings and about evidence in such proceedings;

    (b) enable or require such proceedings to be determined without a hearing; and

    (c) make provision about legal representation in such proceedings.

(2) Rules of court made in exercise of the relevant powers may also, in particular—

    (a) make provision enabling control order proceedings or relevant appeal proceedings to take place without full particulars of the reasons for decisions to which the proceedings relate being given to a relevant party to the proceedings or his legal representative (if he has one);

    (b) make provision enabling the relevant court to conduct proceedings in the absence of any person, including a relevant party to the proceedings and his legal representative (if he has one);

    (c) make provision about the functions in control order proceedings and relevant appeal proceedings of persons appointed under paragraph 7; and

    (d) make provision enabling the relevant court to give a relevant party to control order proceedings or relevant appeal proceedings a summary of evidence taken in his absence.

(3) Rules of court made in exercise of the relevant powers must secure—

    (a) that in control order proceedings and relevant appeal proceedings the Secretary of State is required (subject to rules made under the following paragraphs) to disclose all relevant material;

    (b) that the Secretary of State has the opportunity to make an application to the relevant court for permission not to disclose relevant material otherwise than to that court and persons appointed under paragraph 7;

    (c) that such an application is always considered in the absence of every relevant party to the proceedings and of his legal representative (if he has one);

    (d) that the relevant court is required to give permission for material not to be disclosed where it considers that the disclosure of the material would be contrary to the public interest;

    (e) that, where permission is given by the relevant court not to disclose material, it must consider requiring the Secretary of State to provide the relevant party and his legal representative (if he has one) with a summary of the material;

    (f) that the relevant court is required to ensure that such a summary does not contain information or other material the disclosure of which would be contrary to the public interest;

    (g) that provision satisfying the requirements of sub-paragraph (4) applies where the Secretary of State does not have the relevant court's permission to withhold relevant material from a relevant party to the proceedings or his legal representative (if he has one), or is required to provide a summary of such material to that party or his legal representative.

(4) The provision that satisfies the requirements of this sub-paragraph is provision which, in a case where the Secretary of State elects not to disclose the relevant material or (as the case may be) not to provide the summary, authorises the relevant court—

    (a) if it considers that the relevant material or anything that is required to be summarised might be of assistance to a relevant party in relation to a matter under consideration by that court, to give directions for securing that the matter is withdrawn from the consideration of that court; and

(b) in any other case, to ensure that the Secretary of State does not rely in the proceeding on the material or (as the case may be) on what is required to be summarised.

(5) In this paragraph "relevant material", in relation to any proceedings, means—

(a) any information or other material that is available to the Secretary of State and relevant to the matters under consideration in those proceedings; or

(b) the reasons for decisions to which the proceedings relate.

Application for anonymity for controlled person

5

(1) Rules of court made in exercise of the relevant powers may provide for—

(a) the making by the Secretary of State or the controlled person, at any time after a control order has been made, of an application to the court for an order requiring anonymity for that person; and

(b) the making by the court, on such an application, of an order requiring such anonymity;

and the provision made by the rules may allow the application and the order to be made irrespective of whether any other control order proceedings have been begun in the court.

(2) Rules of court may provide for the Court of Appeal or the Inner House of the Court of Session to make an order in connection with any relevant appeal proceedings requiring anonymity for the controlled person.

(3) In sub-paragraphs (1) and (2) the references, in relation to a court, to an order requiring anonymity for the controlled person are references to an order by that court which imposes such prohibition or restriction as it thinks fit on the disclosure—

(a) by such persons as the court specifies or describes, or

(b) by persons generally,

of the identity of the controlled person or of any information that would tend to identify him.

Use of advisers

6

(1) In any control order proceedings the court may, if it thinks fit—

(a) call in aid one or more advisers appointed for the purpose by the Lord Chancellor; and

(b) hear and dispose of the proceedings with the assistance of the adviser or advisers.

(2) Rules of court may regulate the use of advisers in accordance with the power conferred by this paragraph.

(3) The Lord Chancellor may, out of money provided by Parliament, pay such remuneration, expenses and allowances to advisers appointed for the purposes of this paragraph as he may determine.

Special representation in control order proceedings

7

(1) The relevant law officer may appoint a person to represent the interests of a relevant party to relevant proceedings in any of those proceedings from which that party and his legal representative (if he has one) are excluded.

(2) In sub-paragraph (1) "relevant proceedings" means—

    (a) control order proceedings; or

    (b) proceedings on an appeal or further appeal relating to control order proceedings.

(3) A person may be appointed under this paragraph—

    (a) in the case of an appointment by the Attorney General, only if he has a general legal qualification for the purposes of section 71 of the Courts and Legal Services Act 1990 (c 41); ·

    (b) in the case of an appointment by the Advocate General for Scotland, only if he is a person with appropriate rights of audience in Scotland; and

    (c) in the case of an appointment by the Advocate General for Northern Ireland, only if he is a member of the Bar of Northern Ireland.

(4) In sub-paragraph (3) "person with appropriate rights of audience in Scotland" means—

    (a) an advocate; or

    (b) a solicitor with rights of audience by virtue of section 25A of the Solicitors (Scotland) Act 1980 (c 46) in the Court of Session or the High Court of Justiciary.

(5) A person appointed under this paragraph is not to be responsible to the person whose interests he is appointed to represent.

(6) In this paragraph "the relevant law officer" means—

    (a) in relation to control order proceedings in England and Wales or proceedings on an appeal or further appeal relating to such proceedings, the Attorney General;

    (b) in relation to proceedings in Scotland or proceedings on an appeal or further appeal relating to such proceedings, the Advocate General for Scotland;

    (c) in relation to proceedings in Northern Ireland or proceedings on an appeal or further appeal relating to such proceedings, the Advocate General for Northern Ireland.

(7) In relation to any time before the coming into force of section 27 of the Justice (Northern Ireland) Act 2002 (c 26), references in this paragraph to the Advocate General for Northern Ireland are to have effect as references to the Attorney General for Northern Ireland.

Effect of court orders

8

(1) Where—

    (a) a control order,

    (b) the renewal of such an order, or

    (c) an obligation imposed by such an order,

is quashed, the order, renewal or (as the case may be) obligation shall be treated for the purposes of section 9(1) and (2) as never having been made or imposed.

(2) A decision by the court or on appeal from the court—

(a) to quash a control order, the renewal of a control order or an obligation imposed by such an order, or

(b) to give directions to the Secretary of State in relation to such an order,

does not prevent the Secretary of State from exercising any power of his to make a new control order to the same or similar effect or from relying, in whole or in part, on the same matters for the purpose of making that new order.

Interception evidence

(1) Section 18 of the Regulation of Investigatory Powers Act 2000 (c 23) (exceptions to exclusion of interception matters from legal proceedings) is amended as follows.

(2) In subsection (1), after paragraph (d) insert—

"(da) any control order proceedings (within the meaning of the Prevention of Terrorism Act 2005) or any proceedings arising out of such proceedings;".

(3) In subsection (2) (persons disclosures to whom continue to be prohibited despite section 18), for "paragraph (e) or (f)" substitute "paragraphs (da) to (f)".

(4) In that subsection, before paragraph (a) insert—

"(za) in the case of any proceedings falling within paragraph (da) to—

(i) *a person who, within the meaning of the Schedule to the Prevention of Terrorism Act 2005, is or was a relevant party to the control order proceedings; or*

(ii) *any person who for the purposes of any proceedings so falling (but otherwise than by virtue of an appointment under paragraph 7 of that Schedule) represents a person falling within sub-paragraph (i);".*

Allocation to Queen's Bench Division

10

In paragraph 2 of Schedule 1 to the Supreme Court Act 1981 (c 54) (business allocated to Queen's Bench Division), after sub-paragraph (b) insert—

"(ba) all control order proceedings (within the meaning of the Prevention of Terrorism Act 2005);" .

Interpretation of Schedule

11

In this Schedule—

"legal representative", in relation to a relevant party to proceedings, does not include a person appointed under paragraph 7 to represent that party's interests;

"relevant appeal proceedings" has the meaning given by paragraph 1(2);

"relevant court"—

(a) in relation to control order proceedings, means the court; and

(b) in relation to relevant appeal proceedings, means the Court of Appeal or the Inner House of the Court of Session;

"relevant party", in relation to control order proceedings or relevant appeal proceedings, means any party to the proceedings other than the Secretary of State;

"relevant powers" has the meaning given by paragraph 1(1).

About the Author

Sally Ramage is a lecturer at the University of Wolverhampton, United Kingdom, where she teaches business compliance. She is a regular writer for the legal column of Accounting Technician. She practised as an accountant before going into law.

Sally Ramage has had many articles (36 in 2004) published in the following publications:

1. "The Criminal Lawyer",1. TOTTEL PUBLISHING (ex Butterworths)

2. Lexis-Nexis (US Politics and World News) [http://66.102.9.104/search?q=cache:mmLpA-sA3r0J:www6.lexis-nexis.com/publisher/E…]

3. HEDGEWORLD [www.hedgeworld.com]

4. Accounting Technician [www.accountingtechnician.co.uk]

5. The Securities and Exchange Commission (USA Chief Regulator) [www.sec.gov/news]

6. PoliceOne.com (I wrote (six) ipolice training articles voluntary basis)

7. LAW IN A BOX [www.lawina box.net] They train LLB and LLM degree students externally for University of London exams.

8. Sally Ramage is ALSO A FULL ACADEMIC MEMBER OF "EUROPEAN CORPORATE GOVERNANCE INSTITUTE." [www.ecgi.org].

9. She is also a full Chartered Manager, member of the Chartered Management Institute.[www.managers.org.uk]

10. She is now a Fellow of the Association of International Accountants.[www.aia.org.uk]

11. Most importantly (for the books) she is a full member of the Society of Legal Scholars. [www.legalscholars.ac.uk]

12. She is a full member of the British Institute of international Comparative Law [www.biicl.org]

13. Finally, she is a fully fledged Journalist with the National Union of Journalists. [www.nuj.org]

Links:

http://www.biicl.org/

http://www.nuj.org.uk/

http://www.legalscholars.ac.uk/

http://www.ecgi.org/

http://www.managers.org.uk/

http://www.aia.org.uk/

http://www.vistacomp.com/

http://www.accountingtecghnician.co.uk/

http://www.barnesandnoble.com/

http://www.amazon.com/

http://www.policeOne.com/

http://www.wlv.ac.uk/

http://www.law-office.demon.co.uk/sally/index.htm

978-0-595-35678-2
0-595-35678-8

Printed in the United Kingdom
by Lightning Source UK Ltd.
110101UKS00001B/1-10